Ihya' 'Ulum ad-Din

The Revival of the Religious Sciences

Imam Abu Hamid Al Ghazali

Translated by
Maulana Fazlul Karim

VOLUME II

Nadeem Press

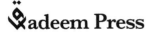

Qadeem Press Edition
Breathing Life into Forgotten Pages
www.qadeempress.com

Find our titles on your favourite online bookstore using the keyword 'Qadeem Press'

The Revival of Religious Learning
THE BOOK OF WORLDLY USAGES

CONTENTS

Preface

PREFACE

The Book of worldly usages is the second book of Imam Ghazzali's world renowned master-piece *Ihya Ulum-id-Din* or 'The Revival of Religious Learnings'. This work is an attempt to translate the second part of the *Ihya* not too literally but in substance from the original written in Arabic. The book II deals with the worldly usages, etiquettes, manners, rules and regulations concerning eating and drinking, marriage, earnings and trade, lawful and unlawful earnings, duties towards Muslims, neighbours, servants and slaves, harms and benefits of seclusion and society, journey, music, enjoining good and forbidding evil and character and conduct of the Holy Prophet.

A literal translation is avoided in order to omit the unnecessary argument of sects and things prevailing in the then world and to omit the sayings of less important sages. But no verse of the Qurãn or saying of Prophet has been omitted in this book.

I pray to the Almighty Allah that He may guide the people of the world in accordance with the teachings of the Holy Qurãn and Sunnah and the spirit in which the *Ihya* was written by Hujjatul-Islam (the Proof of Islam), a title received by Imam Ghazzali and about which it has been said "If all the books of Islam were destroyed, it would be but a slight loss if only the *Ihya* of Ghazzali were preserved."

Fazlul-Karim

December, 1971

بِسْمِ اللّٰهِ الرَّحْمٰنِ الرَّحِيْمِ

نحمده و نصلى على رسوله الكريم

REVIVAL OF RELIGIOUS LEARNINGS

THE BOOK OF WORLDLY USAGES

PART I

CHAPTER I

Rules of Eating and Drinking

All praise is due to God who conducts the whole creation in an orderly manner, Who gives provision according to a measure, Who increases the strength of animals by food and drink and Who nourishes religion and good deeds by good foods and drinks.

The object of the wise is the vision of the Lord in the next world and the only way to gain it is learning and action and there is no other way, but it is not possible to stand constantly on them without a healthy body which is also not possible without food and drink, such food and drink which are absolutely necessary and which are taken according to prescribed rules. For this reason, some learned sages said that food and drink appertain to religion. God said : "Eat pure food and do good deeds (23 : 51). If a man takes food for helping his learning and actions and God-fear, his food and drink are considered as divine service. For that, he should not spend his time uselessly and remain busy like a lower being which roams from field to field in eating and drinking. The modes and the ways of food and drink are the lights of religion. A religious man must stick to these ways and control his passion and greed for food and drink by weighing them in the balance of *Shariat*. The Holy Prophet said: A man can acquire virtues in all his actions, even in a morsel of food he lifts up to his mouth and to the mouth of his wife.

SECTION 1

Rules of Eating alone

The rules of eating alone are of three kinds– (a) rules before eating, (b) rules at the time of eating and (c) rules after eating.

(a) Rules before eating : There are seven rules before eating. **(1)** The food must be lawful. God enjoined eating good and lawful food and prohibited bad and unlawful food. There is benefit in the former and harm in the latter. God says: O believers! don't eat the properties of one another unjustly (2:188). The root of religion is lawful food, which is the basis of all religious actions. **(2)** The hand shall be washed before eating. The Prophet said: 'Wash before eating prevents poverty and wash after eating prevents frivolous thoughts.' Dirts and germs that keep attached in hands as a result of manual labour can be removed by wash. So, wash before eating is necessary as ablution before prayer is necessary. **(3)** Food shall be placed on the ground as it is the way of the Prophet. Whenever any food was taken to the Prophet, he kept it on the ground as it is the sign of humility. The Prophet used not to take food in any plate except in a big dish with others. Four things were innovated after the Prophet – (a) to eat on tables, (b) to sift food–stuffs by sieve, (c) to use soaps and (d) to eat to one's heart's content. These things, though not unlawful, are not good for an humble man. **(4)** One should take food sitting straight. The Prophet said : 'I don't eat leaning as I am a mere slave and I eat as a slave eats and I sit as a slave sits'. To eat leaning is bad for stomach. **(5)** One shall make *niyyat* before eating : I eat to gain strength in worship. He will take promise to eat little and not much as full belly prevents worship. The more the intention is pure for religion, the less is the greed for food. The Prophet said : 'Such quantity of food is sufficient for a man which can keep his backbone erect. If he is unable to do it then one part of the belly is for food, one part for drink and one part for breathing.' If the *niyyat* or intention is true, one should not extend his hand towards food if he is not hungry. **(6)** Be satisfied with the food served and don't be greedy for varieties of curries. Food is honoured only when one does not wait for curry. The Prophet said : When the time of night meal and the time of night prayer come together, first take meal. **(7)** The more are the people to partake food, the better. The Prophet said : Eat all together, as there is blessing in it. The Prophet used not to eat single. He said : The food in which many hands participate is best.

(b) Rules at the time of eating

Begin eating reciting *'Bismillah'* – in the name of God and end it reciting *'Alhamdulillah'*–all praise is due to God. Eat with the right hand and begin and end it with salt. Take little morsels and chew each morsel well. Don't extend your hand to a morsel till you swallow the previous one. Don't speak of the defects of cooking. The Prophet never did it. When he liked a food, he ate, and when he did not like it, he did not eat it. Except fruits, he used to take from the nearest side of the dish. The Prophet said : Eat from the side of your front and not from every side, nor from the middle. Don't cut bread or meat with knife. The Prophet said: Cut meat with your teeth. He said : Honour the principal foods as God sent them from the blessings of heaven. The Prophet said : 'If any morsel of food falls down, take it up and clear of the dust attached to it and don't leave it for the devil. Don't wipe out your hands with handkerchiefs till you lick your fingers, because you don't know in which food there is blessing.' Don't blow breath in hot food as it is prohibited, but be patient till it becomes cold. Eat odd number of dates, grapes and such other fruits which can be counted.

Rules of drinking water : Don't drink water at the time of eating except when thirsty. It is better and keeps stomach sound. Take the name of God and drink slowly. The Prophet said : 'Drink water drought by drought and not at a time.' Don't drink water standing or lying, as the Prophet prohibited it except for an excuse. Don't throw breath into pot or yawn. The Prophet used to recite after drinking water: All praise is due God who has made it delicious and sweet by His grace and has not made it either saltish or distasteful for our sins. Drink water with three breaths and at the end recite *'Alhamdulillah'* all praise is due to God and at the beginning *'Bismillah'*– in the name of God.

(c) Rules after eating

Lift up your hand before the stomach is filled up and lick up the fingers. Then wipe them with a towel and then wash them. Lift up the remnants of food. The Prophet said : 'He who eats what lies on the dining cloth will remain safe, will pass his life in solvency and his children will remain safe.' Then make pick of teeth and don't swallow what comes out of teeth as a result of pick. Thereafter gurgle, lick the dish and drink its water. It has been said that he who licks his dish and drinks its water will get the reward of the manumission of a slave. Express gratefulness to God sincerely for what God has given you to eat and take food as His gift. God says: Eat of the good things which I have produced for you and be grateful for the gifts of God (2 : 168). Whenever you eat a lawful thing, say : All praise is for God for whose mercy good deeds are completed and blessings descend. O God! give us good food and engage us in good deeds. If you eat doubtful things, then say : All praise is due to God under all circumstances. O God! let it not lead us towards Thy transgression. After meal, recite chapters *Ikhlas* and *Lailafe*. Don't rise up till the dining cloth is lifted up. If you take food in the house of another person, pray for him and say : O God! give him abundant good and give him blessings in what Thou hast provided him. The Prophet said : Hell is better for the flesh which has been nourished by unlawful food. If you drink milk, say : Give blessing in what Thou hast provided us and increase it for us. After meal, recite the following: All praise is due to God who provided us with food and drink sufficiently and gave shelter to our leader and chief. Then wash your hand with soap.

SECTION 2

Rules for eating with others

(1) If there is any elderly or honourable man with you, don't begin eating till he begins. (2) Don't remain silent at the time of eating and hold talks. (3) Don't wish to eat more than your friend. It is not lawful for you to eat more when food is equally distributed unless your friends give you out of their own accords. (4) Eat in such a way that there remains no necessity of saying to your companion 'eat, eat.' Eat according to your habit. (5) It is no fault for one to wash hands in the dish and for all in the same pot. If the same pot is used by all for washing hands, the following rules shall be observed. There should be no spitting in the pot, the chief guest should be honoured, beginning should be made from the right hand side, a servant should pour water upon the hands and throwing water from the mouth should be slow. (6) One should not look at the eating of his companions and should withdraw his hand before his companions finish eating. (7) One should not do what appears bad to his companions and talk not such words as may offend them.

SECTION 3

Hospitality

There is a great merit in showing hospitality and in entertainment of guests. Hazrat Jafar Sadiq said : When you sit with guests in the dining cloth, sit for a long time as no account will be taken of that time. Hazrat Hasan Basri said : Accounts will be taken of what one spends for himself, for his parents or for any other person, but no account will be taken of what one spends for food of his Muslim brethren as God will feel shame in taking its accounts. There are many traditions to this effect. The Prophet said : Angels like one till there is food before him. He said : When your Muslim brethren lift up their hands after they finish eating, no account will be taken of one who eats the remaining food. He said : No account will be taken for the food which he gives to his brother Muslim. He also said : No account will be taken for three things - (1) pre-dawn tiffin for fasting, (2) what is eaten for breaking fast and (3) what is eaten with a brother Muslim. Hazrat Ibn Omar said : To take good food in journey and to give it to the companions appertain to generosity. Some companions said : To eat together is the sign of good conduct. There is in one *Hadis* God will say to a man : O son of Adam! I was hungry and you did not give Me food. He will reply : How could I have given Thee food while Thou art the Lord of the universe? God will say : Your certain brother Muslim was hungry, but you did not give him food. If you had given him food, it would have reached Me. The Prophet also said Honour one who comes to see you. He said : There are high places in Paradise, the outer sides of which are visible from the inner sides. These are for those who are modest in treatment, give food and pray at night when the people remain

asleep. The Prophet said : He who gives food is best of you.
He said : If a man gives food to his brother Muslim to his
satisfaction and gives him drink till his thirst is appeased,
God will keep him away up to seven ditches from Hell, the
distance of every two ditches is the path of five hundred years.

Rules of eating

(1) When you enter the house of your friend to take your
meal, don't enter it suddenly as it is prohibited. God says :
Don't enter the house of the Prophet at the time of meal
without permission and don't look at the dish of food. The
Prophet said : He who joins a feast without invitation is a
transgressor.

(2) If a man goes to the house of another man for necessity
and if then the time of meal comes, he should not take meal
without being requested. When the host says : Take meal, he
should see whether it has been said willingly or out of shame.
If it is said out of shame, he should not join it.

(3) It is *sunnat* to demand food from the house of a bosom
friend. The Holy Prophet, Hazrat Abu Bakr and Omar used to
go to the house of Abul Haisam and Abu Ayyub Ansari for
taking meal. They used to take meal in the houses of Ansars
in the beginning. God said : There is no fault in taking meal
in the houses of your friends. Once the Prophet took meal in
the house of Barirah without her permission. When questioned
about friends, Hasan Basri said : He is friend to whom mind
finds peace and is pleased with.

(4) To present food before the guest. Don't take too much
trouble in preparing food. Place before the guest whatever
you have got. If you have got no food and also no money,
don't run into debt and don't inflict trouble on yourself. If
you have got measured food and you have no mind to part

with it, it is not necessary to give food to a guest. Give better food to your guest than what you eat. A certain sage said : If any of my friends comes to me. I don't care to feed him as I don't inflict any trouble on myself for his sake. I present to him whatever I have got. If I take trouble, I don't welcome him. It is said that once when Hazrat Ali was invited, he said: I can accept your invitation on three conditions - (1) don't buy anything from the market for me; (2) don't hoard up what is in your house and (3) don't give trouble to your family members. Hazrat Salman said: The Prophet prohibited us to take trouble for a guest for what is not in our houses and ordered us to present before him what is ready. It has been reported of Prophet Jonah that whenever his friends came to see him, he used to place before them pieces of bread and vegetables of his garden and say : Eat. If God does not curse upon those who take trouble, I would have taken trouble for you. Hazrat Anas said that they used to present before a guest dried bread and dried dates and say : We don't know who is a greater sinner between the two - one who dislikes the food presented before him or one who dislikes to present what is near him.

(5) A guest should not order his host to arrange meal or for a particular item of food. It causes trouble to the host. There is in a *Hadis* that the Prophet used to like the easier of two things. A certain sage said : Feast is of three kinds - (1) to eat with the poor with *I'sar* (sacrificing own interest). (2) to treat with friends with pleasure and (3) to treat with the worldly men with good manners. The host will ask his guest what kind of food he likes. There are merits in giving food to the guest according to the wish of the latter. The Prophet said: The sins of one are forgiven who takes care to fulfil the desires of his brother Muslim. God will please one who pleases his brother Muslim. The Prophet said God writes thousands of

merits and forgives thousands of sins of one who gives taste to what his guest likes. God gives him thousands of ranks and will feed him from three Paradises - *Firdous*, *Adan* and *Khuld*. Don't say to a guest: What food shall I bring for you? Present to him whatever food is ready. The sage Sufiyan Saori said : When your brother Muslim meets you, don't say to him: What food will you eat? What food shall I present to you? A certain Sufi said: When the poor come to you, give them food. When the theologians come to you, ask them about legal decisions. When the learned come to you, show them the praying clothes.

SECTION 4

Rules of entertainment of guests

There are six rules of entertainment of guests - to invite, to accept invitation, to attend at the invitation, to present food, to take meal and then to depart. The Prophet said about the entertainment of guests : Don't take trouble for a guest, lest you think bad of him. He who thinks bad of a guest, thinks bad of God and God also thinks bad of him. He also said = There is no good in one who does not entertain guest. The Prophet once passed by an owner of many camels and cattle who did not entertain him. A woman who had some goats only entertained him by sacrificing a goat. At this, the Prophet said: Look at these two persons and this conduct is in the hand of God. He gives it to whom He is pleased with. Once a guest came to the Prophet who said : As I have got a guest, tell that Jew to give me a loan, I shall repay it in the month of Rajjab. The Jew said : By God! if you do not keep something as pawn, I will not give you the loan. On being informed of it, the Prophet said : By God! I am trustworthy in heaven and trustworthy in the earth. If he gives me loan, I shall repay it. Take my shield and give it to him as a pawn.

Whenever the Prophet Abraham wished to lake meal, he used to seek a guest to take meal with him upto the distance of one or two miles for which he was surnamed *Abu Zaifan* or father of guests. The custom of entertainment of guests is still prevalent by the side of his grave as a commemoration of this attribute of his. Not a single night passes there when one to three hundred guests are not entertained. The manager of this place says that upto this day no night passed there without a guest. The Prophet was once asked : What is faith? He replied: Not to be miserly in giving food and in tendering *salam.* The Prophet said : Giving food and praying at night when people remain asleep expiate sins and increase rank. Being asked about an accepted pilgrimage. The Prophet said: Giving food and talking sweet words. Hazrat Anas said Angels do not enter a house where a guest does not enter. There are many other traditions regarding the merits of entertainment.

To invite and to accept invitations

Don't invite other than religious men and don't invite the transgressors. The Prophet once prayed for a person thus: Let your food be eaten by religious men. He said : Don't eat except the food of religious men and don't give your food to be eaten except by the religious men and invite the poor. The Prophet said : The worst feast is that of marriage where the rich are invited and not the poor. Don't neglect the relatives in feasts as neglecting them produces their displeasure and the evils of the tie of relationship. Treat with the friends and acquaintances in such a manner as no other people are dissatisfied if special persons are invited. Follow the ways of the Prophet in feeding and incur the pleasure of the believers. Don't invite such a person who will not join a feast or the guests may suffer owing to his presence. Don't invite except one who willingly accepts invitation. The sage Sufiyan Saori said : He who invites a person who does not accept it commits sin. If the latter accepts the invitation at last, he commits two sins as he comes to him in spite of his unwillingness. If a religious man is fed, it helps his religion ; and if a sinner is fed, it helps sin.

Five rules of acceptance of invitations

To accept invitation is *sunnat* or the practice of the Prophet. Some say it is compulsory. The Prophet said : If I am asked to eat goat's thigh, I shall accept it. There are five rules of accepting invitation.

(1) Don't distinguish between the poor and the rich. It appertains to pride and is prohibited. For this reason, those who accept the invitation of the rich in comparison with that of the poor appertain to the class of proud people and are opposed to the ways of the Prophet. The Prophet used to accept the invitation of the slaves and the poor. Once Hasan, son of Hazrat Ali, was passing by a group of poor people who were begging by the side of a pathway and were eating food in a dusty place. Hazrat Hasan was riding on a camel. They said : O grandson of the Prophet! join us in our food. He at once got down, sat with them on the ground, ate food with them and then rode upon his camel and said: I accepted your invitation. Now accept my invitation. They accepted it and he entertained them on a fixed date.

(2) Invitation should not be refused for distance. There is written in the Torah: Go to see a sick man even to a distance of one mile. Join a funeral prayer even to the distance of two miles. Join an invitation even to the distance of three miles and meet with a friend for the sake of God even to the distance of four miles. The Prophet said: Had I been invited to a place in the village of Gamim (it is several miles off from Madinah), I would have accepted it. The Prophet once broke fast there in *Ramazan* and made his prayer short.

(3) Don't refuse invitation owing to fast and attend feast and break fast so as to incur the pleasure of the host, as it brings greater rewards than that of optional fast. The Prophet said : Your brother has taken trouble and you say : I am fasting. Hazrat Ibn Abbas said: The best virtue is to eat with friend after breaking (optional) fast. There are signs of entertainment of guests to give antimony and scents or scented oils.

(4) Don't accept invitation where you know or doubt that food unlawfully earned will be served or irreligious acts will be performed such as unlawful food and wine will be placed, gold and silver cups and plates will be used or immoral songs will be sung. Acceptance of invitation is not lawful if the host is a tyrant, transgressor or innovator.

(5) Don't accept invitation for satisfaction of belly, but intend to gain strength for acquiring merits in the next world. Be careful of disobeying God. The Prophet said : He who does not accept invitation disobeys God and His Apostle. According to this *Hadis*, intend to honour your brother believer. Intend to incur pleasure in the minds of the Muslims according to this *Hadis* : 'He who incurs the pleasure of a believer incurs the pleasure of God.' Intend to meet a believer in order that you may love him as the Prophet imposed this condition for it. Therein there is meeting with each other and expense for the sake of God. Intend to be free from defamation, so that it may not be said that he did not attend owing to pride. Don't take pride in it and don't show bad conduct and don't hold in contempt your brother Muslim. If one of the above intentions is observed, it will bring one to the nearness of God. A certain sage said: I wish to have *niyyat* or intention in all my actions, even in food and drink. The Prophet said: All actions are judged by intention. Every man gets what he intends. Whosoever emigrates for the sake of God and His apostle, his emigration is for God and His Apostle, he who emigrates for worldly gain or for marrying a woman will get that for which he emigrates. There is no effect of intention in unlawful things. So don't intend to do an unlawful thing.

Rules of joining in feasts

(1) When you attend an invitation, don't sit in the middle place and don't occupy the best space. **(2)** Don't make delay in attending an invitation, as the guests may be waiting for you. Don't attend it before the fixed time as the host may not prepare food before hand. **(3)** Don't sit in such a manner as causes inconvenience to others. If there is any fixed place for you, don't act contrary to it. The Prophet said : To remain satisfied with a little space for sitting for the sake of God appertains to humility. **(4)** Don't look towards the place wherefrom food comes, as it is against good manners. **(5)** Entertain one who sits by your side and hold talk with him. **(6)** When a guest comes to a host, the latter should show to the former the direction of *Qibla*, places of calls of nature and ablution. **(7)** Make delay after meal to wash your hands. **(8)** If you see anything opposed to *Shariat*, remove it if you are able or else go away expressing your dislike therefore.

Presentation of food before guests

There are five rules in it -

(1) Serve food before a guest without delay as it honours the guest. The Prophet said: Let one who believes in God and the last day honour his guest. God said about Abraham: Have not the news of the honoured guests of Abraham come to you? He honoured them by placing food before them without delay and did not make delay in bringing a cooked beef. In another verse, God said: He hurriedly went to his house and brought the meat of a roasted calf (11: 69). The sage Hatim Asim said : Hastiness comes from the devil except in five cases. These five cases are the ways of the Prophet to give food to a guest, to bury a dead man, to give a grown up daughter in marriage, to clear off debt and to repent for a sin.

Serve first fruits or fruit juice, if any, as they help digestion. The Qurān also gives instruction to eat fruits first. And from what they like out of fruits. Then God said: And what they like out of meat of birds. After fruit meat and *sarid*, which is a mixture of date and curry should be served, as the Prophet said : The superiority of *sarid* over other fruits is like the superiority of Ayesha over other women. After that, sweets should be served. To honour guest by meat is instructed by the Qurãn while narrating the story of Abraham. To serve meat first is a sign of honouring a guest. God said about good things of food : I sent down to you *Mann* (sweet thing) and *Salwa* (meat) (2 : 57). The Prophet said : The best curry is meat. God says: Eat out of the good things I have provided for you (2 : 168). Meat and sweet things appertain to good things. A certain sage said : Sweet things after food are better than many curries. It is said that green vegetables increase beauty.

(2) The best food should be served first before guests, so that they may eat with satisfaction. Don't eat much. The habit of voracious eaters is that they first serve inferior foods and then better foods. This is against the way of the Prophet. It was the custom of the earlier sages that they served all kinds of food before their guests. A menu of food should be given to each guest, so that he may know the particulars of food to be eaten by him. The remnants of food should not be taken away till the guests finish eating. Serve before the guest sufficient quantity of food as it is against gentlemanliness to present insufficient quantity of food before them. One day varieties of dishes were served before the sage Ibrahim b. Adham. At that time, Sufiyan Saori said to him: O father of Ishaq! don't you fear that it is extravagance? Ibrahim said : There is no extravagance in food. Hazrat Ibn Masud said : We have been prohibited to accept invitation of one who takes pride in giving feast. Before going after feast, observe three rules - **(a)** It is *sunnat* to go with the guest upto the door. It is within the ways of the Prophet to go upto the door with a guest. The Prophet said : Let him honour a guest who believes in God and the hereafter. The Prophet said : It appertains to *sunnat* to go upto the door to honour a guest. Hazrat Abu

Qatadah reported that when a deputation from the Negroes of Abyssinia came to the Prophet, he began himself to serve them. His companions said to him : O Messenger of God! we are sufficient for you. He said : Never, they honoured my companions and I wish to repay it. **(b)** To welcome guests with a smiling face and with good words, to give them farewell and to feed them complete honour. The sage Aozayi was asked: What is the meaning of honouring guests? He said : To welcome with a smiling face and to use sweet words. Give farewell to the guest with a pleased mind even though he might have defects. The Prophet said : 'A man can earn the rank of a fasting man and a praying man in this way.' **(c)** A guest should not leave without the permission of the host and without satisfying him. If you are a guest, don't reside with a host for more than three days, as many a time a host is vexed with a guest for his long stay. The Prophet said : 'Hospitality is for three days and if it exceeds that, it will be considered as an act of charity.' If the host requests the guest to stay longer with sincere heart, it is lawful for him to stay. The Prophet said : One bed is for his host, one bed for his wife, one bed for a guest and the fourth bed is for the devil.

Rules and Prohibitions in Feast

(1) To avoid eating in markets is good as far as practicable. Hazrat Ali said : God removes seventy kinds of disasters from one who begins eating with salt. He who eats daily seven dried dates, every worm of his stomach is destroyed. He who eats daily twenty-one raisins of reddish colour will not feel any pain in his body. Meat begets meat. *Sarid* (cooked dates with sugar) is a tiffin of the Arabs. Belly grows large if sweet things are eaten and two testicles hang down. Beef creates diseases, milk has got cure and clarified butter has got medicinal effect. Fat comes out of disease like it. There is no better thing than fresh grapes for a mother who just gives birth to a child. Fish melts the body. Qurãn reciting and tooth-stick remove scum.

(2) He who wishes to live long should eat in the morning, eat very little at night, wear shoes, should not entertain a man with clarified butter, should have little sexual intercourse and should put on simple dress. These are the injunctions also of religion.

(3) Once Governor Hajjaj said to a certain physician: Tell me such a medicine which I shall use. The physician said: Don't marry except a grown-up girl. Don't eat except the meat of a stout and strong animal. Don't eat food unless well-cooked. Don't use medicine except in illness. Don't eat fruits unless ripe. Don't eat food unless it is chewed well. Eat what you like but don't drink water after it. Don't eat anything after drinking water. Don't hold up stool and urine. Sleep a little after breakfast and walk a little after dinner before going to bed but not less than one hundred steps. It is said that if urine is held up, it is harmful to the body, just as everything around a stream is destroyed if it is held up.

(4) The rupture of a vein is a cause of disease and to give up dinner at night is the cause of old age. A certain physician said to his son: Don't go out of the house without eating food in the morning as there is patience in it and it removes thirst and greed for food.

(5) As a diseased man who gives up patient's diet suffers, so a healthy man suffers if he takes a patient's diet. Someone said: He who takes care of his diet has got certainty of no disease and no doubt of sound health. It is better not to be careful at the time of sound health.

(6) It is better to carry food to a house wherein a man has died. When Jafar b. Abu Talib died, the Prophet said: The family members of Jafar are busy owing to his death and cannot cook food. Take to them what they eat. It is *sunnat*.

(7) Don't eat the food of a tyrant and an oppressor. If there is no alternative, eat a little, but don't eat their best foods. It is reported that when the sage Zunnun Misri was sent to prison, he did not take his meal for three days. He had a foster sister who sent food to him through the guard of the prison. He did not eat it. He sent news to her: Your food is lawful, but it has reached me through the hand of an oppressor. This is the height of God-fear.

(8) Imam Shafai said: Four things make the body strong-eating meat, using scents, taking much bath and putting on linen cloth. Four things make the body idle-excessive sexual intercourse, too much thinking, too much drinking of water when hungry and too much pepper. Four things give power of eye - sight - to sit towards the *Qibla* to use antimony before sleep, to look towards green colour and to keep the clothes clean. Four things reduce eye-sight - to look to unclean and impure things, to see one being hanged, to look to the female organ and to sit keeping the *Qibla* behind. Four things increase the power of sexual intercourse - to eat the meat of sparrows, to eat big Atri fruit, to eat pistachio and to eat water-fruit. Sleep is of four kinds - to lie with belly upwards is the sleep of the Prophets, to sleep on the right side is the sleep of the worshippers, to sleep on the left side is the sleep of the rulers and to sleep upon the face downwards is the sleep of the devil. Four things increase wisdom, to give up useless talk, to cleanse teeth, to keep company with the learned and the pious men. Four things appertain to divine service - to take steps with ablution, to prolong prostration, to keep attached to the mosque and to recite the Qurān much. He said also: If a man enters a bathroom after being hungry and makes delay in taking food soon after coming out of it, it is wonder that he is alive, if a man eats soon after cupping, it is wonder that he is alive. He also said: I don't see any better medicine than Banafsha for epidemic diseases. Body is to be besmeared therewith and it is to be taken as a drink. God knows best.

CHAPTER II

SECRETS OF MARRIAGE

Merits and Demerits

Know, O dear readers! that there are differences of opinions among the learned men about the merits of marriage. Some say that for divine service marriage is better, some say that to remain unmarried is a means of increasing divine service. The following are the proofs that marriage is better. God says: Marry your widows. God says: Don't prevent them in taking husbands. God says in praising the Prophets: I have sent Prophets before you and gave them wives and children. By this, God gives superiority to marriage. The prophets also prayed for good children. God says: They pray - O our Lord! give us such wives and children out of our descendants who will console our eyes and make the God - fearing among them leaders. Out of the Prophets, Jesus Christ did not marry but he will marry after his second advent.

Hadis: The Prophet said: Marriage is my *sunnat* (way), whosoever diverts from my *sunnat* is not of me. He said: Marriage is my way, whosoever loves my conduct should follow my way. He said: Unite in marriage tie, your numbers will increase. I will boast justly on seeing your numbers on the Resurrection Day in comparison with the followers of others. He said: He who does not marry fearing poverty is not of me. He said: Let them marry who have got means. He said: 'Let him marry who has got strength as marriage, shuts up eyesight and protects private parts. Let him fast who has got no means to marry as fasting is for him like castration.' Castration means to remove sexual passion. Fasting brings weakness of body. The Prophet said : 'When a man comes to you whose religion and trust please you, give in marriage to him. If you do not do it, there will be disasters and quarrels in the world.' This encouragement has been given fearing disturbance and disorder. He said : He who marries and gives in marriage becomes entitled to God's care. He said : 'He who marries fulfils half of his religion. Let him fear God for the second half.' Generally private parts and belly create disorder in the religion of a man. Marriage removes that disorder. The Prophet said : The actions of a man come to an end except three -(l) a religious issue who prays for him, (2) a recurring charity and (3) a religious book. A religious issue is impossible without marriage.

Wise sayings : Hazrat Omar said : Two things prevent marriage–inability and being a sinner. It appears from this that religion does not prohibit marriage. Hazrat Ibn Abbas said : No divine service becomes complete without marriage. Hazrat Omar married many wives and said : I marry for children. A companion renunciated the world and stayed with the Prophet and passed nights with him. He said to him : Will you not marry ? He said : O Apostle of God! I am a poor man, I have got no means. Shall I be deprived of rendering service to you ? The Prophet remained silent. He again told this to him and he replied as before. The companion then thought within his mind : The Apostle of God is well aware which thing will bring us near God and what will be our good in this world and the next. I shall certainly marry. The Prophet said to him for the third time - Will you not marry ? He said : O Prophet of God! get me married. A certain hermit was superior for divine service to all the people of his time and when his case was mentioned to the Prophet of his age, he said : How good he is, but he has given up one habit. Being grieved, he asked that Prophet about it and he said : You have not married. He said : I am a poor man, I have got no means to bear its expense. He said : I will give my daughter in marriage to you. This he did. It is said that Hazrat Ali had four wives.

In short, marriage is a part of *sunnat* and the practices of the Prophets. A man asked Ibrahim b. Adham : Good news to you. You can engage yourself in divine service as you are alone. He said : Your prayer in the midst of your family is better than my entire divine service. He asked : Then why do you not marry ? He said : I have got no necessity of women. I don't wish to retain connection with any woman. Someone said : The rank of a married man in comparison with that of an unmarried man is equal to the rank of a *Mujahid* in comparison with a worshipper. One *rakát* prayer of a married man is better than seventy *rakats* of prayer of an unmarried man.

Reasons for not marrying

The Prophet said : After two hundred years, a man who will have no wife and children will be better. A time will come over men when he will be destroyed by his wife, parents and children. They will give him such trouble which will be out of his capacity. As a result, he will adopt such measures for which his religion will be ruined and he will be destroyed. The Prophet said : One of the two reasons of wantlessness is a less number of family members. One of the two reasons of poverty is having too many persons. Abu Sulaiman Darani was once asked about marriage and he replied : Patience of not having a wife is better than having patience of duty towards her ; and the patience of duties towards her is better than patience at Hell-fire. He also said : He who searches for three things becomes attached to the world-searching for livelihood, marrying a woman and writing stories. Hazrat Hasan said When God wishes good of a man, He does not keep him engaged in family and property.

Benefits of marriage

There are five benefits of marriage- (1) to have children, (2) to control sexual passion, (3) to find peace of mind - (4) to increase divine service (5) and to get rewards of duties to family.

(1) To have children : This is the root for which marriage is contracted. The object is to preserve dynasty and the earth not existing without men, four objects are fulfilled in having children-: (a) Increase of mankind, (b) the love of the Prophet is searched by increasing his followers, (c) after death, the prayers of religious children are sought, (d) If the issues die before death, their intercession is sought.

First object is very subtle and not within easy comprehension of man. It is a natural truth and the following is its proof. Take for instance that an owner of land handed over the seeds of crops and instruments of cultivation to a servant and gave him also the land for cultivation. The servant did not cultivate it, kept the instruments useless and destroyed the seeds. It is clear that he becomes then an object of wrath of the master. Similarly God created man and woman. He created life germ for production of children in the back of a man and the breast of a woman. The uterus is the fertile field and the male organ and the female organ are the instruments of cultivation. He also created sexual passion in the male and female for creating child by using the instruments of their organs. These prove the objects of God. The Prophet also clearly proved it by saying 'Marry and keep dynasty.' He who does not marry destroys the seeds and keeps the instrument useless and idle and goes against the object of God. For this reason to kill the child and to bury it alive have been prohibited. Question may be asked that when the object of God is to preserve dynasty, then why He prescribed its destruction by death. Life and death though opposed to each other are within the will of God as love and hatred though opposed to each other are within God's will. God says : He does not love infidelity for His servants. There is in a *Hadis Qudsi* that God said : I feel no greater grief for anything than to take the life of My Muslim servant. He considers death as disliking to him and I don't like to trouble him, but there is no escape from death. God says : I have prescribed death among you. He says : I have created life and death. So the words of God - 'I have fixed death among you' and 'I don't wish to inflict trouble on him'. These two verses are not opposed to each other, but they express truth. This is the will of God.

(2) Second object of children : By marriage, love is expressed towards the Prophet and efforts are made to increase his followers as he will boast for the increased number of his followers on the Resurrection Day. The Prophet said : A prison in a corner of a house is better than a childless woman. He said : Among your woman, a lovely woman producing many children is better. He said : An ugly woman with children is better than a beautiful woman having no children. It appears from the above traditions that the object of marriage is to get children and not only satisfaction of sexual passion.

(3) Third object of children : If anybody leaves a religious son or daughter, he or she may pray for his or her dead parents. There is in *Hadis* that the actions of a man end by death except his three actions. He mentioned among them a religious issue. The Prophet said : The invocations are presented like the layers of light to a dead man. If an issue is religious, his parents get the rewards of his pious actions and invocations as he is the earnings of his parents, but his parents are not punished for his sins as nobody bears the burden of another. God says I will attach them to their issues and they will suffer no loss owing to their evil actions but their good deeds will increase owing to the good deeds of their children.

(4) Fourth object of children : If a child dies before his father or mother, he will make intercession for his father or mother. The Prophet said : A child will carry its parents towards Paradise. There is in another *Hadis* : He will draw his parents as I draw your cloth. He said : It will be said to the child : Enter Paradise. He will go to the door of Paradise and say in an angry mood : I will not enter Paradise without my parents. It will then be said to him. Admit his parents alongwith him in Paradise. There is in another *Hadis* : The children will be brought alongwith other men in the place of judgement. The angels will be said : Take their children to Paradise. They will be waiting at the door of Paradise. They will be said : Welcome to the Muslim children. Enter and there is no account on you. They will say : Where are our parents ? The guard will reply: Your parents are not like you. They have got sins and faults for which they will be summoned and they will be called to account. Then they will make tremendous noise before Paradise. God will say : What is this cry for ? They will then disclose the above thing. God will say – Leave them all, so that they can take their parents to Paradise. The Prophet said: He whose two children predeceased him will be safe from Hell. He said : God will admit out of His mercy one whose three issues who have not attained puberty predeceased him. He was asked : O Messenger of God! if two of them predeceased ? He said: Even if two predeceased him.

(II) Second benefit of marriage is to be safe from the devil, to satisfy lust and to save private parts. The Prophet said : If a man marries, half of his religion is saved. Fear God for the remaining half. The Prophet said : Let one who is unable to marry fast, as fast for him is the means of controlling passion. The pleasure which lies in sexual intercourse is only an example of next worldly happiness. There is no benefit in a thing of which there is no pleasure. A minor boy will not get any pleasure in sexual intercourse, nor there is any benefit in it. A boy shall not find any taste in reign, nor there is any taste in it. God created pleasure of the world with this object that if the people have pleasure they will be eager to have lasting pleasure of the next world. To get this pleasure divine service is necessary. The marriage is a means of saving oneself from the oppression of sexual passion.

Heart is the root of all actions of a traveller towards the next world. Hazrat Ibn Abbas said : The worship of a man does not become perfect without divine service. God says that man has been created weak. Hazrat Ikramah and Mujahid explain this that man cannot be patient regarding women. Faiaz b. Nazih said : When the male organ of a man stands erect, two third of his intellect go away. God says : When there falls the darkness of night, seek refuge from its evils. Hazrat Ibn Abbas explains this by saying : Seek refuge from the devil when the male organ stands erect. The Prophet said: O God! I seek refuge to Thee from the evils of my ears, my heart and myself. He said : I pray to Thee for purity of my mind and protection of my private parts. The sage Junaid said: Sexual intercourse is as much necessary for me as food is necessary. The Prophet said : If the look of a man falls on any woman, let him turn it towards himself and cohabit with his wife ; in that case his evil desire will go away. Hazrat Jabir reported that once the Prophet looked to a certain woman. He soon went to his wife Zainab and performed his necessity. After that he came out and said : If a woman comes in front, she comes as a devil. If one of you sees a woman who pleases him, let him come to his wife as what is near that woman is also near his wife. The Prophet said : Don't go to a woman in absence of her husband as the devil runs through your veins like the circulation of blood. We asked him : In your case also? He said : In my case also, but God helped me over him and he submitted to me. This means : I have been saved from the machinations of the devil.

Once a young man asked Hazrat Ibn Abbas : I am a young man, I have got no wife. I fear sin in most cases and many a time I take out semen by hand pollution. Is there any sin in it? Hazrat Ibn Abbas turned his face from him and said : Alas ! it is better to marry a slave girl than it, but it is better than fornication. Sexual passion is so strong in some man that one wife cannot satisfy him and so there is provision of marrying four wives. Hazrat Ali took a wife seven days after the death of Fatima. It is said that Hazrat Hasan took many wives but not more than four at a time. The Prophet said to Hasan : You have got in you my character and appearance. The Prophet said : Hasan is from me and Hussain is from Ali. Some of the companions had three or four wives and those who took two wives were many.

(III) Third benefit of marriage : Marriage brings peace in mind and there grows love between the couple. This peace of mind is necessary for divine service. God says : He created you from a single person and created his mate from him, so that he may find consolation in her. Hazrat Ali said – Give peace to mind as it becomes blind when it becomes disturbed. There is in *Hadis* that there are three special times for a wise man; he speaks secretly with his lord at one time, he takes accounts of his actions at another time and he remains busy with his food and drink at another time. In another narration, a wise man is not desirous except of three matters, to earn the livelihood of the next world, to earn the livelihood of this world and to take taste of lawful things. The Prophet said :

There is effort in every action and there is langour in every effort. He who takes langour goes towards my *sunnat* and guidance. The Prophet said : On complaint to Gebrail about the lessening of my sexual passion, he advised me to take Harisah. The Prophet said : Three things are dear to me among your earthly matters-scent, woman and prayer; the latter is the doll of my eyes. This comfort is necessary for peace of mind.

(IV) Fourth benefit of marriage. Leisure is found for divine service. The wife lessens the duties of a man regarding cooking of food, spreading of bed, cleansing of utensils and other duties of livelihood. A chaste and religious wife helps her husband in this manner. Sulaiman Darani said : A religious wife does not only appertain to three things of enjoyments of the world, rather such a woman is one of the instruments of the next world. She gives leisure to her husband for doing divine service by performing household duties and satisfying his sexual passion. The Prophet said : Let one of you have a grateful heart, a remembering tongue and a chaste wife helping him for the next world. Hazrat Omar said : Nothing better has been given to a man after faith than a virtuous wife. No wealth is compared as valuable to a man as a chaste wife. The Prophet said : I have been given superiority over Adam for two conducts. Adam's wife was his helper in a sinful act but my wives are my helpers in my religious affairs. The devil was disobedient to Adam but he submitted to me and he orders me nothing but truth.

(V) Fifth benefit of marriage : There are some duties arising out of marriage which are considered as divine service to maintain family, to have patience at the character and conduct of the wife, to bear the hardships of the family members, to try to do good to them, to show them the path of religion, to earn for them lawful things and to educate the children. The Prophet said : 'One day of a just ruler is better than divine service for seventy years.' To rule a family is no less task than a king. He said : Be careful, everyone of you is a ruler and everyone of you will be asked about his subjects. The Prophet said : What man spends for his family will be considered as an act charity. Even if he lifts a morsel of food to the mouth of his wife, he will get rewards therefore. A learned man mentioned about his actions regarding his pilgrimage, *jihad* and other good works to another learned man. The latter said : You are far away in comparison with the religious acts of *Abdals*. He asked him : What are those ? He said - Those are lawful earnings and expense for family. The Prophet said : He whose prayer is good, who has got a big family, whose wealth is little and who abstains from defaming the Muslims will live in Paradise with me like these two fingers. He said : God loves the poor man having a big family and refraining from begging. There is in another *Hadis* that if the sins of the family members of a man become large, God tries them therewith that they may be expiations of his sins. A certain wise man said : There is a certain sin of which there is no expiation except patience at the trouble of maintaining a family. The Prophet said : If a man has got three daughters and he spends for their maintenance, God makes Paradise sure for him, except one whose sin is not pardonable.

Harms of marriage : There are three harms of marriage- (I) Lawful earnings become difficult as a result of marriage. There is in *Hadis* that if a man earns virtues to the height of a mountain, he shall have to wait near the balance and accounts will be taken from him of his wealth, of his expenditure, of his maintenance and other matters. The children will say to God on the Resurrection Day : O our Lord! take from him the account of his duties towards us, he did not teach us what we did not know and he gave us unlawful food to eat without our knowledge. Take compensation from him for these. The Prophet said : Nobody will meet God with a greater sin than with a sin of keeping his family members uneducated. Very few people will get release from this danger.

(2) **Second harm of marriage** is the lack of duty towards family members, to lose patience at their character and conduct and not to forbear the hardships inflicted by them. The Prophet said : Sufficient for the sin of a man is not to fulfil his duties of maintenance for which he is responsible. He also said : 'The fleeing of a man from his family is like that of a slave from his master. His prayer and fast are not accepted till he returns.' He who neglects to do his duty of maintenance is like a fleeing man even though he remains present. God says: Save yourselves and your family members from Hell. The sage Ibrahim b. Adham raised objection to marry saying : I don't wish to let any woman do any fault and I have got no necessity for woman.

(3) **Third harm of marriage** is to keep away the family members and children from the remembrance of God, to encourage them to hoard up wealth and to search for objects of pride and boast. Whatever thing diverts attention from God is a cause of misfortune. Ibrahim b. Adham said : He who keeps sticking to the waist of his wife gets no benefit.

These are the benefits and harms of marriage. To marry is better or not depends on the personal character of a man. These benefits and harms are by way of advice and they show path. Marriage is good for one who is not diverted from the remembrance of God and from the path of honesty and virtue. In the contrary case, marriage is bad for him, if there is necessity of controlling sexual passion, marriage is necessary. Jesus Christ did not marry in spite of his high and lofty position as a Prophet. The Holy Prophet, placed in the highest rank

among men, took several wives and yet he did not forget God
for a moment. Even he used to get revelation at the time when
he was in the same bed with his wife Ayesha.

SECTION 2

Rules of marriage

There are some rules of marriage. There are four conditions
of a woman being lawful for a man. **(1)** Permission of guardian
is necessary in case of marriage of minor boy and minor girl
without which the marriage is void. Ruler or his representative
is guardian in cases where there is no guardian **(2)** The consent
of a grown up girl is necessary for her marriage, whether she
is unmarried or widow. **(3)** Two major witnesses are necessary.
They will inform the audience of the girl's consent.
(4) Proposals and acceptances of the bride and bridegroom
are necessary.

Some rules of marriage : **(l)** Proposal of marriage is to
be submitted to the guardian of the girl. **(2)** *Khutba* must be
recited before marriage alongwith proposal and acceptance.
The guardian of the girl will say : All praise is for God and
blessing on God's Apostle, I give my daughter in marriage to
you. The bridegroom will say : All praise is for God and
blessings on His Prophet, I accept her in marriage on this
fixed dower. **(3)** The bride should be informed of the condition
of the bridegroom. It is better that they should see each other
before marriage **(4)** Two witnesses are necessary for marriage.
(5) One should have intention to establish *sunnat* of the
Prophet by marriage and to seek issues. **(6)** It is good to
perform it in the month of *Shawwal*. The Prophet married
Ayesha in *Shawwal* and took her in his house in *Shawwal*.
(7) The bride must be in pure state at the time of marriage.
This means she must not be the wife of another man. It cannot

be performed during the period of waiting. She must not be infidel or retrogade. She must not be a slave of another. She must not be within the prohibited degrees of the husband, mother, mother's mother, daughter, sister, father's sister, foster mother, foster sister, wife's previous husband's daughter, grand daughter, fifth wife, sister of wife who is alive or her mother's sister, a woman who cursed her husband, a woman not in *Ihram* state.

The following qualifications of the bride should be sought:

(1) Religion : The bride should be religious and possess good conduct. This is the main quality of the bride. A man came to the Prophet and said : O Messenger of God! my wife does not repulse any foreign touch. He said : Divorce her. He said : I love her. The Prophet said : Then keep her. The Prophet said : Marry a girl for her wealth, for her beauty, for her qualities and for her religion. You should consider the attribute of her religion. May your hands be covered with dust. There is in another *Hadis* : He who marries a woman for beauty and wealth is deprived of her beauty and wealth, if a man marries for protection of his religion, God gives him, the means of beauty and wealth. The Prophet said - Don't marry a woman only for her beauty, perchance her beauty will be a cause of her ruin. Don't marry her only for her wealth, perchance her wealth will make her disobedient. Marry her only for her religion. He laid a great stress on her religious habits, as such a wife becomes a helper in religion.

(2) Good Conduct : If the wife is harsh and rough and ungrateful, her harms are more than her benefits. One Azdi met Prophet Ilyas who ordered him to marry and prohibited him to have recourse to monkery. Then he said to Azdi - Don't marry four kinds of women - **(1)** a woman who always seeks dresses without any reason, **(2)** a woman who boasts before other women regarding her wealth and riches, **(3)** a woman who is a sinner and unchaste and who has got friends (God says of such women : Don't marry such women who take friends secretly) and **(4)** a woman who takes pride before her husband with haughty words. Hazrat Ali said : There are some conducts which are bad for a male but good for a female– miserliness, pride and cowardice. When a woman is miser, she protects her wealth and her husband's wealth and properties. When a woman is proud, she becomes soft and rejects doubtful talks. When a woman is coward, she keeps separate from her friends and fears to go to any place of defamation for fear of her husband.

(3) Beauty : Beauty is also to be sought of a girl as it saves one from fornication. For this reason, it is *mustahab* or commendable to see a bride before marriage. The Prophet said : When any of you wishes in his mind to marry a woman, let him look at her, as it generates mutual love. The Prophet said : 'If any of you wishes to marry an Ansar woman, let him look at her as there is something in the eyes of Ansars.' It is said that they have got yellow colour in their eyes. Hazrat A'mash said : The result of a marriage which is performed without mutual sight of bride and bridegroom is sorrow and anxiety. The sage Malik b. Dinar said : A man does not marry an orphan girl, but she remains pleased simply with food and clothes and there is less expense for her. The people marry girls of good fortune and wealth, but they demand fine foods and dresses. Imam Ahmad married a deaf woman although he had a beautiful cousin. He did not wish comforts and pleasures. God says : They are beautiful and good. He says : 'They look askance', meaning they are loving to the husbands and eager to have their company. The Prophet said : Of all your women, the best one is she who gives her husband pleasure when he looks at her. She obeys him when he orders her and protects her body and his properties when her husband remains absent.

(4) Dower : The Prophet said : The best woman is she who is beautiful and whose dower is little. He prohibited dower beyond limit and one's capacity. The Prophet gave only ten *dirhams* as dower to some of his wives and some articles of household. He gave some of them dower of two *mudds* of wheat or dates or two *mudds* of maize. Some of the companions of the Prophet fixed dower of a piece of gold for their marriages. It is said that it valued only five *dirhams*. There is in *Hadis* that there is good in a woman who is given in marriage without delay, who gives birth to a child without delay and for whom a small amount of dower is fixed. One should not marry coveting many goods from the bride. Mutual presents are commandable and signs of love. The Prophet said : Give presents, it will beget mutual love and don't seek too much presents from each other. God says : Don't give present in search of excessive presents.

(5) Bride should not be barren if it is known. The Prophet said : Marry lovely and child-bearing women.

(6) Bride should be virtuous : The Prophet said to Hazrat Jabir : Why have you not married a virgin girl, so that you could have played with her and she could have played with you? He married a previously married woman. There are three benefits if a virgin girl is married. She loves her husband. The woman who enjoyed husband is generally addicted to her previous husband. Another benefit is that the love of the husband for his wife becomes perfect and the third benefit is that a virgin girl will not have occasion to grieve for a previous husband.

(7) She must come of a respectable family. If she comes of a good family, she can educate her issues good manners and good conduct. The Prophet said : Choose woman for your semen, as a vein is like an arrow.

(8) Bride should not be a near relative as in that case sexual passion becomes less. The Prophet said : Don't marry a near relative as in that case a child is born weak. The Prophet said: He who gets his daughter married to a transgressor, cuts of his blood tie.

SECTION 3

Some rules after marriage

The husband shall observe twelve rules after marriage. (1) Marriage feast is commendable. Hazrat Anas reported : The Prophet once saw yellow colour on the body of Abdur Rahman b. Auf and said : What is it ? He said : I have married a woman in lieu of a piece of gold. He said : May God bless you both. Give feast with a goat. When the Prophet married Safiyah, he gave feast with grapes and wheat. The Prophet said : Feast on the first day is a duty, feast on the second day is *sunnat* and feast on the third day is for show. If a man who does an act for show, God will disgrace him. It is commendable to give blessing to the bridegroom thus : May God unite you both in good. It is commendable to proclaim marriage. The Prophet said : Distinguish between lawful and unlawful thing by proclamation of marriage by beating '*Daf*'. He said : Proclaim this marriage, perform it in mosque and beat '*daf*' for it.

(2) The husband should treat well with his wife. God says: Treat them with kindness. God says in the fulfillment of their duties : I have taken a solemn oath from you. The Prophet gave three instructions at the time of his death. Soon after that, his tongue was closed and his words stopped. He was saying - prayer. Don't inflict trouble on one whom your right hands posses beyond his capacity. And about your women they are prisoners in your hands. You have taken them as trusts of God and you have made their private parts lawful with the

words of God; The Prophet said : If a man keeps patience at the ill-treatment of his wife, God will give him rewards like the rewards of Ayyub which God gave him for his patience in disasters. If a wife keeps patience at the ill-treatment of her husband, God will give her rewards like the rewards which God gave to Asiyah, wife of Pharaoh. To have patience at the time when the wife gets angry and when she gives trouble is following the Prophet in good treatment with her. It is not merely to restrain oneself from inflicting troubles on the wife. The wives of the Prophet at times argued before the Prophet. Once a wife of the Prophet placed her hand on the chest of the Prophet and gave him a push. At this, her mother rebuked her. The Prophet said - Leave her, as she does more than this. Once there was altercation between the Prophet and Hazrat Ayesha, when they found Hazrat Abu Bakr as their judge. Hazrat Ayesha said to the Prophet : You speak but don't speak except truth. At once Hazrat Abu Bakr gave her such a slap that blood began to ooze out from her mouth. Then he said : O enemy! will he speak but truth ? Then she took refuge to the Prophet.

(3) Make plays and sports with the wife after bearing hardships given by her. This gives pleasure to the wife. The Prophet used to cut jokes with his wives and come down to the level of their intelligence in their manual labours. The Prophet ran races with Ayesha. One day Ayesha won the race and on another day, the Prophet won it and said : This is the revenge of that day. The Prophet said : The most perfect believer in faith is one who is the best of them in good conduct. The Prophet said : The best of you is one who treats best with his wife among you. Hazrat Omar in spite of his sterness said: Stay in the house with your wife like a boy. When the wife demands things from her husband, he should treat like a man. The wise Luqman said : A wise man should live in his house

like a boy and when she stays among people, he should stay like a man. There is in a *Hadis Qudsi* : God dislikes a man who is stern to his family and self-conceited. The Prophet said to Jabir : Have you not found a virgin to marry ? You could have played with her and she with you. A desert woman described her husband after his death: By God! he was fond of sports and when there was darkness, he remained silent.

(4) Don't sport with wife so much that her conduct is ruined and fear goes out of her mind, but take to middle course. Don't give up your duties and strike some sort of fear in her mind at the time of doing evils. Hazrat Omar said : Act opposite to women as there is blessing in opposing them. Someone said - Take advice from them but act to the contrary. The Prophet said: He who becomes the slave of women is ruined. He said for this reason that if a husband acts according to the wishes of his wife, he becomes her slave and is thus ruined as God has made him her master. The right of a husband is that the wife should follow him and the husband should not follow her. God termed the husbands as the maintainers of women and husbands as masters. God says : Both. (Zulaikha and Yusuf) found the master (husband) of Zulaikha near the door. Imam Shafayi said : If you honour three kinds of men, they will disgrace you and if you disgrace them, they will honour you - wife, servant and Nabti. Evils and little intelligence are strong over them. The Prophet said : The example of a religious woman among general women is that of a crow with white belly among one hundred crows. The wise Luqman advised his son : O dear son! fear unchaste wife, as she will make you grow old before you grow old. Fear the harms of women as they do not call towards good. Beware of unchaste women. The Prophet said : Seek refuge to God from three calamities. An unchaste wife will make you old before you get old. In another narration, if you go to her she will

rebuke you. If you don't go to her, she will be treacherous to
you 'When the Prophet fell seriously ill and could not come
out to the mosque for prayer, he said to Abu Bakr to lead the
prayer. Hazrat Ayesha said : The mind of my father is soft.
When he will find your place vacant, he will be perturbed.
The Prophet said : When you prevent Abu Bakr to lead the
prayer, you have swayed towards your low desires being
misguided from the right path. When the wives of the Prophet
disclosed the secret talks of the Prophet, God said : If both of
you make repentance to God, he will unite your hearts. He
said this regarding his good wives. The Prophet said : No
nation prospers over whom a woman rules.

(5) Take middle course in case of anger. Don't make excess
in enquiring into their secret matters. The Prophet prohibited
following the secrets of women. In another narration : He
prohibited to go suddenly to them. Once the Prophet returned
with his companions from a journey to Madinah and said to
them : Don't go to your wives this night suddenly. Two of
them went to their wives without paying heed to his words
and found disagreeable things in their houses. There is in a
famous *Hadis* : 'A wife is like the crooked bone by the side of
a husband. If you go to make it straight, it will break. If you
leave it as it is, it will be more crooked.' It is said for her
correction. The Prophet said : There is an action in anger which
God hates to get angry at the wife without entertaining any
doubt, as it is included within bad conjectures which have
been prohibited. "Some conjecture is sin." Hazrat Ali said :
Don't get angry at your wife, lest evils may come out. To
disclose guilts in proper place is necessary as it is praiseworthy.
The Prophet said : God has got wrath and a believer also has
got wrath. God has got wrath when a servant commits an
unlawful thing. The Prophet said : Do you wonder at the anger
of Sa'ad ? By God! I am more wrathful than him and God is

more wrathful than me. For His wrath, He made unlawful both open and secret indecencies.

The Prophet said : I was taken to Paradise in the night of *Meraj*, I found a palace there. I asked : For whom is this palace? It was said that it is for Omar. I wished to see Omar therein and remembered his anger. Omar wept and said : O Messenger of God! shall I be angry at you ? The Prophet said: There is such anger which God loves and such anger which God hates. There is such pride which God loves and such pride which God hates. The anger which God loves is anger at things of doubt and the anger which God hates is anger at the things beyond doubt. The pride which God loves is the pride at the time of *Jihad* and self-conceit of a man at the first advent of danger. The pride which God hates is pride at an useless thing. The Prophet once asked Fatima : Which thing is good for woman ? She said that she should not look at another man and another man should not look at her. The Prophet drew her close to him and said : This daughter is worthy issue of a worthy father. He considered her reply as good. Hazrat Omar issued order : The females will stay within their houses if they dress well. He said : Habituate your women to stay within their houses. The Prophet once issued order to the women to be present in the mosques. Hazrat Ayesha said: If the Prophet after his death would have seen the condition of women, he would have prohibited them to come out. The Prophet gave permission to women to come out for *I'ds*.

(6) Just expense : Don't make your hand of expense narrow in case of women, nor spread it, but keep the balance between the two. God says : Eat and drink but do not be extravagant. God says : Don't make your hand tied up to your neck, nor spread it to its utmost. The Prophet said : The best of you is who is best of you to his wife. The Prophet said The best in reward of what you spend in the way of God, for the poor and for your wife is what you spend for your wife. Someone said : Hazrat Ali had four wives. He used to buy meat in every four days for one dirham for each of his wives. The sage Ibn Sirin said : It is commendable to give feast every week for family members.

(7) A husband will teach his wife in religious matters, as all men have been given orders to save the members of their families from fire. God says : Save yourselves and your family members from Hell-fire. So to teach religious learnings, articles of faith and all the questions of religion is necessary.

(8) If there is more than one wife, the husband should mete out equal treatment to all. If the husband wishes to take one wife with him in journey, he should select her by casting lottery as the Prophet used to do it. The Prophet said : If a man has got two wives and if he is inclined more to one of them, he will appear on the Resurrection Day with half of his limbs crooked. Spending nights and giving presents to them both must be equal, but equal love is not necessary as mind cannot he divided equally. God says : You will not be able to treat equally among wives though you desire. The Prophet used to divide the nights equally among his wives and said O God! this is my efforts. Don't make me responsible for what is beyond my power and capacity and what is in Thy power and not within my power. The Prophet loved Ayesha more than any other wife. His wives knew it.

(9) Appoint two judges from the side of the husband and the wife to arbitrate between them in case of disputes. If they have got willingness to settle, God will settle between them. The wife should be separated gradually and not all at once. At first, she should be given advice. If it does not bear fruit, she should be separated from bed. This should be done for one to three nights. If it does not bear fruit, beat her mildly but don't inflict physical torture on her, don't shed her blood

or slap her on the face. The Prophet was once asked about the rights of wife over her husband. He said : 'If the husband eats, he shall give her food. If the husband puts on cloth, he shall give her clothes.' Don't change her face, but beat her mildly without causing any wound and do not leave her except in the house she usually spends the nights, get angry at her for not observing her religious duties and for this, be separate from her from ten to even thirty days. The Prophet once remained absent from his wives for one month.

(10) Rules of sexual intercourse : At the beginning of sexual intercourse, take the name of God by reciting '*Bismillah*' and read *Takbir* and *Tahlil* after chapter *Ikhlas* and say : O God! if Thou takest out semen from my back. make it a good issue. The Prophet said : When one of you comes to your wife, let him say : O God! save me from the devil and save the devil from what thou hast provided us. The result is that the devil will not be able to injure the child that is born of such a intercourse. Don't face the *Ka'ba* at the time of intercourse and cover your body and the body of your wife. The Prophet used to over his head, shut up his mouth and say to his wife : Take peace. There is in *Hadis* : When anyone of you comes to his wife, let him not fall suddenly upon her but let him speak words of love and kiss each other. The Prophet said : Let none of you fall suddenly upon his wife like a lower animal. Let him send messenger before cohabitation. Some one asked : What is the messenger ? O Prophet! He said : Kiss and words of love. The Prophet said : In three matters, the weakness of a male is expressed firstly if a lover meets his beloved, both separating without enquiring about their mutual condition and health ; secondly, not to return honour if it is shown to him, or not to do any benefit ; thirdly to cohabit with wife or female without talking with her or without kissing her and to be unable to restrain the ejaculation of his semen before that of the semen of his wife. It is not commendable to cohabit with wife on the first, middle and last dates of the lunar month. It is commendable to cohabit in Friday night. When his semen comes out, let him keep his body sometime upon her breasts till her semen comes out as her semen comes out late. It is painful to her to be separated from her husband when her sexual passion rises high.

A young husband should cohabit with his wife once in four days. To keep the character of the wife, it may be increased or decreased. To cohabit with wife at the time of her menstruation is unlawful. It is, however, lawful to enjoy her without sexual intercourse. God says : 'Come to your field when you wish,' It is also allowed to sleep with her during this time.

(11) Birth-control : It is a rule of cohabitation that the semen should not be thrown out of uterus as what God decreed must come to pass. The Prophet also said so. There are differences of opinion among the learned men regarding *Azl* which means throwing of semen not in the uterus but outside it. One party say that *Azl* is lawful under all circumstances and another party say that it is unlawful under all circumstances. Another party say that with the consent of wife, it is lawful. Another party say that in case of female slaves, it is lawful and not in case of free women. To us, the custom of *Azl* is lawful, but it is not commendable for the reason that the merits of throwing semen in uterus are given up. For instance, it is *Makruh* or not commendable if a person sits idle in mosque without remembering God. The object is that not do a thing for which it is intended is *Makruh*. There is virtue in producing a child but it is given up in *Azl*. The Prophet said : If a man cohabits with his wife, the reward of producing a child is written for him - such a child who becomes martyr fighting in the way of God. He said this in consideration of reward, because if a child is born like this, he will get reward for producing a cause in the way of God. This is possible if semen is thrown into uterus.

That birth-control by *Azl* is lawful is supported by *Qiyas* or inference from the Qurãn. Though there is no clear verse regarding it, yet it can be gathered therefrom by inference. It is this. It is not unlawful to give up marriage, or to give up sexual intercourse after marriage or to give up ejaculation of semen after sexual intercourse. It is true that rewards are given up on these actions, but absence of actions is not unlawful. There is no difference in these three things. A child is born after semen is thrown into uterus. Before it, there are four stages - (1) to marry, (2) then to cohabit, (3) then to have patience to eject semen after intercourse, (4) then to throw semen into the uterus and then to stay in that condition till semen is settled in uterus. The life of a child coming into existence has got some stages - (1) Semen in uterus should be mixed with female ova. If both are mixed, it is sin to destroy· it. There is no sin if they are not allowed to mix. (2) If it is created into a clot of blood and a lump of flesh, it is more hateable to destroy it. (3) If life is infused into that lump of flesh, it is most hateable to destroy it. (4) The last limit of this sin is to destroy the child when it is born. If the male semen is mixed with the blood of menses of a woman, it is condensed, as when something is mixed with milk, milk is condensed. It is just like proposal and acceptance which constitute an agreement or contract. Both things are necessary for a contract. If there is proposal but no acceptance, there is no sin in breaking it. The ejaculation of semen is like a proposal and its throwing into uterus is like its acceptance. If it is thrown outside, the proposal is lost. There is no sin in it. Therefore, to throw semen outside the uterus before it is mixed up with female ova is not sin.

Question. If there is no sin in throwing semen outside uterus, still it is bad as the object of semen is to produce a child and if it is not done, it is a secret *shirk.*

Answer. There are four objects of *Azl* : **(I)** To preserve the beauty and health of the wife and thus to enjoy her always. If semen is destroyed with these objects, it is not unlawful. **(2)** To prevent birth of too many children. It is not unlawful. To maintain too many children is very difficult. The verse of God guaranting maintenance of all creatures means perfection of God-reliance and perfection of merits and rewards but it is no sin to give up the highest stage of merits, just as it is no sin to protect wealth and properties and to hoard up for a limited period. This is the meaning of the following verse of God : There is no animal in the earth of which the maintenance is not upon God. **(3)** To take birth-control for fear of the birth of daughters. This is unlawful. The Arabs before Islam used to bury their daughters alive and they feared the birth of daughters. It was prohibited by the Qurān. If with the above object, marriage or sexual intercourse is given up, it will be committing sin, but these actions simply without that object are not sinful. If semen is thrown not into uterus with the above object, it will be sin. **(4)** To protect the honour of woman, to keep her neat and clean and to save her from maintaining children. To throw semen outside the uterus with these objects is unlawful.

If you question that the Prophet said "He who gives up marriage for fear of child-birth is not of us" the answer is that to do *Azl* is like not to marry and the meaning of "he is not of us" is that our *sunnat* or way is better. The Prophet also said: There is secret murder in *Azl* and he thereafter recited this verse : When those buried alive will be asked for which sin they were killed. The answer to the above verse is that there is an authentic *Hadis* about the legality of *Azl.* Secret murder in the above *Hadis* means secret *shirk.* It is *Makruh* and not unlawful. Hazrat Ali said : Life comes into being after seven stages. Then he read this verse : I have created man from dried clay, then 1 placed it as semen in its resting place, then I created semen into clot of blood, then the clot of blood into lump of flesh, then the lump of flesh into bones, then the bones covered with flesh and then I created it into another creation. In other words, I infused into it life. Then he recited this verse : When one buried alive will be asked for what fault he was murdered. There is in *Sahih Bukhari* and *Muslim* that Hazrat Jabir said : We used to practice *Azl* at the time of the Prophet and the Qurān was then being revealed. When this news reached the Prophet he did not prohibit us from it. There is another *Hadis* reported by Jabir : A man came to the Prophet and said : I have got a slave girl. She serves us and gives water to the palm trees. I cohabit with her but I don't wish that she should conceive. The Prophet said : Practice *Azl* with her if you wish but what has been decreed must come to pass. Then after sometime the man came to the Prophet and said : The slave girl has conceived. The Prophet said What has been decreed must come to pass. This is in *Sahih Bukhari* and *Muslim.*

(12) If the child is born, five rules shall have to be observed. (a) It is not good to be pleased with the birth of a son and displeased with the birth of a daughter. The Prophet said : If a man has got a daughter, teaches her good manners, gives her good food and gives charity to her out of what God has given him, she becomes the cause of fortune to him and makes the path to Paradise easy for him after saving him from Hell fire. The Prophet said : If a man has got two daughters or sisters and teaches them good manners upto their marriage, he and I will be in Paradise like these two fingers. The Prophet said: If a Muslim goes to market, purchases something and

after returning home gives it first to his daughters and not to the sons, God will look at him and God will not punish one to whom He will look. The Prophet said : If a man takes a good thing for his family from the market, its rewards are like those of charity. He should first give it to the hand of his daughter and then to that of his son. He who incurs pleasure of his daughter will get rewards of weeping in fear of God. If a man weeps for fear of God, God makes his body unlawful for Hell. The Prophet said : If a man has got three daughters or sisters and keeps patience at the loss by supplying their demands, God will admit him in Paradise. A man asked him : O Messenger of God! if a man has got two ? He said : Even if he has got two. The man again asked him : If he has got one ? He said : Even if he has got one.

(b) To give *Azan* to the ears of the child. The father of Rafe said : I have seen the Prophet proclaiming *Azan* into the ears of Hasan when he was born. The Prophet said : Give *Azan* to the right ear of the newly born child and *Iqamat* to his left ear. When the child begins to talk, teach him "There is no deity but God." This should be his first word. On the seventh day, make circumcision of his male organ. (c) Give good name to the child. The Prophet said : When you give name, give name of slavery. He said : The best of names are Abdullah and Abdur Rahman (slave of God). He said : Name according to the names of God and do not give surname according to my surname. The Prophet said : Don't unite my name and my surname. The Prophet said : On the Resurrection Day, you will be called by your names or the names of your fathers.

(4) Two goats for a son and one goat for a daughter should be sacrificed which is called *Aqiqah*. There is no harm if only one goat is sacrificed for a son. It is *sunnat* to give in charity gold or silver to the weight of the hairs of the child. The

Prophet ordered Hazrat Fatima to shave the head of Hussain on the seventh day and to give silver after weighing his hairs.

(5) Besmear the vertex of the child's head with dates or sweet things. Hazrat Asma'a said : Hazrat Abdullah b. Zubair was born at Quba. When he was brought before the Prophet, he prayed for him and besmeared dates on his body. Then he threw some of his saliva to his mouth. Then he besmeared dates on the sculp of his head and prayed for him. He is the first child born in Islam.

Divorce

Divorce is lawful, but of all the lawful things, the most detestable to God is divorce. God says : 'If they obey you, don't seek ways regarding them.' If your father dislikes her, give her divorce. Hazrat Ibn Omar said : I loved my wife very much, but my father Omar did not like her. When he ordered me to divorce her, I informed it to the Prophet. He said : O son of Omar! divorc e her. This shows that duty towards father is greater. God says : Don't drive her out of your house till she does indecent action openly. God says: There is no fault in getting release on payment of wealth. The Prophet said : If a woman seeks divorce from her husband without any reason, she will not get the fragrance of Paradise. In another narration Paradise is unlawful for her. In another narration, the Prophet said : The women who seek divorce are hypocrites.

Four matters at the time of divorce

(1) The husband will divorce the wife in her pure state and not at the time of menstrual discharge. Hazrat Ibn Omar divorced his wife at the time of her menstrual discharge. The Prophet said to Omar : Tell him to take her back and keep her till her menstrual discharge ends. Thereafter, she will have monthly menses and she will be pure. Then he may divorce

her or take her back. This is the period of waiting which God ordered. **(2)** Don't unite three divorces at a time. If he is repentant within the period of waiting, she may be taken back. **(3)** After divorce, give maintenance to the wife and presents. This is compulsory on the husband. **(4)** Don't disclose the secrets of wife at the time of divorce. There is such prohibition in authentic *Hadis*.

Duties of wife towards husband

(1) If the husband wants to enjoy her body, she should not refuse. The Prophet said : If the wife of a man dies while he is pleased with her, she will enter Paradise. The Prophet said: When a woman prays five times a day, fasts the month of *Ramazan*, saves her private parts and obeys her husband, she will enter Paradise of her Lord. The Prophet said about women: They bear children, give birth to children and show affection to the children. Even though they do not come to their husbands, they will enter Paradise if they pray. The Prophet said : I peeped into Hell and found that the majority of its inmates are women. It was asked : Why ? O Messenger of God! He said : They take recourse to much curse and deny relatives. There is in another *Hadis* : I peeped into Paradise and found that there are few women there. I asked : Where are the women ? He said : Two things of reddish colour stood as a stumbling block against them gold and *Zafran* (ornaments and varied dresses). Once a girl came to the Prophet and asked: I don't want to get married. The Prophet said : Yes, get married and it is better. A woman of Khasham tribe once came to the Prophet and asked him : I want to marry, but what are the rights of the husband ? He said : When he wants her, she will not refuse it even though she remains on a camel's back. She will not give anything of his house in charity without his permission. If she does it, she will commit a sin and her husband will get rewards. She will not keep optional fast without his permission. If she does it and becomes hungry and thirsty, it will not be accepted from her. If she goes out of his house without his permission, the angels curse him till she returns to his house or till she repents. The Prophet said : If I would have ordered anybody to prostrate before another, I would have ordered a woman to prostrate before her husband, as duties towards him are many. The Prophet said : When a woman stays within her house, she becomes more near to God. Her prayer in the courtyard of her house is more meritorious than her prayer in mosque. Her prayer in a room is better than her prayer in her courtyard. The Prophet said : A woman is like a private part. When she comes out, the devil holds her high. He said : There are ten private parts of a women. When she gets married, her husband keeps one private parts covered ; and when she dies, grave covers other parts. The duties of a wife towards her husband are many, two out of them are essentially necessary. The first one is to preserve chastity and to keep secret the words of her husband and the second thing is not to demand unnecessary things and to refrain from unlawful wealth which her husband earns.

(2) Don't spend extravagantly the properties of your husband but protect them. The Prophet said : It is not lawful to give in charity the food of his house without his permission but give such ready food as would be spoilt. Asma'a said to her daughter at the time of her marriage : You are now going to spend such a life where you shall have to live long and you are going to the bed of such a person with whom you have got no acquaintance. You are going to love one with whom you had no love before. Make for him such a world which will be heaven for you, prepare for him such a bed which will be a pillar for you. Be such a slave for him that he might become your slave. Don't go willingly to him, lest you become

to him an object of hatred. Don't remain far from him, lest he may forget you. When he remains near you, be near him. When he stays distant from you. Save your nose, ears and eyes. Let him not get from you except sweet smile. Let him not hear from you except sweet words. Let him not see in you except beauty.

(3) She would engage herself in good works in the absence of her husband and make enjoyment in the presence of her husband. The Prophet said : If a woman inflicts trouble on her husband, the black-eyed. Hur says : Don't inflict trouble on him. May God destroy you. Now he is with you, perchance he will leave you soon and come to us.

(4) Don't express sorrow for more than four months and ten days when your husband dies. The Prophet said : It is not lawful for a woman who believes in God and the next world to grieve for more than three days except in the case of the death of her husband for whom she should grieve for four months and ten days and she should stay in her husband's house during this time.

(5) She should do all household affairs to her utmost capacity.

CHAPTER III

SECTION 1

Earnings : Trade and Commerce

God made the next world the place of rewards and punishments and this world the place of efforts, troubles and earnings. Earning is not the aim of human life but it is a means to an end. The world is the seed ground for the hereafter and the door to enter it. There are three kinds of men - **(1)** One kind of men forgets the return and makes the earning of livelihood as the sole object of his life. He is one of those who will be destroyed. **(2)** Another kind of men makes the return to the next world as his sole object of life and remains busy in earning his livelihood therefore. **(3)** The third kind of men is near the middle path who keeps his goal of return to the next world as fixed and takes to trade and commerce for livelihood. He who does not adopt the straight path in earning livelihood will not get the pleasure of straight path. He who takes the world as the means of earning the next world adopts the rules and regulations of *Shariat* in search of it and gets the pleasure of the middle path.

Merits of earning livelihood Qurān : God says : I have created the day for earning livelihood. God says : I have placed in it provisions for you. You are grateful but little. God says : There is no fault in searching livelihood from your Lord. God says: A party travel in the world to search for the grace of God. God says: Spread out in the earth and seek the wealth of God.

Hadis : The Prophet said : There is such a sin of which there is no expiation except anxieties of earning livelihood. He said : The truthful tradesman will resurrect on the Resurrection Day with the truthful and the martyrs. He said : He who refrains from begging, making efforts for family members and being kind to the neighbours searches livelihood lawfully and will meet with God with such a face which will be bright like the full moon. One day, the Prophet was seated in the mosque of Madinah with companions, when a stout and strong young man was going to his shop running by the mosque. The companions said : Alas for this young man ! Had his body and health run in the way of God ! The Prophet then said : Don't say like this. If this young man runs with the object of not depending on others and refraining from begging, he is in the way of God. If he makes efforts for livelihood of his weak parents or weak children, he is in the way of God. If he tries to show his health out of pride, he is in the way of the devil. The Prophet said : God loves one who adopts the path of labour to save himself from depending on others. God hates one who learns education thinking it a means of earning. The Prophet said : God loves the believing businessman. He said: The best lawful earning is that which one gets by his own lawful earning. If he obeys the rules of *Shariat* in his business, it is the greatest lawful earnings of his own.

The Prophet said : Take to trade and commerce, because nine-tenths of the source of earnings is in trade and commerce. Once the Prophet Jesus asked a man : What do you do ? He said : I make divine service. He asked : Who gives you food? He said : My brother. He said : Your brother makes better divine service than you. The Prophet said : I have left no such instruction which if obeyed will not bring you near Paradise and keep you distant from Hell. I have left no such prohibition which, if obeyed, will not keep you distant from Paradise and bring you near Hell. The trusted spirit infused into my soul saying : No man will die till his provision does not finish even though he wishes it. So fear God and seek livelihood in a lawful manner. I enjoin you to earn livelihood in a just manner. Let nobody say : Give up to seek livelihood. Then he said at last : Let not the delay in earning livelihood give you encouragement to earn it illegally, because disobedience to God cannot bring what He has got. The Prophet said : The markets are the repositories of food of God. He who comes to them gets something therefrom. The Prophet said : If anyone of you gathers fuels with a rope and searches livelihood by bearing it upon his back, it is better than to beg of men whether they give or not. He said: if a man opens a door of begging upon him, God will open for him seventy doors of begging.

Wise sayings : The wise Luqman advised his son ! O dear son! shut up poverty by lawful earnings, because he who is poor earns three habits - laxity in religious actions, weakness in intellect and loss of manliness. Greater fault than these three is to keep it secret from the people. Hazrat Omar said : Let none of you retrain from earning livelihood and say: O God! give me provision. Know it for certain that the heaven will not shower rain of gold and silver. Hazrat Jabir was once sowing seeds in his field. Hazrat Omar said to him: If you do good, you will not depend on the people. it will save your religion and you will be honoured by them. Hazrat Ibrahim b. Adham was asked : Who is better of the two - a truthful merchant and a worshipper ? He said : A truthful merchant is dearer to me, as he is in *Jihad*. The devil comes to him in the path of weight and measure and buy and sale. He makes *jihad* with him. Hazrat Omar said : No place in dearer to me than that where I search livelihood for my family members and where I buy and sell. When a strong tempest arose in the sea, the passengers of a boat asked Ibrahim b. Adham : Don't you look to this calamity ? He said : I don't consider it a calamity. Depending on men for a necessity is a calamity. Once the Prophet asked about livelihood of beasts and birds. He said : They come out hungry in the morning and return with full belly in the evening. In other words, they come out in search of their livelihood. The companions of the Prophet used to do trade and commerce in land and sea and worked in gardens. It is sufficient to follow them.

Once Hazrat Aozayi saw the sage Ibrahim b. Adham to bear a load of fuels on his back and said : O Abu Ishaq! why are you taking such trouble ? Our brethren are sufficient for you. He said : O Abu Amir! leave me alone in this matter, as I have come to know that if a man waits in a place of disgrace in search for earning lawful livelihood, Paradise is sure for him.

The object of trade and commerce is to gain either necessary livelihood or to gain enormous wealth. The latter is the root of attachment to the world which is the basis of all sins. It is better for four persons not to beg : (1) One who is busy with physical divine service (2) The friend of God who is busy in exercise of soul and spiritual learnings. (3) One who is *Mufti* (gives legal decisions) and one who is *Muhaddis* (one who teaches *Hadis*) and one who is learned and teaches. (4) One who is busy in the administration of the affairs of the Muslims like rulers and kings. These four kinds of persons remain busy in the affairs of the public or in their religious affairs. The Prophet was not commissioned to be a tradesman, rather he was directed to glorify God. For this reason, when Hazrat Abu Bakr became Caliph, other companions advised him to give up his business and they fixed for him a monthly allowance from the State Treasury. He advised his sons to return it to the Treasury after his death.

SECTION 2

Four things are necessary in earnings - lawful earnings, justice, kindness and fear of religion. We shall describe them separately.

Lawful earnings

Earnings can be searched in six ways : (1) Bargaining in buy and sale, (2) Trade on interest, (3) Taking advance payment, (4) To work on wages for labour and to accept pay and rental, (5) To do business through others advancing capital and (6) Joint business in fixing shares. To know the rules of *Shariat* in these concerns is compulsory, as to search knowledge is compulsory for every Muslim. It was reported that Omar used to visit the markets and instruct some inexperienced tradesmen on whipping them and say: Nobody shall carry on business in our markets who has got no knowledge of business.

(1) Bargaining in buy and sale : There are three subjects in it – (a) Buyer and seller. (b) commodities for sale, (c) and contract for buy and sale.

(a) With regard to the first thing, no transaction is valid with a minor, insane, slave or blind man. No minor and insane man have got any sin. No transaction is valid with a slave except with the permission of his master. Transaction with a blindman is not lawful except with the consent of his representative. It is lawful to have transaction with an unbeliever but it is unlawful to sell arms to them.

(b) Commodities for sale : There are six conditions in it– (1) These must not be impure, such as dog, pig, dung, stool, wine, teeth of elephant, fat of impure animals. (2) Things of sale should be beneficial and necessary. Scorpions, rats, snakes and worms and insects under the earth are unlawful for transactions. Instruments of songs, toys and idols of animals are not lawful for buy and sale. Clothes on which there are animal pictures are not lawful for sale. (3) Commodities for sale must be in possession of the seller. (4) These should be fit for transfer according to *Shariat*. A fugitive slave, fish in water, birds in air, foetus in womb of an animal, milk in udder cannot lawfully be sold. (5) Things for sale must be known, fixed and certain and not unfixed and uncertain. (6) Things to be sold must be in the possession of the owner. If the buyer sells it before possessing it, it will be unlawful.

(c) **Contract for buy and sale** : The contract for buy and sale must be expressed in clear and unambiguous terms. Intention plays an important part in it. No condition can lawfully be imposed by one party after agreement is final. Auction sale is lawful if the terms are proclaimed beforehand. Imam Shafayi held such auction as unlawful.

(2) Transaction of Interest

God made interest unlawful and there is strict order of prohibition regarding it. The question of interest arises in only two cases - in transactions of cash money, gold and silver and of food stuffs. Interest occurs in these two cases only under two conditions : (1) If sale is held on credit and not in cash, that is, not to hand in hand transaction and (2) if more in quantity is taken in lieu of less quantity of the same kind of thing. It is unlawful to sell a fixed quantity of gold or silver for a fixed quantity of more gold or silver on credit. It is not lawful to receive in cash the value of a certain thing which is to be delivered in future. Three things are to be observed in case of gold and silver. (1) Counterfeit coins in a great meanuer cannot be taken in lieu of less quantity of pure coins. This kind of transaction is unlawful. An inferior quality of a thing cannot be taken in lieu of a good quantity of the same thing. (2) There is no fault in selling silvers in more quantity in lieu of gold of small quantity, because they are of different kinds of things and not of the same kind. (3) If gold and silver are mixed and the quantity of each is not known, the transaction is not lawful.

Food-stuffs : The food-stuffs of seller and buyer are of different kinds or of the same kinds. When food stuffs are of the same kinds, it is lawful to exchange them and the rules of the same kind of things are applicable in this case. If a man gives a goat and takes in exchange mutton on credit or in cash, it is unlawful. To give wheat and to take in exchange bread on credit or in cash is unlawful. If milk is given to a milk trader and if in exchange clarified butter, butter or cheese is taken, it will be unlawful.

(3) Advance payment

Some conditions are to be observed in advance payment of money and things. (1) The quantity and kind of a thing for which advance payment is made should be fixed. (2) In the place of contract, the principal thing or money shall be paid in advance. If both of them become separate before possessing the thing, the transaction will be unlawful. In the place of contract, the thing or money shall be delivered. (3) The thing that is given in advance must be an exchangeable commodity such as food stuffs, animal, minerals, cotton, milk, meat etc. (4) The weight and quantity of the thing given in advance must be fixed. (5) Time of the delivery of the thing should be fixed. (6) The place should be ascertained in which the thing is to be delivered, as there might be difference of price in case of place where commodity is to be delivered. (7) The thing to be advanced should have no connection with another thing, such as crops of this land, fruits of that garden.

(8) Transaction of rare and precious things on advance payment is not lawful, such as transaction of rare jewel, a beautiful slave or slave girl.

(4) Wages, salary and rental

Wages : There are two rules of wages - remuneration and profit. If wages are in cash, it must be fixed like the price of a thing sold. If the remuneration is salary or rental, its kind and quantity should be fixed. It is not lawful to let out a house on rent on condition that the tenant must construct the building or house as the expense of a house is unknown. To give skin in lieu of taking skin from the body, to give skin in lieu of carrying an animal and to give outer cover for cushing wheat are all unlawful.

(2) Profit : The object of industry in business is to gain profit. (a) The remuneration of a work must be fixed. (b) The remuneration given to a broker is unlawful. To maintain an animal in lieu of milk, to maintain a garden of grapes in lieu of grapes and to take lease of a garden in lieu of its fruits are unlawful. (c) One must possess necessary strength to do a thing for which his salary is fixed. It is unlawful to engage a weak man in a work which is beyond his strength and capacity. (d) It is unlawful to appoint a representative in a compulsory duty, for instance, to appoint warrior in *Jihad,* or to appoint a representative in divine services. But it is lawful to make pilgrimage on behalf of another who is otherwise incapable to observe it, to bury or carry a deadman, to be an *Imam* in prayer for fixed term, to proclaim *Azan,* to teach the Qurān and such other things and to take remuneration for these works.

(5) Partnership business : There are three things in partnership business : (a) Principal, (b) profit, (c) and kind of business. With regard to the principal in business, it will be fixed and paid in cash. Principal is to be handed over to the managing agent. It is unlawful to advance things and not money as principal. **(b)** It should be settled beforehand what share of the profit the capitalists should get and what share the businessman will get. If the profit is fixed for the trade, it is not legal. **(c)** No condition should be attached in a partnership business of fixed commodities and fixed time. The businessman becomes the representative or agent of business who can utilise the capital according to his wish in the business.

Partnership business is of four kinds. Out of them three kinds arc unlawful and the fourth kind only is lawful. It is unlawful to divide the works in a joint business. If a partner advances capital and another partner possessing honour uses only his influence in the business, it will be unlawful. If the capital comes equally from the sharers with the profit divided equally among them, it is lawful.

SECTION 3

Justice to be observed in business

It is unlawful to give trouble to the public by unjust dealings and oppression and by deceit and fraud. There are two kinds of loss by deceit and fraud. One kind of loss is for the general public and another for some special persons. The loss of the public is of many kinds. One kind of public loss arises from hoarding of food stuffs. It is done with the object of getting enhanced price of food stuffs. It is an oppression to the people in general. There is curse of *Shariat* on the hoarders of food stuffs. The Prophet said : If a man hoards up food stuffs when they are dear for forty days to get more price, he is displeased with God and God also is displeased with him. Someone said that he commits sin of murdering all people. Hazrat Ali said : If a man hoards up food stuffs even for a day to gain increased price, his heart becomes hard. The Prophet said : He who takes food stuffs from one place to another and sells them on that day according to the market rate will get the rewards of charity. In another narration : He will get the rewards of setting a slave free. The Qurãn says : If a man intends to transgress the limits unjustly, I will give him taste of a grievous chastisement. This applies to hoarding up for getting more profit.

A certain pious merchant sent food stuffs on a boat in the sea to his agent at Basra with the instruction that he should sell it as soon as they reached him. When the commodities reached Basra, the merchants told him to hoard them for one week and then sell, because they would bring greater profit. His agent did accordingly and sold them after one week with increased price and informed his master. His master wrote to him : You have acted contrary to my wish. It was not my wish to make loss in religion and gain profit in commodities. I have committed sin of hoarding. Therefore, distribute all the proceeds to the poor and the destitute. In that case, I may save myself from the sin of hoarding.

It is, therefore, prohibited to hoard up food stuffs for getting greater profit, but it is connected with the kinds of food and time. It is not prohibited to hoard up such kinds of things which are not principal food stuffs for livelihood. Such as medicine, Za'afran etc. There are differences of opinion with regard to the hoarding of things which are near principal food stuffs, such as meat, fruits and such kinds of food which appease hunger and which are taken as alternatives of principal crops. There are things which become unlawful for hoarding regard being had to the time when food stuffs are not easily available and there are dire needs of men for them. To make delay in selling food stuffs is harmful to the public. But when there are no such circumstances it is lawful to make some delay as the public do not suffer by it. When there is famine, it is harmful then to hoard up even honey, clarified butter, meat and such things. So the legality and illegality of hoarding of food stuffs becomes according to the harms caused or not caused to the public.

Use of counterfeit coins : It is an oppression on the public to use counterfeit coins. The first man who uses such coin will get the sins of every person who subsequently transfers it to other persons. This is like introducing a bad custom. A certain sage said : To transfer a counterfeit coin to another is worse than the theft of a hundred coins, as theft is confined to a sin, while the circulation of a counterfeit coin is not limited and it continues years after years unless they are destroyed. God says : I shall write what they sent in advance (during their life time) and what they will send (after their death). God says : Man will be informed what they sent in advance before and what they will send latter.

Five rules of counterfeit coins

(1) If a man has got such counterfeit coins, he will throw them in wells, rivers and tanks. (2) knowledge of counterfeit coins is necessary to every merchant to save himself and to protect the Muslims from them. (3) If he communicates their nature to others, he will not be absolved from its sin if he knows about its nature at the time of receiving it. (4) He who receives counterfeit coins to destroy them is absolved from its sin and receives the blessings of the Prophet : May God show kindness to one whose buy is easy, whose sale is easy; whose clearance of debt is easy and whose demand is easy. (5) A counterfeit coin is one which has got nothing of gold or silver. The coin in which there is something of gold or silver cannot be called counterfeit. But in a place where a certain kind of coin is prevalent, another kind of coin is not lawful there.

(2) It is an act of impression if a merchant is caused loss. It is justice not to do loss to a Muslim. The general rule is love for others what you love for yourself. This should be observed in four dealings - (l) not to praise one's thing, (2) not to conceal the defects of one's things from others. (3) not to conceal the weights and measures of a thing, (4) and not to cheat in respect of a price of a thing. To say that a thing possesses a quality which it has not got is falsehood. If a buyer purchases a thing on the basis of that description, it will be an act of deceit. Account will be taken of every word uttered. God says : There is a guard over man of what one utters. The Prophet said - In false oath, there is much loss of commodities and there is less profit. The Prophet said : God will not look on three persons on the Resurrection Day - a proud disobedient man, one who deals harshly after charity and one who sells things by oath.

Not to conceal defects of commodities

One who conceals defects is an oppressor, a deceit and a fraud. Deceit is unlawful. Once the prophet saw a man selling food stuffs and it pleased him. The Prophet then entered his hand unto the interior of the food stuffs and found moisture in them. He asked him : Why there are wet things in them ? He said : Rain melted them. He said : Has not the rain fallen on the top of the crops ? The Prophet then said : He who defrauds us is not of us. The Prophet took allegiance of Islam from Jarir and when he was about to go, he took promise from him that he should do good to the Muslims. Thereafter, whenever Jarir was present at the time of transaction of a thing, he disclosed the defects of it and gave him option to purchase. Someone said to him : You will not get profit by it. He said : I made promise to the Prophet that I shall seek good of every Muslim. The Prophet said : It is unlawful to sell a thing without disclosing its defects and one who knows it will commit sin if he does not give precaution to him.

A man had a cow. He milked his cow everyday and sold milk after mixing water therein. One day there was flood which drowned the cow. One of his sons said to him : The waters which you mixed with milk gathered together and washed away the cow by a strong current. The Prophet said : When the buyer and seller tell truth and wish good, blessing is given to their transaction. When they conceal and tell falsehood, blessing is withdrawn from them. There is in another *Hadis* God's hand remains upon two partners till they do not commit treachery to each other. When they commit breach of trust, He withdraws his hand from both.

It becomes easy to seek good of the people if one knows that the profit in the next world is better than the wealth and treasures of the world and that these will end with the end of life, but his sins and virtues will remain. So, how can a man take to evil things instead of good ones ? The Prophet said : The word 'There is no deity but God' will remove the wrath of God from the created beings till they do not give superiority of worldly affairs over their next worldly affairs. There is in another *Hadis* : He who utters 'There is no deity but God' out of sincere faith, will enter Paradise. He was asked : What is sincere faith ? He said : To be careful of what God prohibited. He also said : 'He who regards unlawful thing as lawful does not believe in the Qurãn.' Deceit in buying and selling and in mutual transactions is unlawful.

(3) Don't conceal in weights and measures : Take recourse to just balance and weight. God says : Woe to the defaulters in weights and measures, those who take full measure when they take from men and who give less when they measure out to them or weigh to them (83:1). The way to be rescued from this is the following. Give more when you measure out to others and take less when you take by measure from the people. When the Prophet purchased something, he used to tell the seller : Weigh according to the amount of price and give measure a little more. Hazrat Sulaiman said to his son : O dear son! sin enters between two transactors just as seeds enter into mills. God says : Don't exceed the limit in weights and measures and establish just balance and don't reduce the measure (35 : 8). He who takes more and gives less falls within this verse : Woe to the defaulters who take full measure when they take from men, the verse (33 : 1).

(4) Tell truth in selling commodities and do not conceal anything. The Prophet said : Don't meet the riders who bring commodities. The owner of the commodities has got option to break an agreement after they are brought in the market with those who meet them in advance.

SECTION 4

To do good in mutual transactions

God ordered us to adopt good and just dealings and to do good to the people. God says : Show kindness as God has shown kindness on you. God says : God enjoins justice and doing good (16:90). God says : God's mercy is near those who do good. Doing good means an act which does benefit to another. Though it is not compulsory, it brings rewards and ranks. The rank of doing good can be obtained in one of the following six actions

(a) Not to make much profit : Sale is for profit in a business and there is no profit unless a thing is charged more than the price by which it is bought. To take less profit is '*Ihsan*' doing good but to take greater profit is not unlawful. Once a man bought a bundle of cloth from the salesman of Yunus b. Obaid for 400 dirhams which was to be sold for 200 dirhams to the buyer. He said to his salesman : Why have you not loved for another which you love for yourself ? Return half. Hazrat Ali used to roam in the bazar of Kufa with a stick and say : O merchants! take your dues and return the dues of others. Don't refuse little profit or else you will be deprived of greater profit. Hazrat Abdur Rahman b. Auf was asked What is the reason of your success ? He said : Three things - (1) I never refused any profit, (2) I sold everything in cash and not on credit. (3) I did not make delay in selling a thing.

(b) To suffer loss : If a buyer buys from a poor man, there is no harm to buy at a higher price to show good to him and to enter into this prayer of the Prophet : May God like a person who makes his buy easy and purchase easy ? When he purchases a thing from a rich man, he may search for additional profit. Hazrat Omar did not do any deceit and nobody could ever deceive him.

(c) To show good and to treat well at the time of acceptance of price and realisation of dues. It is expressed in three ways - (1) to accept less price at times ; (2) to grant time when realising the dues ; (3) and to demand in a good manner. The Prophet said : May God show mercy on easy purchase, easy sale, easy payment of price and easy payment of debt. Consider the prayer of the Prophet as valuable. The Prophet said : Forgive and you will be forgiven. He said : If a man grants time to a needy man to repay debt or remits it, God will make his account easy.

In another narration : God will give him shade on the day when there will be no shade except that of the Throne. The Prophet mentioned about such a person who oppressed his soul very much and was engaged in sins. When he will be presented on the Judgment Day, it will be found that he has got no good deeds. He will be asked : Did you no do any good deed ? He will say : No, but I advanced loan to the people. I used to say to my children : Grant time to the solvent and remit the poor. God then will say : I am more fit in this matter than you. Then God will forgive him. The Prophet said: I saw it written on the door of Paradise : One act of charity will bring ten rewards and one act of loan will bring eighteen rewards. It is said here by way of explanation that charity may not always reach the truly poor, but none but the needy bears the disgrace of loan. If a man sells something to a man and does not then realise its price and does not demand it, it is considered as a loan. When Hasan Basri sold his ass for four hundred dirhams, the purchaser said to him : Reduce it by one hundred dirhams. He reduced it so. He again said : Do good to me. He said : I remit you another one hundred dirhams. Then he accepted two hundred dirhams and said : In this way, good is done to a person. There is in *Hadis* : Accept your dues with pardon, whether it is paid up in full or not, then God will make your account easy.

(d) To do good at the time of payment of debt : To pay debt in a good manner is '*Ihsan*' or doing good to another. Clear the debt before demand. Going to the creditor personally and not to wait for its demand is considered as doing good. The Prophet said : He is the best among you who pays his debt in a good manner. Clear it before the time fixed for it and pay something more than the principal. The Prophet said: If a man intends to pay at the time of taking loan, God entrusts him to His angels to keep him safe. They pray for him till he clears his debt. Once a creditor came to the Prophet to demand payment of a debt due from him after the expiry of its time. He had then no means to clear it. The man used harsh words to the Prophet. The companions were about to attack him when he said : Leave him, as a creditor has got a right to say. The Prophet said : Help your brother, be he oppressed or an oppressor. He was asked : How can we help an oppressor ? He said : To prohibit him from oppression is to help him.

(e) To accept return of a thing sold if the buyer thinks that he has suffered loss, as nobody except a repentant or suffering man intends to return a purchased thing. None should remain satisfied with causing loss to his brother Muslim. The Prophet said : If a man forgives the guilt of a repentant man, God will forgive his sins on the Resurrection Day.

(f) To sell things to the needy on credit and not to demand from them when they are in want and do not become solvent. The religious men of yore kept account books. In those books, they wrote the names of unknown poor customers. They were forgiven if they could not pay their dues.

Trade and commerce are the places for trial of religious persons. For this reason, it has been said that when the neighbours of a person praise him, when the companions of a man in journey praise him and when the fellow tradesmen in the market praise him, don't complain against his good character. Once a witness went to depose before Hazrat Omar. He said to him : Bring one to me who knows you. When he brought a person to him, the man began to praise his character. Hazrat Omar asked him : Is he your closest neighbour ? He said : No. He asked him : Were you his companion in a journey? He said : No. He asked him : Did you carry on business with him ? He said : No. He said : So, you don't know him. He then said to the man : Go, take one who knows you.

SECTION 5

Not to be forgetful of religion and the next world in business

Know, O dear readers! that nobody should forget his religion and the next world his destination during the course of his trade and commerce and earning livelihood. If he forgets it, he will then be ruined and he will be then one of those who sell their next world in lieu of this world, but the wise man is he who protects his capital. His real capital is his religion and matters relating to the next world. A certain sage said : The best commodity in this world to a wise man is what is absolutely necessary for him in this world. The necessary things in this world are praise-worthy in the next world. Hazrat Muaz b. Jabal gave his death instruction by saying : What has been decreed for you from the fortunes of this world will surely come to you, but it is more necessary on your part to look to your fortunes of the next world. So begin your actions for the fortunes of the next world. God says : Don't forget your portion in this world. In other words, don't forget the portion of your fate in the next world from your portion of fate of this world, as the world is a seed ground for the next world.

Seven things make the religion of a business man perfect.

(1) Keep your faith firm and perfect and have good intent in business at the start of your business. Do business with the objects of saving yourself from depending on others, to restrain from the greed of what is with the people, to remain satisfied with lawful earnings, to earn keeping on the paths of religion and to maintain family. Intend to do good to the Muslims and love for them what you love for yourself. Follow the path of equity, justice and *Ihsan* as mentioned above and enjoin good and forbid evils you find in the market.

(2) Intend to be upon the duties of *Farze Kifayah* like trade, commerce, industry thinking that, if the various kinds of trade and industry are given up, it will be difficult for the people to manage their livelihood and the majority of the people would be destroyed. One people are responsible for one kind of work. If all remain busy in only one kind of work, all other works would remain idle and hence the people would be destroyed. With this object, the Prophet said : The difference of my people is a blessing. There is in *Hadis*: The business of cloth is the best of all your trades and the work of sewing is the best of all industries. There is in another *Hadis*: Had the inmates of Paradise had trades, they would have the trade of cloth. Had the inmates of Hell had any trade, they would have carried on business of exchange of coins. There are four works in which there is fear of lessening of intellect – weaving of cloth, sale of cotton, weaving of thread and teaching, because in these works mostly women, boys and men of little intellect are engaged. As intellect increases in association of intellectuals, so also it lessens in association of less intellectual men.

(3) Let not the worldly markets be blocks of the next worldly markets which are mosques. God says : There are some men whom merchandise or buying and selling cannot divert from the remembrance of God, from establishing prayer and paying poor rate. God says : God gives order to glorify and remember His name in the houses. So you should work for the next world in the early part of the day till market time, remain attached to the mosque and remain busy in divine service after the division of times. The earlier sages fixed the early and last part of the day for the next world and the middle part for this world. There is in *Hadis* : If the angels who write records of deeds write therein God's *Zikr* and good deeds in the early part and the last part of the day, God forgives sins between these two times. There is in *Hadis* : The angels of day and night meet with one another at the time of morning and *Asr* prayers. God then says : In what condition have you found My servants ? They say : We have seen them praying and came from them in their praying state. God says : I bear witness in your presence that I have forgiven them.

(4) Be attached to the *Zikr* of God in addition to the above duties in the markets. God's remembrance in the markets is better. The Prophet said : One remembering God among the heedless is like a warrior behind a fleeing enemy or like a living man among the dead. In another narration : Or like a living tree amidst dried trees. The Prophet said: If a man says after entering the market the following : 'There is no deity but God, the Single, there is no partner for Him, His is the kingdom and for Him is all praise, He gives life and takes life, He is eternal and will not die, in His hands, there is good and He is powerful over all things'-God rewards him with thousands of merits. Hazrat Omar said: O God! I seek refuge to Thee from infidelity and all the sins committed in the markets. O God! I seek refuge to Thee from the oath of the sinners and the wailings of the losers. The Prophet said : Fear God wherever you are.' Markets, mosques and houses are all the same for those who fear God. They live for God and die for God and God is the corner stone of their life. A certain sage said : He who loves the next world loves a true life. He who loves this world remains thirsty.

(5) Don't be too greedy in markets and in business. There is in *Hadis* : Don't travel in the sea except for Pilgrimage, *Umrah* and *Jihad*. The Prophet said : The worst of places is the market. The sage Hammed used to carry on wool rugs. When he got profit of nearly six annas, he used to close his business. Once Ibrahim b. Adham said to a person who was

going to his business of pottery : You are seeking livelihood but death seeks you.

(6) Keep away from doubtful things even after giving up unlawful things. Leave the places of the earnings of doubt and restrain yourself from eating doubtful things. Once a man brought milk to the Prophet who asked him : Wherefrom has this milk come to you ? He said - We have got it from goats. He asked : Wherefrom have you got goats ? He said - From such and such a place. Then he drank it and said : We are a people of Prophets. We have been forbidden to eat except good things and to do except good deeds. He said : The believers have been ordered to do the things which the Prophet have been ordered to do. God says : O believers! eat of the good things We have provided you (2 : 172). The Prophet asked the source of a thing and the source of its source and not beyond that. The Prophet did not enquire about everything. Don't do business with one who has got connection with oppression, breach of trust, theft and interest. The Prophet said : He who prays for long life of an oppressor, loves to be disobedient to God in His world. He said : When any transgressor is praised, God becomes displeased. He also said: He who honours a transgressor, helps the destruction of Islam.

(7) Adjust accounts of your business with everybody. Accounts will be taken of you on the Resurrection Day of your business with everybody. A wise man said : I saw a merchant in dream and asked him : What treatment has God meted out to you ? He said : Fifty thousand account books have been opened before me. I asked : Are all these records of sin ? He said : You will find one record for each person you have dealt with in the world. All have been recorded in these account books.

CHAPTER IV

Halāl and Harām (lawful and unlawful things)

The Prophet said : It is compulsory on every Muslim to seek lawful earnings. He termed this compulsory subject as a thing of wisdom for a wise man out of other compulsory things. Lawful things are clear and unlawful things are also clear. Between these two, there are doubtful things which are not clear and difficult to know. All things are limited within these three things. This will be discussed in seven sections.

SECTION I

(1) Merits of lawful earnings and condemnation of unlawful earnings

Qurān : God says : Eat of the good things and do good deeds (2 : 168). God ordered for eating good things before doing good deeds. The object of this order is eating of lawful things. God says : Don't eat properties of one another unjustly (2 : 188). God says : O believers! fear God and give up what remains of interest if you are believers (2:278). God says : If you do not do it, then be prepared to fight with God and His Prophet (2 : 289). Then He says : If you repent, then for you is the capital. Then He said : Those who turn away from that are the inmates of Hell. They will abide therein. At first, eating of interest, then call for fight with God and His Apostle and last of all residing in Hell have been mentioned. There are innumerable verses regarding lawful and unlawful things.

Hadis : The Prophet said : It is compulsory on every Muslim to seek lawful earnings. The Prophet said : He who makes efforts to maintain his family out of lawful earnings is like a fighter in the way of God and he who seeks lawful earnings after restraining himself will get the rank of a martyr. The Prophet said : If a man eats lawful food for forty days, God illumines his heart and lets flow wisdom from his heart through his tongue. In another narration : God grants him renunciation in the world. Once Hazrat Sa'ad said to the Prophet : Pray to God that He may accept my invocation. The Prophet said : Eat lawful food and for that your invocation will be accepted. The Prophet mentioned the worldly addicted men and said : There are many men who have got dishevelled hairs, dust laden dresses, are tired in journey, whose food is unlawful, whose dress in unlawful, and who have been maintained by unlawful food. If they raise their hands and say : 'O Lord! O Lord!' how can their invocation be accepted? The Prophet said : An angel residing in Baitul Muqaddas proclaims every night : *Saraf* and *Adal* will not be accepted from a person who eats unlawful food. *Saraf* means optional and *sunnat* actions and *Adal* means compulsory duties. In other words, compulsory duties and optional duties will not be accepted from him. The Prophet said : If a man purchases a cloth with ten dirhams and if one dirham out of them is unlawful, his prayer will not be accepted till a portion of that cloth remains in his body. The Prophet said : The fire of Hell is fit for the flesh which has been grown by unlawful food. The Prophet said : If a man does not care wherefrom he earns his wealth, God will not care by which path he will enter Hell. He said : There are ten shares of worship, nine of which are in lawful earnings. The Prophet said : He who passes times upto evening in search of lawful earnings passes the night in a state of his sins being forgiven and rises at dawn when God remains pleased with him.

The Prophet said : If a man earns by sinful acts and gives it in charity or action of kindness or spends it in the way of God. God will throw him into Hell after collecting everything. The Prophet said : The best of your religion is to keep away from unlawful things. He said : If a man meets God after refraining from unlawful things. God will give him reward of the entire Islam. In an earlier scripture, God said with regard to those who refrained from unlawful food : I feel ashamed to take their accounts. The Prophet said : One dirham of interest is more serious to God than thirty fornications. The Prophet said : Stomach is the fountain of body and the veins come out of it. When the stomach is sound, the veins come out with health, and when it is unsound, they come out with disease. Food in religion is like the foundation of a building. When the foundation is strong and firm, the building stands straight and it can be raised up, and if the foundation is weak and curved, the building inclines to a side. God says - Is not he who establishes God-fear and God's pleasure in the foundation of his religion better than he who lays foundation by the side of Hell fire ? The Prophet said : The wealth which a man earns from unlawful things will not be accepted from him even if it is given in charity. If he leaves it after his death, he will increase the fire of Hell therewith. Many traditions have been mentioned in this chapter on earnings and I don't wish to repeat them here.

Wise sayings : It has been reported that once Hazrat Abu Bakr drank a little milk given by his female slave and asked her about it. She said : I prophesied to a people who gave it to me for that. Then he thrust the fronts of his fingers into his throat and vomited in such a way that his life was in danger.

Then he said : O God! I pray to Thee for forgiveness of what remains attached to my throat and to my stool. In another narration, it is said that when the Prophet was informed of it, he said : Don't you know that Abu Bakr does not allow anything to his belly except lawful food ? In a similar way, Hazrat Omar drank the milk of a camel of *Zakat* through mistake. He thrust his fingers into his throat and vomited it. Hazrat Ayesha said : You are heedless of the best divine service. That is to be safe from eating unlawful food. Hazrat Fuzail said : He who takes care of what thing he admits in his belly, God records him as *Siddiq*. So, O needy man! look with what thing you break fast. Sufiyan Saori said : He who spends in charity out of unlawful wealth is like the person who washes impure clothes with wine. Impure things cannot be purified except with water and there is no expiation of sins without lawful things. Hazrat Yahya b. Muaz said : To perform religious duties is God's secret treasure, invocation is its key and lawful food is its teeth. Hazrat Ibn Abbas said : The prayer of a man in whose belly there is unlawful food is not accepted by God.

Hazrat Sahal Tastari said : The truth of faith does not reach a man who does not possess four qualities- (a) Performance of compulsory duties alongwith *sunnat*, (b) carefulness in eating - (a) giving up the prohibited things openly and secretly and (d) observing those rules with patience upto death. He said : He who likes that the signs of a *Siddiq* should be opened up for him should not eat except lawful things and should not follow except the ways of the Prophet. It is said that the heart of a man who eats doubtful things for 40 days becomes enveloped with darkness. That is the meaning of the following verse: Never, rather rust has fallen upon their hearts on account of what they earned (83 : 14). The sage Abdul Mubarak said: To return a coin of doubt to its owner is better than charity of one lac dirhams. Sahal Tastari said : The limbs of a man become disobedient who eats unlawful food willingly or unwillingly, knowingly or unknowingly. The limbs of a man who eats lawful food become obedient to him and help him in doing good deeds. There is a well-known *Hadis* : There is account of lawful things in the world and punish for unlawful things. The narrator added to it : There is rebuke for a doubtful thing.

A certain religious man served food before an *Abdal*. Without eating it, the latter asked him about it and said : We don't eat except lawful food for which our hearts remain firm, our conditions become lasting, the affairs of heaven are disclosed to us and we see the next world. If we eat only three days what you eat, knowledge of our sure faith will disappear, and fear and actual vision will go from our hearts. The man said to him : I fast throughout the year and recite the Qurān 30 times every month. The *Abdal* said to him : The water which I drink at night and what you see are dearer to me than your reciting the Qurān thirty times in three hundred *rakats* of prayer. The milk of deer was his drink. There is written in the Torah : If a man does not care wherefrom he eats food, God also will not care by which door of hell He will throw him in Hell.

Classes of Halāl and Harām

(1) Things which are naturally unlawful. (2) and earnings which are unlawful.

(1) The things which are naturally unlawful are wine, blood, meat of pigs, dead animals, etc. The things fit for eating in the world are of three kinds: (a) minerals, such as salt, (2) vegetables and (3) animals.

(a) First kind - Minerals : Minerals are of different kinds. What grows out of earth is not unlawful for eating except what causes harm. There are things which have got the effect of poison. They are unlawful as they are injurious things.

(b) Second kind - Vegetables : They are not unlawful for eating except those vegetables which remove intellect, take life and ruin health. The things which destroy intellect are wine and intoxicants. The things which destroy life are poisons. The things which ruin health are medicines used out of time.

(c) Third kind - Animals : They are of two kinds - (1) what is eatable (2) and what is not eatable. Birds, beasts and animals in land and water which are fit for eating and which, if sacrificed according to the rules of *Shariat*, become lawful. What is not sacrificed according to the rules of *Shariat* and what is dead are unlawful. Out of dead animals, two kinds are lawful - fish and locusts. The following animals are lawful according to this rule - worms in food-stuffs and fruits, etc. What is not liking to a particular person is *Makruh* for eating. The Prophet said: 'Immerge a fly if it falls in food.' If an ant falls in food, it does not become impure. If a portion of flesh of a dead man falls in food, the whole food becomes unlawful. It is not on account of impurity, as man does not become impure after death, but it is out of horror. Animal, if sacrificed according to *Shariat*, becomes lawful except its blood and what is attached to its impurities. Regarding vegetables, what produces intoxication is unlawful and what removes intellect is unlawful. One drop of an impure thing renders food unlawful.

(2) Second kind-unlawful things by earnings : There are two kinds of earnings. What is taken willingly or unwillingly and what comes to the owner spontaneously. What is taken willingly or unwillingly are of two kinds (a) One kind is what is taken without the knowledge of the owner, such as minerals underneath the ground. Another kind is what is taken from the owner himself. The latter is of two kinds: (1) What is taken by force from him, (2) and what is taken with his permission'. What is taken by force is again of two kinds : (a) What is taken from the maintenance and care of the owner, such as quadrupeds. (b) What is taken from him by virtue of power of the ruling authorities, such as *Zakat* and other economic liabilities. What is taken with the permission of the owner is of two kinds : (a) What is taken from him in exchange, such as buy and sale, dower, wages, and what is not taken in exchange, such as gift, *wasiat*. Thus the things of earnings are of six kinds

(1) To become owner of the things of which there is no owner, such as minerals, to make barren land fertile, to gather fuels and woods from jungles, to take water from river, to take grass, etc. To take these things are lawful provided there is no owner of these things.

(2) What is taken by force and what is not prohibited are the properties gained after battle and without actual battle. They are lawful for all Muslims when one-fifth is taken out from the war booties and divided justly among those who are entitled to them. It is unlawful to take booty from those unbelievers with whom there is treaty.

(3) What can lawfully be taken by force in spite of prohibition of the owner, such as *Zakat*. It can only be taken by the ruling authorities. (4) What is taken in exchange of things with the consent of the owner is lawful, such as buy and sale transactions. (5) What is taken simply with permission without exchange of things, such as gift, will, etc. is lawful. (6) What comes spontaneously in possession, such as properties by inheritance after deduction of necessary expenses, such as funeral expenses, death instructions by will

or otherwise, expenses of expiations of religious duties, expenses of pilgrimage, etc. They are lawful.

Different stages of Halāl and Harām

Know, O dear readers! that every thing unlawful is bad, but there are different stages of illegality of things of which one is worse than another. All lawful things are good and there are different stages of legality therein and one thing is better than another. There are **four stages** of legality of things-

(1) First stage is lowest and it is forbearance of just and ordinary Muslims. It is to save oneself from the unlawful things prescribed by *Shariat*. This is the lowest stage of piety.

(2) Second stage is the forbearance of the pious. They refrain from lawful things bounding on illegality. A *faqih* will give its decision as lawful as it is a subject of doubt but the pious men keep away even from these doubtful things.

(3) Third stage : This is the stage of forbearance of God-fearing men. God-fearing men keep aloof from even such things as are lawful and free from doubt. If these are always practised, these may turn into Halāl and as a result they have chance of falling into doubtful things. For this, God-fearing men keep aloof even from things free from doubt. The Prophet said : A man cannot reach the stage of God-fearing men till he gives up things free from doubt for fear of falling into things of doubt.

(4) Fourth stage : In this stage, these God-fearing men give up even lawful things free from doubt even if there is no fear of falling into doubtful things, because they fear that those things may not be for God. They are called *Siddiq*.

Examples of the above four-stages

(1) No example is necessary in the case of the first stage,

as the unlawful things are clear and a religious man must keep himself distant from these unlawful things.

(2) In the second stage, there is the forbearance of the pious from every doubtful things bordering on illegality. It is not compulsory to give them up, but it is commendable. The Prophet said : Give up what raises doubt in your mind and take what does not raise doubt in you. The Prophet said : Eat the games of hunting on which there are marks of shooting and which die in presence. Don't eat what goes beyond sight being wounded and then it is presented dead in front.' Though it is not unlawful, it is the forbearance of the pious men. It is an order of the Prophet : Give up what raises doubt in your mind.

(3) In the Third stage, it is the forbearance of the God-fearing people. This *Hadis* bears witness : A man cannot reach the stage of a God-fearing man till he gives up things free from doubt for fear of things of doubt. Hazrat Omar said : We have given up nine portions of lawful things out of ten portions for fear of falling into unlawful things. Hazrat Abu Darda'a said : God-fear gains perfection at the time when a servant fears a very small thing. Even when he sees a lawful thing, he gives it up for fear of falling into unlawful things. Some examples are given below

(1) A certain religious man took loan of one hundred dirhams. When he brought the dirhams for payment, the creditor took only 99 dirhams. Ali b. Ma'bad said : I took a house on rent. I wrote a letter and thought that I should take a little earth from its wall and soak the ink of the letter and I did accordingly. When I slept, I dreamt that a certain man was saying : O Ali b. Ma'bad! you will know tomorrow on the Resurrection Day that the owner of the house will demand the little earth you used. By this act, he fell from the rank of God-fear.

(2) During the Caliphate of Hazrat Omar, the musk of Bahrain gained as a result of battle reached him. His wife began to measure it when Hazrat Omar said : I don't want that you should place your hands on it and say afterwards that something of it remained in your hands on account of touch. This is the property of the Muslims in general and you can't get more than what you are entitled to from the property of the general Muslims.

(3) Once musk was measured before Caliph Abdul Aziz. He kept his nose shut up lest its smell entered his nose. He said : What benefit has it got except its scent ? This benefit only is sought from it.

(4) Once the Prophet's grandson Hasan put into his mouth one dried grape out of the grapes of *Zakat*. The Prophet said: Throw it off, throw it off.

(5) Once a man went to see his friend at night. Soon after his death, he put out the light and said : The right of inheritance has occurred in the oil.

(6) Hazrat Omar gave to his wife some musk for sale. She sold it to another seller. At the time of sale, she began to break one piece by her teeth for which something was attached to her fingers. Hazrat Omar smelt scent from her hand and said : You have taken the scent of the Muslims in general. This he did to become a truly God-fearing man though it is not unlawful.

(7) Imam Ahmad b. Hanbal said : To smell sent of a tyrant ruler destroys the piety of a man.

(8) When Hazrat Omar became Caliph, he had only one wife whom he loved very much. He, however, divorced her for fear that she might intercede to him for an unlawful thing and perchance he might accept her intercession. For this reason, things free from doubt were even given up for fear of

falling into doubtful things. Being habituated to many lawful things, one is led to unlawful things, such as too much eating, excessive use of scent etc. If too much food is eaten, sexual passion rises high and it leads to unlawful cohabitation. Similarly to look at the beautiful buildings and the pomp and grandeurs of the rich may tempt one to follow them.

(9) There is no benefit to white-wash the walls of a building. Imam Ahmad held it as *Makruh* or abominable. When the Prophet once was asked about painting in the mosque, he said : There is no Arish like the Arish of Moses. Arish is a pearl-like antimony with which a thing is painted. The Prophet did not hold it lawful.

(10) The ancient sages said : The life of religion of a man whose cloth is thin is also thin.

(4) Fourth stage is the forbearance of the *Siddiqs*. To them, those things are lawful in which there is no transgression and which do not help the commission of sin. The object of their every action is to please God and they have God-fear in all their deeds. They live for God and they think that what is done except for God is unlawful. They follow this verse : Say God and then leave them sporting in their useless talks. This is the rank of those who follow *Tauhid*. The following are some examples of their piety.

(1) Once the sage Yahya b. Qusan used a medicine. His wife said to him : Walk for a while within the house, so that the medicine may work. He said : I don't know of such walk. I am counting my breaths for the last thirty years. He did not consider it connected with religion.

(2) Hazrat Sufiyan Saori said : Once I got upon a hill and saw a fountain and vegetables. I wished to eat something of the vegetables and drink water. Then I thought that I would eat a lawful thing today. An unseen voice said : Wherefrom

has the strength which has taken you to this stage come ? Then I became repentant and begged forgiveness.

(3) The sage Zunnun Misri was once imprisoned and began to pass time without food. He then became hungry. A woman sent some food to him through the hand of one of the men of the prision, but he did not eat it on the ground that the hand of an oppressor took it to him.

(4) The sage Bashar Hafi did not drink water of a canal dug by a tyrant ruler although this was lawful. For this reason, Hazrat Abu Bakr vomited the milk he drank for fear that the strength of unlawful thing would increase therefore.

(5) Once a servant of a sage took some fuel from the fuel of a transgressor. He put it off on the ground that the fuel was unlawfully earned.

These are some of the instances of God-fear of the early sages and pious men. God-fear reaches its climax in the fourth stage of the *Siddiq* or greatly truthful man.

SECTION 2

Different stages of doubtful things

The Prophet said : Lawful things are clear and unlawful things are also clear and between them there are the doubtful things. Most of the people do not know them. He who saves himself from doubtful things purifies his honour and religion. He who falls in doubtful things may fall in unlawful things like the shepherd who has got chance of falling into reserved grazing ground. If he grazes his flock of sheep round it. What is troublesome and unknown to the majority of the people are the doubtful things which should be discussed.

A lawful thing is what is naturally free from unlawful things, such as the water of sky. Before it goes into the possession of others, the people take it and store it in their lands. An unlawful thing is that which is naturally unlawful for its own defect, such as intoxicant, wine, stool or that things which is earned by unlawful method, such as the earnings by oppression, interest etc. These are fixed, open and clear. In between these Halāl and Harām or lawful and unlawful things, there are doubtful things which change the condition of Halāl and Harām. A lawful thing becomes unlawful when it goes into possession of another for which doubt arises in most cases. If a man gets a fish and thinks that it has come from the possession of another, there arises doubt in his mind whether it is lawful or unlawful for him. This doubt should have reason and not only mere conjecture. Doubt arises out of two conflicting beliefs which come into clash with each other.

Doubt arises out of four places

(1) First place is doubt in the course of Halāl and Harām.

It has got four classes: (1) A man knows a thing to be unlawful before but doubt arises in the matter of its being lawful. It is compulsory to give up this doubt and to take it as unlawful. For instance, an hunted animal falls into water and it is lifted up as dead from water. To eat its meat is unlawful. There is no place of doubt in it. The Prophet said to Adi : Don't eat it, your dog perchance has not killed it. Whenever anything was brought to the Prophet, he used to enquire if doubt arose in his mind, till he knew whether it was present or *Zakat*. (2) Though a thing is lawful, yet one doubts that it may be unlawful. The thing is basically lawful but owing to peculiar circumstances, one doubts whether the legality of that thing still remains. For instance, two men quarrelled with each other, one man said to another : You are a hater. A God-fearing man should leave them on doubt. (3) A thing is basically unlawful but a cause prevails upon it so strongly that it becomes awful. It becomes a subject matter of doubt and becomes strong of its being legal. For instance, an animal after being shot disappeared. Afterwards it was found with signs of only shooting in its body. It might be that it died owing to other reasons. Thus doubt arises whether its meat is lawful. A God-fearing man refrains from eating its meat. The Prophet said : Eat it although it disappears from you till you find the signs of your arrow on its body. (4) A thing is knowingly lawful, but it becomes unlawful at last owing to the decision of *Shariat*. For instance, a pot is lawful but doubt arises whether there is any impurity in it. So to drink water from it becomes unlawful.

(2) Second place of doubt - mixture of Halâl and Harâm

Halâl and Harâm become mixed and are not kept separate and therefore doubt arises whether it is lawful or unlawful. There are three kinds of this mixture of lawful and unlawful things : (1) One unlawful thing is mixed up with limited number of lawful things, for instance the meat of a dead goat is mixed up with the meat of some sacrificed goats. Doubt in these things are to be given up, as there is no sign therein that the meat of a dead goat has been mixed. If there is reasonable doubt that the meat of a dead goat has been mixed, it will be unlawful. (2) The second kind is the mixture of limited number of unlawful things with unlimited number of lawful things, for instance two foster sisters mix with the women of a town. One can marry any woman of the town if the foster sisters cannot be identified, or if there is prevalence of interest in a certain town, it is not unlawful to accept coins of that town. (3) The third kind is the mixture of unlimited number of lawful things with an unlimited number of unlawful things. In such a case, if the unlawful things can be identified, it will he unlawful to enjoy them, otherwise not, but to give up a doubtful thing is a sign of piety. The soldieres of Yezid looted the properties of Madinah for three days, but yet the companions did not prohibit the people from buy and sale of the goods of the Madinah market which consisted also the looted goods. If there is impurity on the pathways, prayer can be said on them, as the earths of pathways are pure. The companions sometimes prayed with their sandals and shoes.

(3) Third place of doubt : Any sin found in any cause making a thing lawful relates to the thing itself, or to its end, or to its beginning or to another thing in exchange of the thing, but it is not such a sin which nullifies an agreement or any cause which makes a thing lawful. Sin relating to a thing itself is, for instance, buy and sale after *Azan* for *Juma* prayer, cutting wood by a stolen axe, selling over the sale of another. These are not unlawful things. Sin relating to the end of a thing is all extravagant expenses which show the path towards sin, for instance, to sell grapes to those who prepare wine, to sell instruments to dacoits. There is difference of opinion among the jurists whether these are lawful or unlawful. Sin relating to the beginning of a thing relates to three stages - highest, middle and lowest. The most detestable is to eat the meat of a goat which has eaten then the grass taken illegally. The less detestable than the former is not to use water of a canal dug by a tyrant. Still less detestable is to restrain oneself from lawful thing that has come through the hand of a tyrant. Sin relating to a thing of exchange has got also different stages, highest, middle and lowest. The most detestable is to purchase a thing on credit and to pay its price by unlawfully acquired money. The less detestable is to give grapes to a drunkard, to give instruments to a dacoit in lieu of price. The least detestable is to accept the price of an unlawful thing, such as wine.

(4) Fourth place of doubt : This arises out of diversity of proofs of *Shariat* in order to distinguish between a lawful thing and unlawful thing. This doubt is of three kinds (a) Contradictory proofs of *Shariat*, (b) contradictory signs, (c) and contradictory doubts. With regard to the first, the verses of the Qurãn or the sayings of the Prophet contradict each other. This creates doubt in mind. In this case, what is strong prevails and if any proof does not become strong, it reverts to its original proof. If illegality of a thing is not strong, it becomes lawful. If there is doubt, it is better for piety to give it up and it is the subject matter of dispute between jurists and theologians. It is better to accept the opinion of a *Mufti* who is well-known in a locality for learning and piety, just as it is better to go to a physician who is well-known in a locality for his knowledge of medical science. If the theologians are unanimous with regard to a certain question, all should accept it. If any proof of legality of a thing is not strong, he should better give it up. There are three stages with regard to this matter.

First stage : It is better to give up a matter which has got a weak proof in favour of a matter which has got a strong proof. The Prophet is reported to have said : A believer sacrifices in the name of God. Whether he utters *'Bismillah'* or not. This is contradictory to a clear verse of the Qurãn and some traditions in which it is said that to utter the name of God at the time of sacrifice is compulsory. So the former tradition shall have to be given up.

Second stage : It is near baseless conjecture. For instance, to give up eating the young one of an animal found in its womb after lawful sacrifice. There is in authentic *Hadis* that the sacrifice of mother should be considered as also the sacrifice of its young one in its womb. So the former conjecture is to be given up.

Third stage : A thing is authenticated as legal by only one tradition. It is better not to come to a decision relying on only a single *Hadis* on a particular subject if there are differences of opinion. It is not unlikely that the narrator might have committed mistake in narrating it or he might have committed mistake in hearing it. But there is no reason to oppose the tradition without a cause. There is no mention of a grandson becoming an heir to his grandfather in the Qurãn, but the companions are unanimous in holding that a grandson becomes an heir to his grandfather in absence of his father. When difficulty arises in these matters, one should take decision according to his conscience as it does not dictate without truth. The Prophet instructed us to take decision according to our conscience in case of doubtful things.

(2) Second kind : If there is greater proof towards illegality, it should be considered as unlawful; and if there is greater proof towards legality, it should be considered as lawful.

(3) Third kind : Proof is equal towards legality and

illegality and doubt is also equal in both the cases. For instance, a man is to distribute some many among the poor. There are poor persons who have got something but they are not rich. So doubt arises whether such persons are really poor fit for acceptance of the money. This is a very subtle question. In this case if one possesses only necessary things, he can accept the charity but if he possesses more than what is necessary for him, it is prohibited. There is also no limit to necessity. For this reason, the Prophet said : Give up what raises doubt in your mind and take to what is free from doubt. For this reason, it is written in the Zabur that God revealed to David : Tell the children of Israil : I do not look to your prayers and fasts. I look to the person who gives up a thing when doubt arises in his mind for My sake. I help him with My help and take glory for him before My angels.

SECTION 3

Arguments and questions

Know, O dear readers! that whatever comes to you as food or present or whatever thing you wish to buy or to make gift, you should not raise questions in all cases or say this : I shall not accept it as lawful till I enquire about it. On the other hand, don't give up enquiry in some matters. In some cases, therefore, it is compulsory to enquire, in some cases unlawful, in some cases praise-worthy, in some cases not commendable. So there is place of doubt in case of questions and enquiries. The place of doubt has got connection either – (1) with the owner of a thing or (2) with the thing itself.

(1) Connection with the owner of a thing : It has got three states – (a) The first state comes when the owner is unknown. (b) The second state comes when there is doubt about the owner. (c) The third state is to know the condition of the owner by some sort of proof.

(1) First state : When you enter an unknown town or place, you meet with strangers and unknown persons and do not know their character and conduct and so you entertain doubt about them. Yusuf b. Asbat said : I used to give up doubt whenever it arose in my mind for the last 30 years. The rule is that if any of them gives you food or drink, you should enjoy it without doubt and you should not entertain evil conjecture about him, as some conjectures are sins, if there is sufficient cause of doubt, it is unlawful to enjoy them. The Prophet used to accept any invitation without enquiry. Once a tailor invited him and he accepted it. Once a Parsee invited the Prophet to which he asked him: I and Ayesha ? The Parsee said : You and not Ayesha. The Prophet did not accept the invitation but when he invited both, he accepted it. Hazrat

Abu Bakr enquired about the earnings of a slave when a strong doubt arose in his mind. It is not good to ask : Wherefrom has this thing been procured, as it gives pain to the mind of a Muslim. God says : Give up most conjectures. Some conjecture is sin. Don't spy and let not some of you backbite others. Once the Prophet ate the food of Barirah. He was informed that it was *Zakat* property. The Prophet said : It was *Zakat* property for her but for us, it is present. So baseless doubt should be given up.

(2) **Second State** : It occurs when there is doubt about the owner owing to the causes of proof. The causes of proof that a thing is unlawful are the character of the owner, his dresses, his actions etc. or he is a well known dacoit, thief, tyrant or his actions are opposed to the fundamental principles of *Shariat*. In such cases, two sorts of doubt arise in mind. One sort of doubt arises from the fact of possession of a thing which indicates ownership of the thing. It is lawful to accept the thing from such possessor. The second sort of doubt arises strongly from the sign of a thing that it may not be lawful. In such a case, it is better to give it up. The Prophet said : Give up what raises doubt in your mind for what does not raise doubt. It is commendable. The Prophet also said : Doubt of mind is a sin. The Prophet also enquired in case of doubt whether a thing is *Zakat* or present. Hazrat Omar enquired about milk and Hazrat Abu Bakr about the earnings of a slave in case of doubt.

(3) **Third state** : Experience or news give indication of a thing being lawful or unlawful. If a man is honest, pious and trustworthy, his thing can be considered as lawful, even though it may be otherwise. In this case, it is unlawful to enquire about such a thing in his possession. To eat food of the pious was the rule of Prophets and friends of God. The Prophet

said: Don't give your food to be eaten except by the pious and don't eat food except of the pious.

(2) Second place of doubt in connection with things :

In this place, lawful and unlawful things become mixed. In the market where the looted properties and properties gained by theft and dacoity are mixed with lawful properties. A buyer should not enquire about the legality or otherwise of the properties of the market. If however, it is disclosed that most of the properties of the market are unlawful, the enquiry becomes compulsory, otherwise not. The companions used to do it. They did not enquire except in doubtful cases. Hazrat Ibn Masud said : You are the inhabitants of such a town where there are the Magians also. So look to the meats of sacrificed animals and the hides of dead animals. If most of the properties are unlawful, it is not lawful to take them. If the meat of a sacrificed animal is mixed with the meat of ten unsacrificed animals, it becomes compulsory to give up the meat. Hazrat Ali said : Take what a ruler gives you, as he generally gives from lawful things. Hazrat Ibn Masud was once asked by a man : Shall I take loan from a man whom I know to be a bad man ? 'Yes' he replied. He was once asked by another : Shall I accept the invitation of a man who takes interest ? 'Yes' he replied. Hazrat Ali did not accept anything from the state treasury. He had only one wearing cloth and he had no other cloth even for his bath. Once Hazrat Abu Hurairah produced before the Caliph Omar abundant wealth of the state to which he enquired : Are these properties lawful? In a similar way Hazrat Ali said : There is nothing dearer to God than the justice and kindness of a leader and nothing more hateable than injustice and oppression of a leader.

SECTION 4

Knowledge of lawful and unlawful things

If any man has got in his possession unlawful things mixed with lawful things, he should adopt two means - (1) To separate the unlawful things from the lawful things and (2) to know the modes of spending the lawful things. With regard to the first means, it has got two conditions : (a) mixture of lawful and unlawful things of the same kind, for instance crops, money, oily things etc. (b) mixture of unlawful thing with a different kind of thing, such as dresses, houses etc. In such cases, quantity is either known or unknown. If, for instance, half of the thing is unlawful, it should be separated. It is lawful to keep doubtful thing but to give it up is better and piety. The repentance of a man is not accepted till the total income of a property taken by oppression is returned to the rightful owner.

(b) The mode of spending unlawful things taken out of lawful things. It is compulsory to return the unlawful things to the rightful owner and in his absence to his heirs. It is also compulsory to return the income and profit arising out of these properties to them. If the owner or his heirs are unknown, they may be given in charity to the poor.

Question may arise how can an unlawful thing be given in charity when he has got no right to do it ? In support of this, there are traditions of the Prophet. When cooked mutton was presented to the Prophet, the mutton informed him that it was unlawful. The Prophet then ordered it to be given in charity saying : Give it to the war prisoners for eating. Once the property of gambling was brought by Abu Bakr to the Prophet who said: It is unlawful. Give it in charity. Hazrat Ibn Masud purchased a slave-girl but he could not find her master in spite of continued search. Then he gifted away her price to the poor on behalf of the master. Imran, Ahmad, Haris and Mohasabi supported this view. Where the owner is not found, either such an unlawful property shall be destroyed or spent for the good of the people. The latter method is better. The Prophet said: A cultivator or a planter of trees will get rewards for the crops and fruits which the people and birds and beasts eat. The rule that except the lawful things nothing can be given in charity applies to the case where we seek rewards for charity. In the case of charity of unlawful things, we seek salvation only for ourselves. The saying - what we love for ourselves, we should love for others is true, but in case of charity of unlawful things, it is unlawful for our enjoyment, but lawful for the poor. If the receiver of unlawful property is himself poor, and the owner is not traceable, he can legally use it up to the limit of necessity for himself and for his family members. The Qurān also allowed eating of unlawful foods like wine in case of extreme necessity to save life.

SECTION 5

Allowances and gifts of rulers and kings

A man is required to look to three things in accepting the allowances and gifts from the rulers and kings - (l) the source of wealth, (2) the right of acquiring it, and (3) the quantity of lawful and unlawful things there in.

(1) **The source of wealth of the rulers** : The ruler has got right along with his subjects in reclaimed lands, booties gained in war and without war against the unbelievers, properties that have got no heirs and *waqf* properties which have got no *mutawallis* or managers. Besides these, all other properties are unlawful for him, such as revenues, fines, taxes and other sources of income to the state. If a ruler gives any *Jagir*, gift or rewards to any man, he gives them generally out of eight kinds of properties-poll-tax, heirless property, *Waqf*, reclaimed land, purchased property, revenue realised from the Muslims, wealth out of merchandise or specially fixed revenue. With regard to poll-tax on the unbelievers four-fifths will be spent for the good of the people and one-fifth only for special purpose. With regard to the heirless property, it is to be spent for the good of the Muslims. *Waqf* property is to be spent for the purposes as fixed by the *waqf* or donor. In the lands reclaimed by the ruler, he has got freedom to spend it in any way he likes. Similar is his freedom in case of landed properties - dresses, horses and other things purchased by the ruler. The taxes imposed upon the Muslims, the booties, fines etc, are all unlawful for a ruler except in case of the profits arising out of his personal business with others. The taxes specially imposed upon a person are unlawful for a ruler.

(2) **Right of acquisition** : Some learned men say that if it

is not established that there is any illegality in a property, it may be accepted. In support, they cite the following instances. There were many among the companions who lived up to the time of the tyrant rulers and used to accept properties from them. Such were Abu Hurairah, Abu Sayeed Khudri, Zaid b. Sabit, Abu Ayyub Ansari, Jarir b. Abdullah, Anas b. Malik and others. Some of them received from Caliphs Marwan and Yezid b. Abdul Malik, some from the tyrant governor Hajjaj. Imam Shafayi received once from Caliph Harun Rashid one thousand dinars. Imam Malik also received them from different Caliphs. Hazrat Ali said : Whatever a ruler gives you, he gives out of lawful things. He himself did not accept it out of a greater sense of piety. When Imam Hasan came to Caliph Muawyiah, the latter gave him four lakh dirhams which he accepted. These sages used to accept the properties of tyrant rulers. The supporters of the above opinion say that some of the sages did not accept them out of greater sense of piety. This does not show that it is illegal. Such men were the rightly guided Caliphs, Abu Zarr and other sages who renunciated the world.

Four stages of piety : There are four stages of piety in relation to the acceptance of properties from rulers.

First stage : In this stage of highest piety, the rightly guided Caliphs and a party of extremely pious men did not accept anything from the state treasury and rulers. The allowance which Hazrat Abu Bakr received from the state treasury as a ruler amounted to six thousand dirhams after accounting. He afterwards deposited it in the Treasury. Once when Hazrat Omar was counting the wealth of the State Treasury, his young daughter concealed a dirham therefrom. When he found it on enquiry, he deposited it in *Baitul-Mal*. Hazrat Abu Musa Ash'ari found a dirham at the time of sweeping the house of the Treasury and gave it to the young daughter of Hazrat Omar. The latter took it from her and deposited it in the Treasury. Hazrat Omar said in connection with the wealth of State Exchequer : I see myself in connection with this wealth as a care taker of an orphan's property. If I am solvent, I refrain from taking anything from it. If I am in want, I enjoy from it in a just manner.

Second stage : Take from the ruler when you know that his wealth is legal. He will not suffer if anything unlawful in it is disclosed afterwards. This is supported by the companions. The companion Ibn Omar said about the tyrant ruler Hajjaj : I have not eaten to my satisfaction since he captured the seat of *Khilafat* till today. It is related of Hazrat Ali that he had some wheat in a sealed cup out of which he used to eat and drink. On being questioned, he said : I don't wish to fill up my belly except with pure things.

Third stage : You can accept the gifts from a ruler and give them in charity to the poor or divide them among those who are entitled to them, even though the ruler is a tyrant. For this reason, many persons used to accept gifts from the rulers. Whatever Ibn Omar got from the rulers was distributed by him among the poor. One day he distributed sixty thousand dirhams among the poor. After this, a poor man came to him and he gave him some dirhams after taking loan from a man. Hazrat Ayesha also used to do like that. Imam Shafayi accepted gifts from Caliph Harun Rashid and distributed them among his relatives without keeping anything for him.

Fourth stage : In this stage, the properties of the rulers have been established to be illegal and therefore cannot be accepted, nor can be given in charity. Accept from the rulers such properties as are mostly lawful.

These are the four stages of piety. In our times, most of the properties of the rulers are unlawful, as Islamic State Treasury consisted of only *Zakat* and the properties gained by war and without war but now nothing of these items is found in the present State Treasuries. Besides there is difference of the people who received gifts from the rulers of past ages and the people who receive gifts now from the present rulers. The rulers of past ages used to make gifts to the learned and the sages who attracted their minds in their favour while the present rulers make gifts to the people who can make flattery to them by falsehoods.

Second matter

The receivers of gifts should be qualified to receive them according to *Shariat*. For instance, there are definite persons prescribed by the Qurãn to receive *Zakat*, war spoils one-fifth of properties gained without war, heirless properties. The properties fixed for the Muslims in general must be spent for them only and it will be illegal to spend them for others. Hazrat Omar said : Every Muslim has got right to get money from *Baitul-Mal*, because he is a Muslim and he increases the number of Islamic Brotherhood.

The wealth of *Baitul-Mal* is for good of the people. The good is connected with the religion and with the State. The learned men of the religion are the guards of the religion and the soldiers are the guards of the State. The religion and the state are interconnected, one cannot be separated from the other. So the learned men of the religion as well as soldiers of the state are entitled to receive wealth from the State Treasury. The officers of the state come under the category of the guardians of the state and so they have got right in it. The rightly guided Caliphs used to give allowances to the Refugees and Ansars from the State Treasury and did not see their wants. It rested on the wishes of the rulers regarding the amount. Hazrat Muawiyah gave Hasan one day four Lakh dirhams. Hazrat Omar fixed twelve thousand dirhams yearly for particular persons including Ayesha, ten thousand dirhams for some persons and six thousand dirhams for some persons. Even there remained nothing after distribution in *Baitul-Mal.* Hazrat Abu Bakr used to distribute equally. Hazrat Omar amended it and used to give more or less as he wished. He used to give to Ayesha twelve thousand dirhams, Zuwairiyah six thousand, Zainab ten thousand, Hazrat Ali a *Jagir*, Hazrat Osman five gardens. All the companions agreed to the distribution of these two Caliphs as they believed in their sense of justice and honesty of purpose.

SECTION 6

Frequenting the Darbar of rulers

In this section, it will be discussed when frequenting to rulers is lawful and when unlawful. Three conditions arise in frequenting the rulers - (1) evil effects of frequenting them, (2) the manner to be observed, (3) and to keep aloof from them.

(i) First condition : It is not commendable to frequent the rulers and administrators according to *Shariat*. A great deal of warnings to this effect was given by the sages and learned men of the religion.

Hadis: The Prophet mentioned about the tyrant rulers and said : He who keeps away from them will get salvation. He who keeps separate from them will be safe or near safety. He who falls with them in their worldly passions will belong to them. The Prophet said : There will be false and oppressive rulers after me. He who supports their falsehood as true and helps their tyranny does not belong to my followers and I am also not of him. He will not be able to take drink from my Fountain. The Prophet said : The learned man who frequents the rulers is an object of hatred near God. He said : The rulers who frequent the learned are good and the learned men who frequent the rulers are bad. The Prophet said : So long as the learned men do not mix with the rulers, they become guardians of trust of the Prophet for the servants of God ; when they mix with them, they commit treachery with the Prophet. So be careful of them and keep away from them.

Wise sayings : The sage Huzaifa said : Be careful of ruinous places. He was questioned : What are those places ? He said : The *Darbars* of the rulers. Hazrat Abu Zarr said to

Salma : Don't frequent the *darbars* of the rulers, as the harms of religion will be greater than the benefits you get from them. Hazrat Sufiyan said : There is a valley in Hell. The learned men who frequent the rulers will live in it. Hazrat Obadah b. Swamit said : If a pious learned man loves the rulers, he commits hypocrisy and if he loves the rich he commits show. Hazrat Omar b. Abdul Aziz appointed an officer. He was then informed that he was an officer of tyrant Hajjaj. He dismissed him on this ground. The sage Fuzail said : The nearer a man goes to the rulers, the distant he becomes from God.

From the above traditions and wise sayings, it appears that many dangers and difficulties arise out of mixing with the rulers and frequenting their darbars. He who frequents them faces sin, as by his actions, silence, words and invocations, he commits disobedience to God. If he bends his head to a tyrant ruler, or kisses his hand and does actions like that he commits sin. If he sees actions in the *Darbar* of the ruler which are unlawful, he commits sin by his silence as it is his duty then to protest against such illegal actions. If one praises him and supports his illegal actions, he commits sin. If he invokes God for the long life of a tyrant, its illegal. The Prophet said : He who prays for long life of a tyrant loves sins. The Prophet said : When any man praises a transgressor, God hates him. He said When a man honours a transgressor, he helps the destruction of Islam. The sage Sayeed b. Musayyib was asked by Caliph Abdul Malik to swear allegiance to his two sons - Walid and Sulaiman. He said : I will not take allegiance to them till night and day turn as the Prophet prohibited allegiance to two persons. As a result, he was flogged and made to wear dress of disgrace.

(2) Second condition : Salute a tyrant ruler and stand up in his honour as in the contrary case, disturbance may occur among the subjects. After interview, give him sound advice and inform him of the injuntions and prohibitions of *Shariat*. Once Caliph Muhammad b. Sulaiman went to the sage Hammad b. Salam who had then before him a mat for sitting, one copy of the Qurān, one bag for keeping books and a pot for ablution. The Caliph said : Whenever I see you, my mind is filled up with fear. What is the reason? Hammad said : The cause is this tradition of the Prophet : Everything fears a man who seek's God's pleasure by his learning ; but he fears everything who seeks wealth by his learning. The Caliph then placed before him forty thousand dirhams as a gift which he refused to accept.

(3) Third condition : The learned men should not frequent the *darbars* of the rulers. If anybody remembers their rewards and presents, he should recall to his mind the sayings of the sage Hatim Asim. He said : There is the difference of only one day between me and the rulers. They did not get the joys of yesterday and they and myself have got the fear of tomorrow. Only today remains. What is possible to occur by today?

Once Caliph Hisham b. Abdul Malik went to Mecca for pilgrimage. When he entered the sanctuary of *Ka'ba*, he called for the sage Taus Yemeni. When he came to him, he took off his shoes and kept them by the side of the royal carpet. He said : O Hisham! peace be on you. He then sat by the side of the Caliph and asked him : O Hisham! how arc you ? At this conduct of the sage, he was about to kill him but as he was in the sanctuary, he was not killed. The Caliph asked Taus : Why have you treated me like this? (1) You have placed your shoes by my carpet. (2) You have not kissed my hand, (3) You have not addressed me : O Commander of the Faithful! (4) You have taken your seat by me without my permission, (5) you have asked me by my name : How are you ? The sage Taus replied : Regarding the placing of my shoes by your

carpet, I put off my shoes daily five times when I go to my
Lord for prayer. He does not punish me for it. Regarding the
kissing of your hand. I heard Hazrat Ali say : Let nobody kiss
the hand of anyone except his kissing his wife's hand out of
passion and his kissing of his parents hand out of reverence.
Regarding addressing you as Commander of the Faithful, the
people are not satisfied with your rule and I don't wish to tell
lies. Regarding my addressing you by your name, God even
addressed His dear friends and Prophets by their names.
Regarding my sitting by your side, I heard Hazrat Ali say : If
you wish to see anyone of the inmates of Hell, look to one
who keeps himself seated with the people standing around
him. Then Taus went away from him.

Hazrat Sufiyan said : I went once to Caliph Mansur. I said
to the Caliph : You have reached to this honour by the help of
Muhajirs and *Ansars* but their descendants are dying of
starvation at present. So fear God and give them what they
are entitled to.

The sage Ibn Abi Shamilah went once to the *Darbar* of
Caliph Abdul Malik who said to him : Give me some
instruction. He said : The people will not get salvation from
the severe chastisement of the Resurrection Day. Only those
will get salvation who incur the pleasure of God causing
displeasure to their baser selves. Abdul Malik wept and said:
I will keep this advice before my eyes until my death.

Once Caliph Sulaiman came to Madinah and called the
sage Abu Hazim. When he came to him, he said : O Abu
Hazim! why is death so disliking to me ? He said : It is because
you have destroyed your hereafter and adorned your world
with numerous adornments. The Caliph said : How shall we
approach God ? He said : O Commander of the Faithful! the
pious men will return to the families in happiness like one
absent, and the sinners like a fugitive slave to his master. The

Caliph then burst into tears and said : What will be my condition ? Abu Hazim said : Look to this verse : The pious will be in bliss and the transgressors in Hell. Sulaiman asked: Where is the mercy of God ? He said : Near the pious. The king asked : Who among God's servants is the most honourable ? He said : The pious and the God-fearing. He asked Who among the believers is the wisest ? He said : The believer who obeys the religion of God and calls the people towards it.

The Caliph Omar b. Abdul Aziz said once to Abu Hazim: Give me advice. He said : Place death near your head when you go to bed and then look to what you love ; you will then give up what you do not like.

Once a desert Arab came to the Caliph Sulaiman who said to him : Give me some advice. On being assured of his safety, he said : O Commander of the Faithful! there are some men among your special friends who have adopted dishonest ways and purchased the world in lieu of their next world and look to your pleasure by incurring the displeasure of their Lord. They fear you in the matters of God and they do not fear God in your matters. You are in good terms with the world after forgetting the next world. You have not given security to the people about the matters from which God has given you security. They are in dire wants and needs. You will be asked for what they do. You will not do good to your world by selling your hereafter, as he is fool who sells his hereafter for his world. Sulaiman said : O desert Arab! beware, the sharpness of your tongue is more than that of your sword. He said : O Commander of the Faithful! that is true, but it is for you and not against you.

Once Hazrat Abu Bakr said to Hazrat Muawiyah : O Muawiyah! fear God and know that the day which goes out from you and the night which comes take you away from this world and near the hereafter. There is such a searcher behind you from whom you can never save yourself. You have got a fixed limit which you cannot cross. The sooner you reach the limit, the searcher will arrest you : The properties we are in will all pass away and what we proceed to still remains. Take to what is good and give up what is bad.

The Prophet said : This community will not cease to be in the help and protection of God so long as the learned in the Qurān are not attracted towards the rulers. God says: Don't be inclined towards the oppressors. In other words : Don't remain satisfied with their actions. Sufiyan Saori said : Don't mix with the rulers and don't mix with those who mix with the rulers. The owners of pens, the owners of ink and the owners of papers are co-sharers. What he said is true, as the Prophet cursed ten persons in connection with wine. Hazrat Ibn Masud said : Those who devour interest, those who give interest, those who are witnesses to it, those who write it are all cursed by the tongue of the Prophet. God said : 'When the angels will take the lives of those who have oppressed themselves'. This verse was revealed in connection with those Muslims who increased the numbers of polytheists by mixing with them. It has been narrated that God revealed to the Prophet Ushu : I will destroy forty thousands of the good people and sixty thousands of other people from among your followers. He asked God : What sin have the good people committed ? God said : They do not become displeased with actions of My displeasure. They eat and drink with the unbelievers. This proves that to love for God and hate for God is compulsory. The Prophet said : God cursed the children of Israil as they lived with the transgressors.

SECTION 7

Some legal decisions

The Prophet said : 'Give present to one another, you will then beget love for one another.' Any present is lawful provided nothing is expected in return. If present is given to a man knowing that he is a poor man but in fact he is not poor, the latter's acceptance of the present is unlawful. So is the case in all similar matters. If any person has got any administrative and official power, such as judge, magistrate, *Zakat* collector, revenue collector, tax collector and others, and if any present is given to him, it will be considered as bribe, as it is given for a special purpose. When any such officer is transferred, he is not given such present. The Prophet said : A time will come over men when they will consider an unlawful present as lawful and will kill innocent people as being lawful in the form of carefulness, so that the general public become cautious.' Two sons of Hazrat Omar accepted some loans from the State Treasury. Hazrat Omar took the profits of the loans from them and deposited them in the Treasury saying : These loans have been given to you as you are the Sons of the Caliph. The wife of Hazrat Abu Obaidah sent a casket of otto as present for the queen of Byzantium. In return, the queen sent him a valuable necklace decorated with jewels. Hazrat Omar took it from her and deposited it in the State Treasury after giving the price of the casket to her. When the Caliph Omar b. Abdul Aziz returned back his present, it was said to him that the Prophet used to accept present. He said : It was present for the Prophet, but it is a bribe to us.

The Prophet sent a man to collect *Zakat* from the tribe of Azad. When he collected *Zakat* and returned it to the Prophet, he kept something which was given to him as present. The Prophet then said to him : Tell me with truth, whether it would have been given to you if you kept seated in your parents' house. By one in whose hand there is my life, let nobody take from you except what is due to him. Beware, he will come to God with the thing he accepts. Let nobody come on the Resurrection Day bearing a high sound-making camel on his back, or a bellowing cow or a sound-making goat. Then he raised his hands so high that the whiteness of his armpit was visible and he said : O God! have I communicated Thy message ?'

CHAPTER V

Love and Brotherhood

Love for one another and friendship and brotherhood for one another is the best way for nearness to God. We shall describe in this chapter (1) love and friendship for God and its conditions and rules, (2) duties of companionship and its rules and (3) duties to the Muslims, relatives, neighbours and rulers.

SECTION 1

Merits of friendship and brotherhood

Know, O dear readers! that friendship is the result of good conduct and enmity of bad conduct. Good conduct is the root of love for one another and bad conduct is the root of hatred, envy and enmity. The result of good conduct is praiseworthy. The merits of good conduct in religion are not secret. God praised His Prophet : You are certainly upon a sublime character (68 : 4). He said : Attributes which will take the majority of people to Paradise are God-fear and good conduct. Hazrat Osamah-b-*Shuraik* reported : We asked : O Messenger of God! what good attribute has been given to man ? He said: Good conduct. The Prophet said : I have been sent to perfect good conduct. He also said : What will be heaviest in the Balance will be good conduct. He said : God has not made the conduct and constitution of people such that fire will burn

them. In other words, Hell-fire will not be able to burn one
whose character and constitution are beautiful. The Prophet
said : O Abu Hurairah! you should take to good conduct. Abu
Hurairah asked : O Messenger of God! what is good conduct?
He said : Keep the tie of relationship with one who cuts it off,
forgive one who oppresses you, give charity to one who
deprives you.

Some traditions have come in praise of friendship. When
the tie of friendship is love for God, its merits are high as
seen from the Quran and traditions. God says after showing
kindness over the entire creation : If you spend everything
what is in the earth, you cannot create love in their minds, but
God has placed love in their hearts (3 : 102). He said : By His
grace, you have been united in brotherhood. He condemned
separation and disunity by saying : Hold fast to the rope of
God unitedly and be not separate (3:102). The Prophet said :
One who is the best of you in good conduct is nearest to me.
The Prophet said : A believer loves and is loved. There is no
good in one who does not love and is not loved. The Prophet
praised brotherhood among the Muslims and said : God gives
a friend to one whose good He intends. If he forgets, he
reminds him. If he does not remember, he helps him. The
Prophet said : If two brothers meet with each other, they are
like two hands one of which clears the dust of the other. If
two believers meet with each other, God gives benefit to one
from another. To give encouragement of friendship for God,
the Prophet said: If a man makes brotherhood for God, God
will increase his rank in Paradise and will not reduce anything
from his actions. Hazrat Idris Khaolani said to Hazrat Muaz :
I love you for God. He said : It is good. I heard the Prophet
say: Chairs will be placed round the Throne for one party of
men. Their faces will be bright like full moon. The people
will be afraid, but they will not be afraid. The people will be
perturbed, but they will not be perturbed. They are the friends

of God and they will not have any fear or sorrow. The Prophet was asked : O Messenger of God! who are they ? He said : Those who love one another for God.

The Prophet said : There are pulpits of light around the Throne. A party of men will be seated therein. Their dress will be of light. They are not Prophets or martyrs but the Prophets and martyrs will envy their rank. They asked : O Apostle of God! narrate to us their qualities. He said : They love one another for God, they sit together in an assembly for God and meet one another for God. The Prophet said of the two men who love each other for God : The more beloved of God is one who loves his friend more. God says : I shall make their children attached to them and nothing will be reduced from their actions. The Prophet said that God says : My meeting becomes sure for those who meet one another for Me. My love becomes sure for those who love one another for Me. My help becomes sure for those who help one another for Me.

The Prophet said : God will say on the Resurrection Day: Where are those who loved one another for Me ? There is no shade today except My shade. I will give them My shade. The Prophet said : On the day when there will be no shade except the shade of God, He will place seven persons under His shade - (1) a just ruler, (2) a young man engaged in divine service, (3) a man who is attracted towards the mosque after he comes out of it, (4) two persons who love each other for God, meet each other for God and keep company with each other for God, (5) one who remembers God in loneliness and as a result his eyes shed tears, (6) a man who does not respond to the evil temptation of a beautiful woman coming from a respectable family and says : I fear God, and (7) a charitable person who keeps his charity secret, so much so that his left hand does not know what his right hand gives.

The Prophet said : If a man meets another for love of God and hoping to meet Him, an angel proclaims from behind him : You are blessed, your foot steps are blessed, Paradise for you is blessed. The Prophet said : Once a man wished to meet his friend for God. God sent secretly an angel to him who asked him : What do you intend ? He said : I intend to meet my brother. He asked him : Have you got any necessity to him ? He said : No. The angel said : Has he done any benefit to you ? He said : No. The angel said: Then why are you going to meet him ? He said : I love him for the sake of God. The angel said : God sent me to you with this news that He loves you as you love him and that Paradise is sure for you. The Prophet said : Love for God and hate for God are the firmest faith. For this reason a man should have enemies so that he may hate them and should have friends so that he may love them.

Once God revealed to a Prophet : You have hastened the happiness of Paradise for you for your renunciation of the world. You have got honour near Me for having renunciated the world to come to Me. Have you done enemity for Me or have you made friendship for Me ? The Prophet said : O God! let no sinner do any benefit to me, as my love may grow for him. God revealed to Jesus Christ : If you do alone the divine services of the inmates of the heaven and earth but do not love for Me and hate for Me, it will do no benefit to you. Jesus Christ said : Be dear to God by having enmity against the sinners and be near to God by keeping away from them and seek pleasure of God by displeasing them. They asked him : O the Spirit of God! with whom shall we keep company? He said : With such people who remind you of God if you see them, whose words increase your actions and who arouse eagerness in your mind for the actions of the next world when you see them. Once God revealed to Moses : O son of Imran!

if your heart is awake, seek friends for you. The friend who does not meet you with My pleasure is your enemy.

God revealed to David : O David! why are you in loneliness after giving up the society of men ? He said : O God! I have adopted loneliness for Thee. He said: O David! beware, seek friends for you and do not take those friends who do not help you for My pleasure, they are your enemies. They will make your heart hard and keep you farthest from Me. David once said to God : O Lord! how is it possible that all the people will love me and obey the message of religion? It was said : Treat with the people according to their nature and make good what is between you and Me. In another narration - Treat with the people of the world with the nature of the world and treat with the inmates of the next world with the nature of the next world. The Prophet said : Those people among you are dearest to God who love and are loved, and those people among you are objects of greatest hatred of God who roam with slanders and create disputes among brethren.

The Prophet said : There is an angel of God whose half-body was created of fire and half of ice. He says : O God! as Thou hast created tie between fire and ice, create love in the hearts of Thy pious servants. He said : If a man makes friendship for God, He creates for him a rank in Paradise. The Prophet said : The mutual lovers of God will live on the long pillars of red emeralds. There will be seventy thousand rooms on that pillar. From them, they will peep at the inmates of Paradise. The brilliance of their look will illuminate the inmates of Paradise as the rays of the sun illuminates this world. The inmates of Paradise will say to one another : Take us to see those who loved one another for God. On their foreheads, it will be written - Lovers of God.

Wise sayings

Hazrat Ali said : You should take to friends. They will be counted in this world and in the next. Have you not heard about the inmates of Hell (1-1). We have got no intercessors or bosom friends ? Hazrat Abdullah b. Omar said : By God, if I fast all days and pray all nights, spend all my wealth in the way of God without account and if I die on the day with no love for those who obey God and with no hatred for those who do not obey God, it will be no use to me. Hazrat Hasan Basri said : O children of Adam! let not the following word deceive you - "He who loves one will be with him", because you cannot earn the rank of the pious people without doing their actions. The Jews and the Christians love their Prophets, but they do not act according to their injunctions. This shows that only love without actions will be of no use. The sage Fuzail said in one of his sermons : It is strange that you wish to live in the Paradise or Firdous and in the neighbourhood of the Merciful with the Prophets, truthfuls, martyrs and pious men, but what actions you have done for it, what passions you have given up for it, what tie of relationship you have united after it was severed, what faults of your brother you have forgiven, and what distant persons you have brought near for God.

God revealed to Moses : What actions have you done for My pleasure ? He said : O Lord! I have prayed to Thee, kept fast, paid charity and *zakat*. He said : Prayer is a clear proof for you, fast is a shield for you, charity is your shade, *zakat* is your light, but what actions have you done for Me ? Hazrat Moses said : O Lord! show me such an action which will be only for Thee. God said : O Moses! have you taken any friend for Me and have you made any enemy for Me ? Then Moses came to know that the best action is love for God and hatred for God. Hazrat Hasan Basri said : To hate the sinners is a means of nearing God. A man once said to the sage Ibn Wase: I love you for God. He said : He loves you for whom you love me. Then he said : O God! I seek refuge to Thee from a person who loves me for Thee, as I do not know Thy love. Hazrat Omar said : When one of you gets love from his brother, let him stick to it. Such a man is rarely found. The sage Mujahid said : When two lovers meet with each other and express gratefulness, their sins drop down from them as the leaves of trees drop down in winter season. The sage Fuzail said : If a man looks to his brother with affection and kindness, it becomes his divine service.

Distinction between love for God and love for world

Know, O dear readers! that love for God and hate for God are secret. What we will discuss will lift the curtain therefrom. This friendship is of two kinds - (1) love for God and (2) love for the world. It is not love for God if there is love for a neighbour, love for reading together, for trading in the same market or travelling together in a journey. But if there is intention of love for the sake of God, it will be love for God. There is no doubt that there is no merit unless a work is done willingly, and love begets from willingness.

Love has got two conditions : Firstly, a thing is loved for its merits and not to reach the beloved by its help or for no other object behind it. Secondly, it is loved to reach the goal by its help. This object also is not confined to this world only but is connected with the next world or with God. In this way, love is of four kinds.

(1) First kind : A man is loved for his own merits. It is possible that a man can become an object of love of another in a natural way, when he sees him, knows him and thinks him good after seeing his character and conduct. Everything beautiful is an object of pleasure to a man who loves beauty. There is another thing for love. That is the internal qualities.

The Prophet said : Souls are the arrayed soldiers. Out of them, those who know one another love one another and those who do not know one another have got differences of opinion. The cause of difference is absence of knowledge of one another and the cause of love is knowledge of one another. Love grows out of acquaintance. In another narration, the Prophet said : Souls are arrayed soldiers, one soul meeting with the other soul in the horizon becomes near. Some learned men explain it by saying that God, after creating souls, let them off in the air and they are roaming round the Throne. The souls which know one another in the air meet one another in the world and love one another. The Prophet said : The souls of two believers meet with each other from a distance of one day's path though one soul has not seen another soul. The Prophet said : When a believer enters an assembly of one hundred hypocrites and only one believer, he will sit near the believer. If a hypocrite enters an assembly of one hundred believers and of one hypocrite, he will sit near the hypocrite. It is seen from this that the same nature attracts one another though they have got no acquaintance. The sage Malik b. Dinar said: Out of ten persons, two cannot agree, but if the nature of the two is the same, they agree. This proves that a man loves another man of the same nature not for gaining any benefit, not for acquiring wealth, but for their nature being the same and for their internal qualities being the same.

(2) **Second class** : A man loves another for gaining the love of a third person. The thing which becomes the means of a dear thing becomes also dear. For this reason, gold and silver are dear to men although they have got no attribute of their own, as they cannot be eaten, nor used as clothes but they are the means of getting these things. These are men among the people who are loved like gold and silver, as they become the means of reaching the destination or gaining the goal and by their help, wealth, name and fame are earned.

(3) Third class : A thing is not loved for its sake, but for another thing which is not for good of this world but for good of the next world. It is open and not secret, as for instance, to love a spiritual guide who becomes the means of gaining spiritual knowledge. His object is to get success in the next world. Jesus Christ said : He who acquires knowledge, acts according to it and teaches it to others is termed noble in the spiritual world. Knowledge is not complete without students. So students are the means of the teacher for perfection. The teacher loves the students as a father. It is a step towards progress. He who spends his wealth for his friend, dresses him with cloth, maintains him with food, keeps him in a house to live in and helps him in all affairs and whose object in doing these things is to give him leisure for divine service is an object of love for God. In days of yore a party of rich men used to supply food to the religious men and loved them. He who marries with the object of getting such a son who will pray for him and for that loves his wife, is also an object of love for God. For this reason, there are ample rewards for spending money for the members of the family ; even for a morsel of food which a husband lifts up to the mouth of his wife. Jesus Christ said in his invocation : O God! don't allow my enemies to become pleased with me, don't create trouble in the way of my religion, don't make the world a great object of my anxiety and remove the pleasure of my enemies from the wealth of the world. He did not pray : Don't make the world the root of my anxiety. Rather he said : Don't make the world a great object of my anxiety. The Prophet said in his invocation : O God! I pray for Thy mercy, so that I may gain the glory of Thy honour in this world and in the next. He also prayed : O God! save me from the calamities of this world and the next.

This world and the next world mean two conditions of

which one is nearer than the other. So if a man does not love the happiness of today, how can he love the happiness of tomorrow? Surely he should love the happiness of tomorrow as tomorrow will turn into a lasting condition. So it is necessary to enquire into the lasting condition. The pleasures of this world is of two kinds - (1) One kind of pleasure is opposed to the pleasure of the next world and is a stumbling block. The Prophets and friends of God were careful of this kind of pleasure. (2) Another kind of pleasure is not opposed to that of the next world and this was not prohibited for them, such as marriage, lawful eating etc.

(4) Fourth class - Love for God and hate for God

It is selfless and disinterested love. This is the highest kind of love, most secret and subtle. Love of this kind is possible, as if this love surpasses beyond limit, it spreads towards the things which have got connection with the beloved. A lover even loves the things of the beloved and he even loves those whom the beloved loves. A lover loves also those who serve the beloved. He loves those who praise and glorify the beloved and try to please him. Baqiah b. Walid said : When a believer loves a believer, he even loves his dog. The lover Majnu, therefore, sang

> When I went to the house of Laila,
>
> I kissed its wall.
>
> Love is not for the wall,
>
> But for its owner.

If love is strong, it spreads more. Love for God is similar. When love for God envelopes the heart, it rules the heart and it even spreads over everything. The lover then sees His power in everything. He who loves a man loves his handicrafts, his letters and all his actions. For this reason, when a fresh fruit was brought to the Prophet, he placed it upon his eyes, honoured it and said : It has come with the help of my Lord. Love reduces the pangs of lover. The love of a party of men reaches such height that they say : We don't distinguish between sorrow and happiness as all come from God. We feel happiness at His pleasure. The sage Samnun said :

I am happy at Thy pleasure,

I have got none near or distant,

So do to me what Thou art pleased with.

He who loves a king, loves also those persons whom the king loves and even his servants. A sage said : when pain gives pleasure, can there remain the pangs of wound ? The proportion of love for a man is known in proportion to the giving of dear things for him. The reason is that when love for a person envelopes his entire heart, love of other things does not remain in his heart. Therefore, a friend of God gives in charity to please God everything he has got. For this reason, Hazrat Abu Bakr left nothing for his family when the Prophet called for charity. Even he sacrificed his little daughter for the Prophet.

Hazrat Ibn Omar said : Once the Prophet was seated with Hazrat Abu Bakr who put on long shirt tied on the chest with a bell. Gabriel got down and said to the Prophet : O Prophet of God! why shall I see Abu Bakr covered with a long shirt ? He said : Because all his wealth he gave in charity before the Conquest. Gabriel said : Tender salam to him from God and tell him that his Lord is saying to him : Are you satisfied or dissatisfied on account of your want ? The Prophet looked to Abu Bakr and said : O Abu Bakr! he is Gabriel. He tendered you salam from God on account of your want. He said: Then Abu Bakr wept and said : I am satisfied with my Lord.

Hatred for God

He who loves God has got no alternative but to hate for God, because one who loves a man for any of his good works hates him for any act contrary to it. These two things - love and hatred, are connected with each other and cannot be separated. When these two things are expressed in words, they are named friendship and enmity. God said to Moses Have you made friends and enemies for My sake ? You love one whose nothing is disclosed to you except allegiance and you hate one whose nothing is disclosed to you except sin and bad conduct. Different conducts are united in a person for some of which he is loved and for others he is hated. He is loved for one reason and hated for a different reason. A beautiful wife who is a sinner is loved for her one attribute by her husband and hated for another. A Muslim can be loved for his religion Islam and can be hated for his sins.

Hate is to be expressed by words and actions. If hate is expressed by words, you stop talking with a sinner and sometimes use harsh words. If hate is expressed by action, you sometimes harm a sinner and destroy his evil design. That occurs in proportion to his sins. When he is repentant, you keep his sin secret. When you love a person, you hate him also for his fault in these ways you protest against his evil actions, you go away from him, you do not look at him etc. These are modes so far action is concerned. One stops his help and sympathy and another tries to destroy his necessary works, so that he may not commit any sin. Mustah b. Asasah once spread a slander against the character of Hazrat Ayesha. Hazrat Abu Bakr used to help him by giving him charity. When it reached his ear, he stopped his help with a promise that he won't help him further. Then this verse was revealed : Those who possess wealth and sufficient means among you should not swear that they would not give in charity to their near relations, the poor and the refugees in the way of God but let them forgive and pardon. Don't you like that God should forgive you? (24 : 22) Though the sin of Mustah was great, yet Hazrat Abu Bakr felt restless in his mind for that event. It is the habit of a Siddiq to forgive one who oppresses.

Classes of sinners and treatment with them : There are two classes of sinners, either (1) they have got no faith or (2) they commit sins in their actions and deeds. Those who have got no faith are either unbelievers or innovators. Innovators are of two classes-one class call towards the views opposed to *Shariat* and another class remain silent. Those who remain silent are compelled to do so or do it willingly. So there are three classes of sinners in the matter of faith.

(1) Unbeliever : If he is at war with the Muslims, he can be killed or made a slave. There is no other punishment except these two for him. A *Zimmi* (one who has been given protection) cannot be given trouble, but if he protests against Islam, he can be given trouble. To make him humiliated is to make his livelihood narrow, not to salute him first, not to mix or to carry on trade with him, not to make enjoyment with him like friends. God says : You will not find a people who believe in God and the next world to make friends with those who oppose God and His Prophet even though they may be their parents, children, brothers or relatives (58 : 22). The Prophet said : O those who believe! don't take my enemy and your enemy as friends.

(2) Innovators : Innovators call towards innovation. If innovation leads towards infidelity, its law is more severe than that of a *Zimmi* as he cannot be given the advantage of a *Zimmi*. If it does not lead to infidelity, its law is lighter. The innovator calls the people towards misguidance as he believes his views to be correct. So his evil is also unlimited. The best way to express hate for him is to give up his company and rebuke him for his innovation. The Prophet said : God fills up the mind of a man with peace and faith who rebukes an innovator. God will keep one safe on the most grievous day who disgraces an innovator.

(3) Ordinary innovator : If the people do not follow him or he is unable to bring them his views, his affair is easy. It is better to treat him harshly at the very beginning. It is better to advise him first with humility. If it is not effective, it is better to turn away from him.

(4) Sinners : The sinners who disobey the injunctions of God by their actions and not by their faith are of two kinds, a sinner who gives trouble to another by actions, such as oppression, misappropriation, false evidence, slander, back-biting etc. and a sinner who does not give trouble to another by such actions. Such a sinner also has got two conditions - (a) either he invites others towards sinful acts or (b) he does not invite others towards sinful acts, for example, a man drinks wine but does not call others to drink it. Thus there are three kinds of sinners - (1) The actions of the first kind of sinners are injurious to a great extent, such as back-biting, false evidence, oppression, etc. It is better not to mix with them and not to transact with them. They are of three classes - (1) those who murder men, (2) those who take movable properties of men by oppression, and (3) those who take immovable properties of men by oppression. It is better not to mix with them. The greater the guilt, the greater the punishment.

(2) The second class sinners create the causes of disturbance and make easy its different paths to the people. They do not give any trouble in the mundane affixis of the people but injure their religion by their actions. Such a sinner is to be humiliated and his connection should be cut off.

(3) Third class sinner : He who commits a great sin by

drinking wine, by giving up compulsory duties or doing unlawful things has got light measure. If a man sees him to commit these sins, it is compulsory on him to prohibit him, be it by beating him or by taking other measure, because it is compulsory to prohibit an evil action. If he is habituated to do it, he should be given advice if there is possibility for him to give up those actions. If there is benefit in treating with him harshly, it should be done. If it is useless to give him advice, one should be led by his conscience to take a suitable measure against him. It has been narrated that a drunkard was beaten several times before the Prophet but still he did not give up drinking wine. One of the companions said : God's curse on this drunkard. The Prophet said : Don't be a helper of the devil regarding your brother. This means that the devil is sufficient for the man. You should not rebuke him.

Conditions of friendship

Know, O dear readers! that every man is not fit for friendship. The Prophet said : 'A man is upon the religion of his friend. So let him look with whom he befriends.' Make friendship having a look to one's character, conduct and qualities. Make condition to get benefit of the qualities of your friend and search to get temporal and spiritual benefits. Wealth, name and bargain are the temporal benefits. This is not our object. The benefits of religion are the following – (1) to get education and learn action, (2) to get benefit of saying oneself from name and fame which cause anxiety of mind, (3) to gain wealth to maintain oneself, (4) to seek help in necessary actions, in dangers and difficulties and in many other actions of life, (5) to get blessings of the invocations of a friend, (6) to hope for getting intercession of a friend in the next world. A certain sage of yore said : Increase the number of friends, as every believer has got the right of intercession and you may hope to fall in the intercession of your friend.

God says : Those who have faith and do good works will seek intercession and He will increase His favours on them. To explain this verse, there is a *Hadis* that believers will make intercession for their friends and God will admit them in Paradise along with them. It has also been said in explaining it that when a man is forgiven, he will get right of intercession for his friends.

There are some conditions of these benefits which we shall describe now. The man with whom companionship is to be kept should have five qualities in him. Intellect, good conduct, not to be a sinner, not to be an innovator, not to be a worldly addicted man.

(1) Intellect : It is the root of wealth and there is no good in the company of the fools and the illiterate. Hazrat Ali said in poems :

Keep no company with the fools
Break friendship with the fools
When a wise friend keeps up patience,
Illiterate friend becomes then impatient.
A wise friend is known in danger,
Illiterate friend leaves him in disaster.

An illiterate friend leaves him in disaster. Though he wants to do benefit, he will do you harm, as he is ignorant. For this reason, a certain wise man said :

You will remain safe,
If a wise man becomes your enemy
If a fool loves your friend
the better may fall in danger
How many insane there are,
who know only to commit murder.

Imam Sufiyan Saori said : It is sin to look at the face of a fool. A wise man is he who understands all his actions and a fool is he who has got no sense of right and wrong and who does not understand it even if it is dictated by others.

(2) Good conduct : A friend should have good conduct as many wise men take things as they are in their normal mood; but when they get angry, sexual passion, miserliness and cowardice gain supremacy, and he conducts himself according to his whims and acts contrary to his wisdom. There is no good in having friends like him.

(3) Religious nature : A friend should have religious nature to give benefit. There is no good in keeping company with a sinner. He who fears God cannot be engaged in great sins, but if a man does not fear God, you can't be safe from his harms and can't trust in his words. He changes according to the change of necessity. God says : Don't follow one whose heart I have made forgetful from My remembrance and who follows his passions. God says : Let him not turn to one who does not believe it and follows his passions. God says : Turn away from one who turns away from My remembrance and intends nothing but this world's life : God says : Follow the path of one who turns to Me. You will understand from this that it is lawful to turn away from the great sinners.

(4) Innovation : It is the duty of one to have no connection with an innovator. What benefit will accrue from his help? Hazrat Omar gave encouragement for religious nature of a friend. He said : You should make friendship with the truthful, because in that case you will live under their care, as they increase happiness in time of joy and remove difficulties at the time of sorrow. Bear well the affairs of your friend, keep your enemy distant and warn your friend, but don't keep a trusted man of a people distant. He who does not fear God is not a trustworthy man. Don't keep company with a great sinner. Don't give clue to your secrets to him. Consult with those in all your affairs who fear God.

The sage Alqamah Attar advised his son at the time of his death. O dear son! if you feel necessity of making friendship, make friendship with such a man who will save you if you save him, who will increase your beauty if you keep company with him, who will help you when you fall in a trouble. If you extent your hand of good towards him, he will also extend his hand of good towards you. He will help you in any good work you undertake. He will remove any evil if he sees in you. He will give you if you want something from him. He will begin with you when he remains silent. He will be sorry when any disaster falls on you and gives you pain. He will confirm your word as true when you speak. He will advise you when you intend to do an action. He will place your opinion above when there arise differences of opinion among you.

The sage Jafar Sadiq said : Don't keep company with four persons - (1) a liar, you will get deception from him and he will make the distant near and the near distant ; (2) a fool, you will not get any benefit from him, he will do you harm if he goes to do your benefit ; (3) a miser, he will forsake you at the time of your dire necessity ; (4) a coward, he will flee away after surrendering you in the hands of the enemies ; (5) a great sinner, he will sell you in lieu of a morsel of food for a thing of lesser value. Hazrat Junaid said : The friendship of a transgressor with good conduct is dearer to me than that of a learned man with bad conduct. The sage Bashar Hafi said : Friends are three- (1) a friend for your next world, (2) a friend for your present world, (3) a friend to console your mind. The Caliph Mansur said : Friends are of three kinds- (1) One kind of friends are like food and there is no alternative but to get their help. (2) Another kind of friends are like a medicine and their help is necessary at times. (3) The third kind of friends are like an epidemic disease and there is no necessity of them at any time.

It is said that a party of men are like some trees which have got shade but no fruits. Those trees are like those persons who come of no use for the next world except for this world and the benefits of this world disappear soon like the disappearance of shade. Out of them, there are some trees which have got fruits but no shade. They are like the persons who come of no use for good of this world except good of the next world. Some trees have got both fruits and shade and some trees have got neither fruits nor shade like Bakul trees whose thorns pierce clothes and which have got no eatable things. They are like snakes and rats. Hazrat Abu Zarr said : Loneliness is better than a bad companion and a good companion is better than loneliness God says : When the illiterate call them, they say salam. It means : We are safe from your sins and you are safe from our evils. Hazrat Ali said : If a man gives life to your action, keep your religion alive by keeping company with him. Luqman advised his son: O dear son! keep company with the learned, as heart is then enlivened with wisdom as a land is enlivened with rain-water.

SECTION 2

The rights of friendship and brotherhood

The tie of friendship and brotherhood is like that of husband and wife. As some rights and obligations arise out of wed-lock, so also some rights and obligations arise out of the tie of friendship and brotherhood. These rights are eight -

(1) Right in wealth and properties : The Prophet said : Two friends are like two hands, one of which washes the other. Similarly friendship is completed when one of them keeps the other, as if they are one and the same and they share the enjoyments of each other. There are three stages of self-sacrifice for each other. **(a)** The lowest stage is to bring down his friend to the level of a servant and to give him charity at the time of his need from his excess wealth. When a friend falls in want, he should give charity to him without asking from the excess of his wealth. If he drives him to the level of asking, he will then transgress the limit of the demands of friendship. **(b)** The second stage is to bring his friend down to his stage and remain satisfied by making him sharer in his properties. He will also come down to his stage till he becomes equal partner with him. Hazrat Hasan Basri said : Once a friend divided his shirt into two portions and gave one portion to his friend. **(c)** The third stage is to place the needs of a friend above his own needs. This is the rank of the truthful and is the last limit of the three stages of friendship. The result is *I'sar* or the sacrifice of one's need for the other. It has been reported that a party of bad people made defamation against a party of religious men. As a result the Caliph passed order for the execution of the religious people. There was the sage Abul Hasan Nuri was one of them. Before all of them, he advanced towards the gallows and said : Hang me first. On being asked the reason of his desire for death, he said : I wish to save the lives of my friends even for some minutes in lieu of my life. This was the cause of the saving the lives of the religious men. Mamun b. Mahran said : He who is pleased with his friend by giving up good things, made friendship as it were with the inmated of grasses.

Stage of the world : It is not pleasing to the religious men. It is said that the sage Otbatul Golam went once to the house of his friend and said : I have got need of four thousand coins from your wealth. He said : Take two thousand coins. He turned his face at this and said : I adopted God in lieu of this world. Don't you feel ashamed that you claim friendship for God but place the love of the world over friendship ? The sage Abu Hazim said : When you have got a friend for the sake of God don't engage him in your affairs of the world.

Highest Stage : God praised the believers in this verse : Their affairs are settled by mutual consultations and they spend out of what I have provided them with. In other words, they mixed their wealth and did not distinguish it. If anybody said among them "This is my shoe", they did not keep company with him as he uttered this keeping his own connection with his prosperity. It is said that the sage Father Musali went once to the house of his friend in his absence and said to his maid-servant : Take to me the cash box of your master. When she brought it to him, he took therefrom some coins necessary for him. The maid-servant informed her master about it and he said : If you speak the truth, I set you free, because what you informed me is a good news. One day a man came to Hazrat Abu Hurairah and said : I wish to make friendship with you for the sake of God. He said : Do you know the rights of a friend ? He said : One of the rights of friendship is that your right in your properties and wealth is not more than that of mine. He said : I have not as yet reached this stage. He

said : Then go away. Hazrat Zaiynul Abidin, son of Hazrat
Hussain said to a man : Does anybody amongst you take
anything what he wished after placing his hand in the pocket
of his friend or in his purse ? He said: No. He said : Then you
are not friends. A party of man came to Hasan Basri and said:
O Abu Sayeed! have you prayed ? He said : Yes. They said :
The market people have not yet prayed. He said : Who has
taken religion from the market people ? I know that nobody
among them gives charity.

Once a man came to Ibrahim b. Adham who was to go to
Baitul Muqaddas (holy Mosque of Jerusalem). He said : I
wish to go there with you. Hazrat Ibrahim said to him. Yes, I
agree with this condition that I shall have greater right in your
money. He said : That will not be. Then he said : Your
truthfulness pleased me. Whenever Ibrahim wished to have
any companion with him, he never acted contrary to his
wishes. He never accepted anybody as his companion if he
did not agree with him. Once Ibrahim b. Adham gifted away
an ass belonging to his friend without his permission. When
his friend returned, he became pleased with him. Hazrat Ibn
Omar said : Once a man presented to a companion a fried
goat's head. The latter sent it to his friend as he was more in
need. The latter again sent it to another man. Thus it turned
round seven persons and came to the first friend.

It is narrated that Hazrat Masruq fell in a heavy debt and
his friend Khaisan also had debts. Hazrat Masruq cleared off
the debts of the latter without his knowledge. Khaisan also in
return cleared off the debts of Masruq without his knowledge.
The Prophet cemented brotherhood between Abdur Rahman
b. Auf and Sa'ad b. Raby. Then Abdur Rahman gave option
to his friend about his properties and said : God has given me
abundant wealth. So take therefrom what you wish. Hazrat
Sa'ad had the quality of equality and Hazrat Abdur Rahman

had the quality of *I'sar* or self-sacrifice which is better than equality. Hazrat Ali said : To spend 20 Dirhams for a friend for the sake of God, I consider better than to give charity of one hundred dirhams to the poor and the destitute. Follow the Holy Prophet in the matter of self-sacrifice. He entered once into a jungle with some of his companions and took two pieces of wood for tooth stick, one straight and another crooked. He gave the straight tooth-stick to a companion who said : O Messenger of God! by God, you are more simple than me. Therefore you are more entitled to the straight tooth-stick than myself. He said : If anybody keeps company of a man for little while of the day, question will be put to him about the rights of his companionship, whether he established it or destroyed it.

Once the Prophet went out to a well for bath. His companion Hazrat Huzaifa covered him with a screen of cloth till he finished his bath. After his bath, the Prophet was going to cover Huzaifa with the screen when he said to the Prophet: O Messenger of God! may my parents be sacrificed to you, don't do it. The Prophet held the screen till Huzaifa finished his bath. Then the Prophet said : If two men keep company with each other, he who is more kind to his companion is dearer to God.

It is narrated that Malik b. Dinar and Muhammad b. Wase went to the house of Hazrat Hasan Basri in his absence. Muhammad took out a cup of food which was under his bed and began to eat. Malik said : Hold out your hand till the owner comes. Suddenly Hazrat Hasan Basri came there and said : O Malik! we used first to give trouble to one another in this way. God ordered us to treat well with our friends. God said : Treat well with your friend. At that time, a friend handed over the key of his house to his friend who had option to spend whatever he wished. His friend, however, refrained from enjoying it for fear of God, when God revealed : Give them order to regard brothers as friends and to give them food to their satisfaction.

(2) Second right : To help a friend before asking in times of need. There are different stages of this help. The lowest stage is to fulfil with pleasure and kindness the needs of a friend at the time of his asking for it. A certain wise man said: When a man requests his friend to fulfil his certain need and he does not fulfil it, let him remind him second time. If he does not fulfil it without delay, let him recite this verse : God will resurrect the dead. This means that he and the dead are equal. A sage of yore maintained the family members of his friend after his death for forty years. The Prophet said : Behold, God has got cups in the world. Those are hearts. The dearest of hearts to God is that which is the most clean, firm and soft. 'Clean' means clean of sins, 'firm' means firm in religion and 'soft' means kind to friends and relatives.

In short, consider the needs of your friend as your own or more than this. As you are not indifferent to your needs, so don't be indifferent to the needs of your friend. Relieve him from asking you to fulfil his needs. Try to remove his difficulties and dangers. Hazrat Hasan Basri said : My friends are dear to me than my wife and children, as my family reminds me of this world, but my friends remind me of the next world. He said : If a man spreads the fame of his friend for the sake of God, God will send His angels of the Throne on the Resurrection Day to spread his fame in Paradise. There is one *Hadis* : If a man meets with his friend for the sake of God, an angel proclaims from behind : Good news, good news of Paradise for you. Hazrat Atta said : Enquire of your friends once in every three days. If they are ill, meet with them. If they remain busy in works, help them. If they forget, remind them. The Prophet once said to Ibn Omar : If you love anybody, ask him his name, his father's name and his address. If he is ill, go to see him. If he remains busy, help him. Once Hazrat Abbas was asked : Who is dearest to you? He said : My friend. He said : If a man comes to my assembly thrice without any necessity and does not get any benefit from me, I can understand that his object of search is not the world. Hazrat Sayeed said : I have got three duties for my friend. When he comes, I shall entertain him. When he speaks, I shall turn my face to him. When he sits, I shall give him good place. God says : They are kind to one another.

(3) **Third right about tongue :** Sometimes you will talk with a friend and sometimes not. Don't disclose any secret talk which your friends tell you, even to their close friends. Don't disclose any secrets of your friend even though there is separation from him, as it is a sign of bad conduct. Don't speak of any bad things about his friends, wives and children. Hazrat Anas said : The Prophet did not say anything he felt bad of the talk of anybody in his presence as he who repeats it to anybody is considered as rebuke. You should not keep secret the praise of your friend. To keep it secret is considered as envy. Don't back-bite your friend or any member of his family. Hazrat Ibnul Mubarak said : A believer searches for excuses and a hypocrite searches for faults. The sage Fuzail said : It is the rule of religion to pardon the faults of a friend.

The Prophet said : I seek refuge to God from a bad neighbour. If he sees any good, he keeps it secret and if he sees any bad, he discloses it. There is no such a man who cannot be called good for some of his conducts and cannot be called bad for some of his conducts. There is a *Hadis* that once a man praised another before the Prophet. On the following day he began to defame him. Then the Prophet said: You have praised him yesterday and you are defaming him today. He said : By God! I told the truth yesterday about him and I have not told a lie about him today. He pleased me yesterday and I said what I knew about him as good. Today he enkindled my anger and then I have said what I know about him as bad.

The Prophet said : There is certainly sorcery in oratory. He compared it with sorcery. The Prophet said in another *Hadis* : Oratory and harshness are two branches of hypocrisy. There is in another *Hadis* : God hates full description of anything. Imam Shafayi said : There is no such Muslim who obeys God and at the same time does not obey God, and there is no such Muslim who disobeys God and at the same time does not disobey Him. He is a just man whose virtues are more than his sins. Don't hold bad conjecture about your friend, because it is the back-biting of mind which is prohibited. Many conjectures remain upon mistakes. The Prophet said : God made unlawful four things for a believer - to shed the blood of a believer, to destroy his properties, to mar his honour and to harbour evil conjectures against him. The Prophet said: Beware of evil conjecture, because evil conjecture is the worst false talks. To search the faults of others and to harbour evil conjecture show the evil path.

The Prophet said : Don't disclose the secrets of one another, don't seek the secrets of one another and don't cut off the connections of one another and unite the servants of God in brotherhood. The object of pleasure to God is the man who imbues himself with divine attributes, as He is the keeper of secrets, pardoner of sins and kind to His servants. So how can you remain without forgiving one who is above you or who is lower than you?

Jesus Christ said to his disciples : What do you do when the wind blows off the wearing cloth of your friend in his sleep and makes him naked ? They said : We cover his private parts with cloth. He said : Rather I see that you uncover his private parts. They said : Glory be to God, who does this ? He said : If anybody amongst you hears any secret word about your brother, he adds to it other words and discloses it in a big form. Know that the faith of a man is not perfect till he loves for others what he loves for himself. The lower state of friendship is that you will respect for your friend the treatment which you expect that he should mete out to you.

God says : Woe to those who take full measure when they take from men and who reduce it when they give it to others? Hope to do justice to others as you expect that others should do justice to you. The Prophet said : If a man conceals the faults of his brother in this world. God will conceal his faults in the next. There is in another narration : He gives life as it were to a buried man. The Prophet said : The discussions of an assembly are trust except those of three assemblies (1) the assembly where unlawful murders are committed, (2) the assembly where unlawful fornications are made lawful, (3) and the assembly where wealth is made lawful except by lawful means. The Prophet said : The consultations of two friends are like trust. It is not lawful to disclose to another what one does not like. One wise man was asked : How can you keep matters secret ? He said : I am like a grave for these matters. The heart of a fool is in his tongue and the tongue of a wise man is in his heart. In other words, the fool cannot keep secret what is in his mind and discloses it in such a place which he does not know.

Hazrat Abbas said to his son Abdullah : I see that Hazrat Omar has given you superiority over the elderly companions. Remember my five instruction – (1) Don't disclose his (Omar's) secrets ; (2) don't vilify anybody in his (Omar) presence ; (3) don't take courage to tell falsehood before him; (4) don't disobey his orders ; (5) and let him not see you committing any act of treachery. The sage Shubi said : Each sentence of these five instructions is better than one thousand sentences. Hazrat Ibn Abbas said : Don't argue with a fool lest he gives you trouble. Don't argue with a wise man, lest he envies you. The Prophet said : If a man gives up dispute over a useless matter, a house will be built for him in a corner of Paradise. If a man gives up dispute of a matter to which he has got right, a house will be built up for him in a high place of Paradise.

The Prophet said : Don't envy one another, don't cut off connections from one another and make brotherhood among the servants of God. One Muslim is brother to another Muslim. He does not oppress him, he does not deprive him and he does not dishonour him. Ibn Omamah Baheli said : The Prophet once came to us. We were then arguing with one another. He got enraged and said : Give up arguing as there is little good in it. Give up dispute as it has got little benefit and it grows enmity between two friends. A certain wise man said: If a man disputes with his friends, his manliness goes away and his honour also goes away. The Prophet said : Don't dispute with your brother, don't ridicule him, don't break promise with him. He said: You give in charity ample wealth to the people, but it does not come out in a cheerful mood and in good manners.

(4) Accord good treatment to your friend in words and deeds : As is the friendship, so the treatment should be. Tell such words which your friend loves. Use words of love and share his sorrows and happiness. The Prophet said : When one of you loves his brother, he should inform him of his love. It increases love. If he knows that you love him, he will surely love you. When you come to know that he also loves you, your love for him will increase. So love will increase from both sides. The existence of love among the believers is the object of *Shariat* and religion. So send presents to one another. For this the Prophet said : Send presents to one another, you will then love one another. The Prophet gave simile of two friends as two hands, one of which works for the other. In other words, one friend helps another in all affairs.

The Prophet said : One Muslim is brother to another Muslim. He does not treat him bad, he does not spoil his honour and does not surrender him to the hands of his enemy. Don't back-bite your friend as God likened back-biting to eating the flesh of a dead brother. God says : Does one of you like to eat the flesh of his dead brother ? An angel presents before the soul of a man what he sees in the guarded Tablet in the form of a figure in dream. He shows back-biting in the form of eating the flesh of a dead animal. A back-biter sees in dream that he is eating the flesh of a dead animal. It means that he roams about back-biting. The sage Mujahid said : Don't remember your friend by back-biting him as you wish that no person should remember you with back-biting.

The Prophet said : Accord good treatment to your neighbour, you will be good Muslim. Accord good treatment to one who keeps your company, you will be a believer. The Prophet said : One believer is a mirror to another believer.' The substance of this *Hadis* is that you should conduct yourself in such a way that your friend may correct himself by looking at your actions. The sage Masar was asked : Do you love one who tells your faults ? He said : If he advises me with regard to the faults that are in myself and him, it is good, but when he defames me before a party of men, it is not good. What he said is true, because to advise before the people is dishonourable.

The saint Zunnun Misri said : Don't keep company with God without obeying His commands. Don't keep company with the people without advice to one another. Don't keep company with your passion without differing from it. Don't keep company with the devil without being his enemy. Hazrat Omar said : If a man holds out the faults of his brother before him, God will show kindness to him. For this reason, Hazrat Omar said to Hazrat Salman : What are the actions of mine which appear disliking to you ? Hazrat Salman said : Pardon me for this. When he pressed Salman, he said : I heard that you have got two shirts, one of which you wear during day time and another at night time. I heard also that two kinds of curries are served before you at the same time. Hazrat Omar said : Neither of these two matters is true. Have you heard any other thing ? Hazrat Salman said : No. Hazrat Huzaifa wrote to Hazrat Yusuf b. Asbat : I heard that you sold your religion in lieu of two pieces. You said to the milk-seller : What is its price ? He said: Six pieces. You pressed for lesser price. The milk seller said : Let it be so. The man was cognisant of your God-fear and hence he sold the milk at reduced price to you. Uncover your head from the screen of passion and give up the urge of passion.

(5) To forgive the faults of a friend : If your friend commits sin and continues therein, advise him with sweet words. If he turns back, it is better. If he does not turn back, connection should be cut off according to Hazrat Abu Zarr. According to Abu Darda'a, connection with him should not be cut off, as he will walk once in a straight path and another time in a crooked way. Hazrat Ibrahim Nakhyi said : Don't cut off connection with your friend and don't leave him at the time of his commission of sin as he may commit a sin today and give it up on the following day. There is in *Hadis* : Fear the slip of a learned man and don't boycot him and hope for his return.

One friend of Hazrat Omar went to Syria and stayed there for long. Hazrat Omar took this news from a certain man of Syria. He said : He has become the brother of the devil and he has begun to drink wine. Hazrat Omar wrote to him a letter saying : In the name of the Most Compassionate, the Merciful (40 : 1). He rebuked him in this letter. When he read it, he wept and said : God said the truth. Omar advised me. He then repented and turned back.

It has been narrated that one of two friends fell in love with a woman and informed it to his friend. He said : If you wish, you may cut off friendship with me. His friend said : Shall I lose a friend for his one sin ? Then he promised that he would fast till his friend came out of his love for the woman. He fasted for forty days, as a result of which his friend's love for the woman went away from his heart. Then he look his meal and drink.

One of two friends went astray. One friend asked him : Have you not forsaken him ? He said : I wish to remain with him more now. I shall have to lift him up by catching him by his hand. I shall have to rebuke him with sweet words and I shall have to call him to his former condition.

It has been narrated that two friends of Banu Israil engaged in divine service in a hill. One of them one day got down and went to a market to buy meat. He saw there an unchaste woman and fell in love with her. He called her in a lonely place and satisfied his lust. This continued for three days. His friend in the hill came down to search for him and found him following a woman. He embraced and kissed his friend and said : I have come to know your condition. Now let us go to the hill for divine service. So his friend went with him to the hill being repentant.

One should not cut off the relationship from his relative who is seen engaged in a sin. God said to His Prophet in connection with his relatives : If your relatives disobey you, say : I am displeased with what you do (26:216). He did not say : I am pleased with your actions. Rather he said : I am

displeased with your action. When Abu Darda'a was asked :
Why do you not hate your friend who is doing this sin ? He
said : Surely I hate his sinful act, but how can I hate him as he
is my brother in religion ? Brotherhood of religion is greater
than that of relationship. A wise man was asked : Who is
dearer to you, a friend or a brother? He said : If my brother is
my friend, he is dearer to me. Hazrat Hasan Basri said : How
many friends there are who are not born of your mother. It
has, therefore, been said : Love is necessary for relationship
but relationship is not necessary for love. Hazrat Jafar *Sadiq*
said : Connection is made out of love of one day and
relationship is made out of love of one month and near
relationship is made out of love of one year. God severs
connection with one who severs connection with his relatives.
It is compulsory to keep the tie of friendship. One should not
make friendship with a great sinner from the very beginning,
but when it is done, it should not be cut off.

The Prophet said : The worst servants near God are those
who roam with slander and create separation in friendship.
When one man committed a sin, his friend rebuked him. Then
the Prophet said to him: Stop, don't rebuke him. Don't be a
helper of the devil in the matter of your friend. So it is better
to keep away from the great sinners from the very beginning
than to servere friendship with them after it is made. Imam
Shafayi said : If a man's anger is aroused but his anger does
not arise, he is an ass. If a man's pleasure is incurred but he
does not get pleased, he is a devil. So don't be an ass or a
devil. Rather be an agent of your friend and bring pleasure to
yourself, and adopt precaution of being a devil by not accepting
it. A certain wise man said : I never rebuked anybody. The
cause is that if an honourable man rebukes me, I pardon his
fault as it is pardonable, but if a man of dishonour rebukes
me, I save myself from his attack without replying to his

rebuke. Whenever your friend raises excuse, accept it, be it true or false.

The Prophet said : He who does not accept the excuse of his friend commits sin like the tax collector in the street. The Prophet said : A believer suddenly gets angry and his anger is soon appeased. He did not mention that he does not get angry. God says : Those who appease anger etc. He did not say about the absence of anger. Now-a-days anger does not appease till harm is not done to a friend, but have patience at the trouble inflicted by him. To remove anger from the soil of heart is not possible as it is a natural attribute of man. To appease it and to act contrary to its nature is possible. To act in agreement with anger is to take retaliation but to act contrary to its nature is not to take retaliation. The Prophet said : Love your friend in a moderate manner, perchance he may become someday your enemy. Get angry at your enemy in a moderate manner, perchance he may turn to be your friend sometime. Hazrat Omar said : Let not your love exceed the limit and let not your hatred lead you to the path of destruction.

(6) Pray for your friend in his life time and even after his death : As you like to pray for yourself and the members of your family, so you should pray for those after the death of your friend with whom your friend had connection. The Prophet said : If a man prays for his friend in his absence, the angels say : Similar prayer is for you. In another narration God says : O My servant! I will accept your prayer in your matter. There is in *Hadis* : If a man prays for his friend, it is better accepted than that for himself. The Prophet said : If a man prays for his friend in his absence, it is not rejected. A good friend will follow you after your death with the angels, as there is a *Hadis* : When a man dies, the people say : What thing he has left behind, but the angels say : What actions he has sent in advance ? They are glad for his good actions, they ask about his condition and intercede for him. The Prophet said : A dead man in grave is like a drowning man in water. As a drowning man catches whatever he gets to save his life, so a dead man remains anxious to get the prayer of father, children, brothers, friends and near relatives. The prayer of a living man enters into the grave of a dead man like a hill of light. A certain sage said : The prayer of a living man for the dead is like a present. The angel takes a handkerchief of one bundle of light and comes to the dead man and says : This is a present to you from that friend of yours, this has come from that relative of yours. He then becomes pleased with it as a living man becomes pleased with a present.

(7) *Wafa* and *Ikhlas* : *Wafa* means to remain firm on the rights of friendship, to keep it lasting till the death of friend and to keep it even after his death with his wife, children and friends and relatives and to take care of them. *Ikhlas* means to fulfil the duties of friendship selflessly for the sake of God. The object of friendship for the sake of God is to get benefit in the next world. The Prophet said that seven persons will get shade under the shade of the Throne on the Resurrection Day. There are two persons out of them who love each other for the sake of God. A certain woman once came to the Prophet who showed respect to her. On being asked the reason, the Prophet said : This woman used to come to our house during the life time of Khadija. To honour the right of friendship appertains to faith. Accord good treatment to friends. God says : Tell My servants that they should say those things that are best, for the devil sows dissensions among them (17 : 53). God says about Joseph that he said : When God took me out of prison. He was indeed good to me and took you all from the desert even after the devil had sown enmity between me and my brothers (12 : 100). Friendship becomes lasting when it is done for the sake of God. If one makes friendship for a

certain purpose, it ends when the purpose is fulfilled. The result of friendship for God is not hatred for any matter, temporal or spiritual. God says of this love for Him : They don't find any necessity (hatred) in their hearts for what they are given and they take to self sacrifice for friends. Finding any necessity means here hatred.

(8) Not to give trouble to a friend : Don't inflict trouble to your friend and give up the giving of trouble and taking of trouble. Don't ask anything from his wealth and properties. Don't hope to get any benefit from his name and fame. Don't tell him : Take my care and fulfil the duties towards me. Hope for the rewards of his prayer, meet with him and help in his duties of religion and seek nearness of God by fulfilling duties towards him. A certain wise man said : The friend who places his honour above the honour of his friend and thinks himself superior to his friend, commits sin and allows another to commit it. The man who considers his friend as his equal suffers mental agony. The man who considers himself inferior to his friend keeps himself and his friend safe. Hazrat Ayesha said : A believer is brother to another believer. He does not seek advantage over him and does not inflict trouble on him. Hazrat Junaid said : I kept company with four classes of Sufis. There were thirty Sufis in each class. They are Haris Mohasbi and his party men, Hasan Majusi and his party men, Sirri Saqti and his party men, Ibnul Karabi and his party men. Those who made friends out of them for the sake of God, did not inflict trouble on one another and did not keep company with one another without any reason. A certain sage said : Live with the worldly people with good manners. Live with the people of the next world with knowledge and live as you wish with the God-fearing people.

Know, O dear readers! that there are three classes of people. You will gain benefit by association with only one

class of people. You can do some benefit to the second class
of people and you receive no harm at their hands, nor you
will receive any benefit from them. You cannot do any benefit
to the third class of people, rather you will receive harm as a
result of your association with them. These people are fools
and ill tempered. Don't give up the second class of people as
they will do you benefit in the next world by their intercession
and invocation. God sent revelation to Moses : If you obey
Me, you will have many friends. In other words : If you show
sympathy to them, bear patience at their harms and do not
hate them, you will have many friends. A wise man said : The
love of one is lasting who has got no outward show. A certain
companion said : God curses those who inflict trouble on
others.

The Prophet said : I and the God fearing men of my
followers are free from inflicting troubles. A wise man said :
When a man does four works in the house of his friend his
love becomes perfect - (1) when he eats with him, (2) when
he does necessary works with him, (3) when he prays with
him, (4) and when he sleeps with him. The Prophet said : 'A
man is upon the religion of his friend. There is no good in the
company of a friend who does not consider good for his friend
what he considers good for himself.' Look to your friend with
such a look of love that he can know your love. Look to his
good deeds and not to his faults. It has been reported that
whoever sat before the Prophet, he used to show his face to
him. Every man thought that he was honoured more by the
Prophet. Even his sitting, his hearing, his dissension and
arguing with him in sweet words are held in the same
assembly. His assembly was that of shame, humility, modesty
and trust. The Prophet wore a smiling look before his
companions and remained satisfied with what the companions
remained satisfied.

Summary of duties towards friends

If you wish good company, meet with your friends and enemies with smiling countenance and do not dishonour them. Don't fall into fear from them. Take to gravity without pride. Be modest without meanness. Adopt middle course in all your actions. The two extremes of every action is condemned. Don't look to both sides of your own. Don't look long towards anything. Don't keep standing in the assembly of many men. When you sit, sit comfortably. Don't make sound by your fingers. Don't move your beard and ring, don't make pick of your teeth, don't enter your finger into your nose, don't spit much, don't cleanse teeth off and on, don't drive flies and mosquitoes very much, don't yawn much before the people in prayer and in other deeds, make your assembly as guide, make your decision in an orderly manner. Use sweet words with one with whom you discuss, don't be too much pleased in any matter. Don't request for repetation of any word. Be silent near those who arouse laughter and tell stories.

Don't discuss about your satisfaction with your children, servants, poetry, composition and books and other things. Don't be engaged in telling stories like servants and slaves. Don't use oil or antimony in great quantity. Don't pass urine and stool off and on. Don't term an oppressor as brave. Don't keep informed your wife and children of the amount of your wealth and other properties, because if they see your little wealth, you will become humiliated to them, and if they see your too much wealth, you won't be able to satisfy them. Don't fear them so much as they can treat with you harshly. Don't be so much soft to them as they should sit on your head. Don't keep laughing with the servants or else your gravity will reduce thereby. Keep honour at the time of disputes and be careful of your ignorance. Give up haste and think of your proof. Don't hint much with your hand, look at those who remains behind you or else don't look much at your back. Don't sit on your knees. Speak when anger is appeassed.

If the ruler appoints you as one of his near advisers, keep sharp look like edges of teeth. If he is at laugh with you, don't be safe at his sudden change to you. Treat with him like a boy. Speak according to his wish till he commands to commit a sin. If he shows kindness on you, don't treat unjustly with his wife and children taking its advantage. Be careful of the solvent friend as he is the greatest enemy. Don't honour your wealth more than your honour. When you enter an assembly, salute them first. Don't go in front of one who goes forward. Sit wherever you get space. Salute those who come to you when you sit. Don't sit in the middle of the pathway. If you sit there, shut up your sight, help the oppressed and the weak, show path to the misguided, respond to salutation, give charity to the beggars, enjoin good and avoid evil, spit in its proper place, don't spit towards the *Ka'ba*, nor to the right side but to the left side or under your left foot.

Don't sit together with the kings and rulers. When you sit, give up back-biting, falsehood and secret things, speak very little to them about your necessities, treat with them with words of a gentleman and mention their qualities. Don't cut jokes with them. Don't fear them too much. If their love for you is expressed, it is better. Don't yawn before them and don't make pick after meal. Hear every word in front of a ruler but don't break secrets and pursue honour of his inmates. Don't sit with the people in general. If you sit with them, give up useless talks. Be indifferent to their evil words. Meet with them rarely even in times of necessity. Don't cut jokes with the wise and the fools as the wise will hate you and the fools will go against you. Fear goes away at jokes and laughter, honour is disobeyed, hatred increases, taste of love goes away, defects fall in the wisdom of a learned man, it gives encouragement to the fools, honour is endangered before the wise, hatred increases and for that heart becomes dead. It makes God distant, and carelessness is earned. The Prophet said : If a man sits in an assembly where much useless talks are held and he says before he gets up from the assembly : Glory to God, O God! Thine is all praise, I bear witness that there is no deity but Thou. I seek forgiveness to Thee and I turn to Thee, he is forgiven of the sins he commits in that assembly.

CHAPTER VI

Duties to Relatives, Neighbours, Slaves and Muslims

Man is a social being and he is to observe certain rules and regulation if he lives in society. I am going to discuss these rules and regulation to be observed by a Muslim while dealing with persons of various types.

Duties towards a Muslim

(1) The following instructions have come in the Qurān and *Hadis* : When you meet a Muslim, give him Salam. When he invites you, accept his invitation When he sneezes respond to him. When he falls ill, call on him. When he dies, join his funeral prayer. If he seeks your advice, give him advice. If he is absent, guard his properties. Love for him what you love for yourself. Don't love for him what you do not love for yourself. The Prophet said : There are four duties on you to help the pious, to seek forgiveness for the sinners, to invoke good for the unfortunate and to love those who make repentance. God says : They are sympathetic towards one another. Hazrat Ibn Abbas explained it by saying : The pious among them seek forgiveness for the sinners. When a sinner among the Muslims looks to a pious man, the latter should say : O God! give him the blessing of good of which you have decreed for him and keep him firm over it and give him benefit therewith. When a pious man looks to a sinner among them, he should pray for him thus: O God! give him guidance, accept his repentance and forgive his sins.

(2) Love for the believers what you love for yourself and dislike for the believers what you dislike for yourself: The Prophet said: The Muslim society is like a body in respect of mutual love and sympathy. If a limb of the body suffers pain, the whole body responds to it by sleeplessness and fever. The Prophet said: One believer is like a building to another believer a portion of which strengthens another portion.

(3) Don't give trouble to a Muslim by your words and actions. The Prophet said: A Muslim is he from whose tongue and hands other Muslims remain safe. The Prophet advised the people to do good deeds in a long sermon. He said in the midst of his sermon: If you are unable to do it, advise the people to give up evils, because it is a charity. It will be considered for you as an act of charity. The Prophet said: The best Muslim is he from whose tongue and hands other Muslims remain safe. The Prophet once was asked: Do you know who is a Muslim? The companions replied: God and his Apostle know best. He said: A Muslim is he from whose tongue and hands other Muslims are safe and a believer is he in whose hand the lives and properties of the believers remain safe. The companions asked : Who is a refugee? He said: One who gives up sin. A man asked : What is Islam? He said: Your sacrifice of heart for the sake of God and the Muslims remaining safe from your tongue and hands. The Prophet said: I saw a man loitering freely in Paradise for rewards of cutting a tree which was obstructing the path of the Muslims.

Hazrat Abu Hurairah asked the Prophet one day : O Messenger of God! give me such advice as will do benefit to me. He said : Remove the injurious things from the path of the Muslims. The Prophet said : If a man removes an injurious thing from the path of the Muslims, God writes for him a virtue. Paradise is sure for one for whom God writes a virtue. The Prophet said: It is not lawful for a Muslim to cast such a look on another Muslim which gives him trouble in mind. He said: It is not lawful for a Muslim to threaten another Muslim with fear. He said : God does not like that the believers should be given trouble.

(4) Be modest to every Muslim : Don't treat harshly with him, don't take pride near him as God does not love the proud and the self-conceited. The Prophet said: God revealed to me: Be modest to one another and don't be proud to one another. If anybody shows pride to you, keep patience. God ordered the Prophet: Take to pardon and enjoin good and keep away from the illiterate. The Prophet was modest to every Muslim, he was not harsh to them and did not dislike to do the necessary works of the poor and the widows.

(5) Don't hear back-biting and don't take it to others: The Prophet said : The back-biter will not enter Paradise.

(6) Give up disputes and quarrels : When you get angry with another, don't give up his association for more than three days. The Prophet said : It is not lawful for a Muslim to remain aloof from his brother for more than three days, nor should he turn away his face from another if both of them meet. The better of the two is one who greets first with salutation. The Prophet said : if a man pardons the faults of a Muslim, God will forgive his faults on the Resurrection Day. Hazrat Ayesha said : The Prophet never took revenge for personal wrongs. The Prophet said : Wealth does not reduce by charity. God does not increase but honour in case of pardon. God raises a man who becomes modest for the sake of God.

(7) Do good to every one either deserving or undeserving : The Prophet said: Do good to everyone, pious or impious. if you do good to one who is fit to receive, it is good. If he is not fit to receive it, you are fit to do good. The Prophet said : The root of wisdom after religion is to love for men and to do good to everyone, pious or impious. Hazrat Abu Hurairah said that the Prophet did not withdrew his hand from another till the latter withdrew his own hand.

(8) Treat well with all and speak to everyone according to his intellect : If you go to meet an illiterate person with words of wisdom and with theology and dispute with the fools, you will get trouble.

(9) Honour the dead and show affection to the juniors: The Prophet said: He who does not show affection to our juniors is not of us. He said: 'To honour an aged Muslim is to honour God.' The honour of an aged man does not become perfect if without his permission one talks with others of the party. Hazrat Jabir reported: A deputation of Juhaina tribe once came to the Prophet. A young man among them stood on their behalf to talk to the Prophet. The Prophet said : Stop, where is your aged man? The Prophet said : 'If a young man shows honour to an aged man, God will create for him such one in his old age who will show him honour.' This means that he will live up to old age. So if you show honour to the aged, God will prolong your life. The Prophet said that the Hour will not come till a son gets angry at his parents, till there is profuse rain, till the back-biters come out from every place, till the honourable men will be unseen, till the juniors will not show honour to the aged and till the wrong doers will not be doing wrong against the honourable men. So treat affectionately with the boys according to the habit of the Prophet. Whenever the Prophet returned from a journey, the boys used to meet him and he waited for them standing in their front. He used to make some boys sit in his front and some in his back. He used to take the little children in his lap and some of them even passed urine in his cloth.

(10) Live with all men with smiling face and kind heart:
The Prophet said : Do you know for whom Hell has been made unlawful ? The companions said : God and his Apostle know best. He said : Those who are modest, simple and neighbours of God. He said : God loves the simple and those having smiling countenance. A certain man asked : O Messenger of God! give me clue to such an action which will send me to Paradise. He said : To give salutation and to speak sweet words are means of forgiveness. The Prophet said : Save yourself from the fire to Hell by giving in charity even half a seed of dried grapes. If you cannot do it, save yourself in lieu of a sweet word. The Prophet said : There are rooms in Paradise of which the inner sides can be seen from the outer sides. A desert Arab said : 'O Prophet of God! for whom are these rooms?' He said: For those who use sweet words, give food and remain busy in prayers when the people remain asleep. The Prophet advised Muaz b. Jabal saying : Fear God, tell the truth, fulfil promise, break not trust, take care of neighbours, show kindness to the orphans, be modest in talk, greet with salam and spread peace. Hazrat Anas narrated : A poor woman came to the Prophet and said : I have got some necessity to you. Some companions were then present there. He said: Sit down in this lane and I shall also sit with you. She sat down and the Prophet also did so. She said to the Prophet what she had to say.

(11) Fulfil promise with the Muslims : The Prophet said: Promise is like charity. He said : There are three faults of a hypocrite – (1) when he promises, he breaks it, (2) when he speaks, he speaks lies, (3) and when he is entrusted with a thing, he does not return it. The Prophet said : He in whom there are these three faults is a hypocrite though he prays and fasts.

(12) Do justice to the people willingly and come to them with what they love. The Prophet said : The faith of a man does not become perfect in whom three qualities are not found– (1) to spend till he becomes poor, (2) to do justice to oneself, (3) and to greet with *salam*, The Prophet said : He who hopes to keep Hell distant and to enter Paradise shall testify at the time of death that there is no deity but God and Muhammad is the Messenger of God and treat with the people in such a manner as he wishes to get from them. The Prophet said : 'O Abu Darda'a! treat well with your neighbour, you will then be a believer. Love for men what you love for yourself, you will then be a Muslim'. Hazrat Moses asked God : 'O Lord! who is the best judge among Thy servants? He said : That servant who does best justice to himself.

(13) Honour those to whom honour is due : Honour one who is understood to be honourable in rank from his nature, conduct, appearance and dresses and his status and rank. It is reported that when Hazrat Ayesha was in her tent in a journey, a beggar came to her when food was served to her and begged some food. Hazrat Ayesha said: Give him a piece of bread. Thereafter a man came to her riding on a horse. Hazrat Ayesha said: Call him to this feast. She was asked : You have given a bread to the beggar, while you called the horseman to a feast. What is the reason ? Hazrat Ayesha said: God has given different persons different ranks. We should entertain them according to their ranks. This poor man will be pleased with a piece of bread, but to give to this rich man a piece of bread is out of etiquette.

It has been reported that once the Prophet entered a room and the people came there and the room was full. Then Zarir b. Abdullah, the chief of the tribe, came there but finding no place to sit. He sat upon the door. Seeing this, the Prophet gave him his shirt to sit thereon. He began to kiss it and handed it over to the Prophet and said : May God honour you as you have honoured me. The Prophet said : When any honourable man of a people comes to you, honour him. The foster mother of the Prophet, Halima, once came to him and the Prophet gave her his own shirt to her to sit on and said: Mother, you are welcome. Your intercession will be accepted. You will be given what you want. She said : I intercede to you for my own people. The Prophet said: You are the owner of my dues and the dues of the people to Hashemite dynasty. Then he gave the entire booty gained in the battle of Hunain to her. Halima sold it to Hazrat Osman for one lac *dirhams*.

(14) **Compromise disputes among the Muslims if you have got means :** The Prophet said : Shall I not inform you of a greater rank than that of prayer, fasting and *Zakat* ? The companions said : Surely. The Prophet said : It is to compromise disputes. Dispute between two persons is destructive. The Prophet said : To settle dispute between two persons is the best charity. The Prophet said : Fear God and settle disputes among you, God will then compromise disputes among the believers. The Prophet said : He who settles dispute between two persons is not a great liar. He also said : Every lie is recorded except three lies – (1) the lie of a man in a war battle as it is a deception, (2) the lie of a man to settle disputes between two persons, (3) and the lie of a husband to please his wife.

(15) **Keep the secrets of Muslims Secret :** The Prophet said : If a man keeps the guilts of a Muslim secret, God will keep his guilts secret both in this world and the next. He also said : If a man keeps the sin of a man secret in this world, God will keep all of his sins secret on the Resurrection Day. The Prophet said: If a believer keeps the fault of his brother secret, he will enter Paradise. When Ma'az disclosed the condition of his fornication to the Prophet, he said : Had you

kept it concealed under your cloth, it would have been better. Hazrat Abu Bakr said : If I see a drunkard, I entertain such a hope in my mind that God will keep this sin secret. Hazrat Omar one night went out in the city in disguise and saw a man and a woman in obscene action. In the morning he told the people : If a certain Ameer sees a man and a woman committing fornication and if he metes out prescribed punishment in the Qurãn to them, what is your opinion about it? They said : You are a ruler. You have got freedom in this action. Hazrat Ali said : Punishment in this case is unlawful, rather you are to suffer punishment for this for slander. This punishment cannot be meted out without the evidence of four persons. After this, Hazrat Omar kept silent for some days. Again he questioned them and they replied as they had said. He became inclined towards the opinion of Hazrat Ali and decided not to mete out the punishment. This is a good proof that the sins of the Muslims should be kept secret and that four eye witnesses are necessary for the capital punishment for fornication which is practically impossible in a case of sexual intercourse. The Prophet said : 'When God keeps the sin of a person secret, He is more honourable to disclose it in the next world'.

Hazrat Abdur Rauf b. Auf narrated : We came out with Hazrat Omar secretly to travel in the city of Madinah in the grim midnight. We saw a light in a house and proceeded towards it. When we came near, we found that in a closed door Rabia b. Omayya was intoxicated with drinking wine. I said : Don't spy. So Hazrat Omar returned from there. The Prophet said to Muawiyah : If you enquire into the secrets of the people, you will ruin them. The Prophet said : O people (who have faith by tongue but in whose heart the light of Islam has not yet entered) don't back-bite the Muslims, don't roam about to enquire into their secrets because he who roams about to enquire the secrets of his brother, God will enquire about his secrets. God humiliates one whose secrets He follows, even though he remains within the house. Hazrat Abu Bakr said : If I see anybody to commit prescribed offence, I will not arrest him nor I will tell anybody to arrest him till some person remains with me. A wise man said : I was seated one day with Hazrat Abdullah b. Masud. At that time a man brought another man to him saying : This man is a drunkard. Abdullah b. Masud said : Take smell from his mouth. The people took smell from his mouth and it was found that he drank wine. He then arrested him and whipped him. He asked the man who brought him : Is this man your relative? He said: I am his uncle. He said: You have not given him training and good manners and did not keep his sin secret. When any sin of a person is mentioned to a ruler, he has got no other alternative but to punish him. God is forgiving and loves forgiveness. Then he recited : Take to pardon and forgiveness. I will mention to you with regard to a thief who was brought to the Prophet for the first time. He ordered for cutting of his hands which were cut off. But then the colour of his face became changed at this. The companions asked : Are you dissatisfied with the cutting of his hands? He said : Why should not I ? Don't be helpers of the devil against your brother. The companions asked : Then why have you not forgiven him ? When a man is brought to a ruler for being guilty of a prescribed crime, it becomes compulsory on him to inflict the prescribed punishment on him. God is forgiving, He loves forgiveness. Then he recited : "Let them pardon and forgive. Don't you like that God may forgive you? God is forgiving, merciful".

Once Hazrat Omar, while going at night in the city, heard sounds of songs in a house. He got over the wall and found that there was a woman with them and a pot of wine near a man. He said: O enemy of God! have you thought that God will keep your sin concealed ? He said: O Commander of the faithful! you have come yourself! Don't be hasty in judgment. I committed one sin this time, but you have committed three sins. God said : 'Don't spy.' You have committed spying and therefore committed one sin. God says : 'It is not righteousness that you should come to the houses by their back-doors.' You have come overstepping the wall and so you have committed another sin. God says: Don't enter a house other than your own houses till you seek permission and greet their inmates (25 : 27). You have entered my house without permission and greeting. Hazrat Omar said : if I pardon you, will it do any good to you? He said: By God! O Commander of the faithful! it will do me good. If you pardon me, I will never do it. Then he pardoned him and went away.

The Prophet said : God will take a believer near Him, spread His mercy on him and keep his faults secret on the Resurrection Day. God will say : O My servant! I have kept it secret for you in the world and I wished to pardon you today. Then the book of good deeds will be given to him. The Prophet said : Every person of my followers will be forgiven except *Muzahir* who is a person who commits, sins and then discloses them. He also said : If a person hears the news of a people secretly but they dislike it, molten brass will be put into their ears on the Resurrection Day.

(16) Keep away from places of slander and back-biting so that the minds of the people remain free from cherishing evil ideas about you. God says: Don't abuse those whom they worship besides God, lest they abuse God out of enmity. The Prophet said : "Do you see a man who rebukes his parents"? The companions said : Is there anybody who rebukes his own parents? He said : Yes, someone rebukes his parents and he in turn rebukes his parents. In order to avoid evil conjecture or the people, one should not even talk with his wife before the public on the path way. Once Hazrat Omar passed by a man who was talking with a woman on the road. When Omar was about to whip him, he said : She is my wife. Hazrat Omar said : Why have you not talked with her in a place where people will not see you ?

(17) Intercede for everyone : Make intercession to one who has got authority to remove the needs of a Muslim and try hard to meet his requirements. The Prophet said : If anybody amongst you seeks something from me, I wish I should give it to him at once, but if anyone among you remains present near me, I like that he should intercede for him, as he gets rewards for that. So make intercession, you will get rewards. God does through His Prophet what He loves. The Prophet said : Intercede to me, you will get rewards. I make delay to do a thing though I wish to do it, so that you may get rewards by interceding for it. The Prophet said : No charity is better than oral charity ? He was asked : What is oral charity? He said : A just pleading which saves the life of a man, benefits a man or saves a man from a calamity.

(18) Greet every Muslim with salam before talk and before greeting handshake with him : The Prophet said Don't respond to one who begins talk before *salam* till he begins talk with *salam*. A wise man said : Once I went to the Prophet but did not greet him with *salam* and did not seek permission. The people said : Go back and say : 'Peace be on you' and then enter. The Prophet said : When you enter your house, greet its inmates with *salam*, because when one of you greets, the devil does not enter his house. Hazrat Anas said : I have been serving the Prophet for the last eight years. He said to me one day : O Anas! make ablution well, your life will be prolonged. Greet with *salam* to any of my followers whom you meet, your rewards will increase. Greet with *salam* the inmates of a house when you enter in, that will be good for you. He also said : When two believers meet and handshake with each other, seventy virtues are divided among them. He who meets out of them with smiling countenance, will get sixty nine virtues therefrom. God says When you are greeted with a greeting, greet them with a better greeting than it or similar to it. The Prophet said : By One in whose hand there is my life, you will not enter Paradise till you believe, you will not believe till you love one another. Shall I not inform you of such an action for which you will love one another if you do it? The companions said : Yes, O Messenger of God. He said : Spread peace among you. He said: When a Muslim greets another Muslim with *salam* and the latter responds to it, the angels bless him seventy times. The Prophet said : The rider will salute one siting. When one of a party salutes, it is sufficient for them.

Handshaking with *salam* is *Sunnat*. A man came to the Prophet and said : Peace be on you. He said : For him, ten rewards have been written. Another man came and said : Peace be on you and God's mercy. He said : For him twenty rewards have been written. Another came and said : Peace be on you, God's mercy and His blessings. He said : For him thirty rewards have been written. Hazrat Anas saluted the boys while passing by them. The Prophet said : Don't greet the Jews and the Christians first. If one of you meets any of them on the path, lead him to the narrow corner of the path. The Prophet said: Don't handshake with the *Zimmis* and don't greet them first. When you meet any of them, take him to a corner of the pathway.

Hazrat Ayesha reported : A party of the Jews came to the Prophet and said: *Sa'm* (death) on you. The Prophet said : On you too. Hazrat Ayesha said : On you also death and curse. The Prophet then said: O Ayesha! God loves kindness in everything. Hazrat Ayesha said : Have you not heard what they said ? He said : I also said on you too. The Prophet said: The rider will salute one who walks, one who walks will salute one seated, a small party to the big party, the juniors to the seniors. The Prophet said: Don't follow the Jews and the Christians, because the greeting of the Jews is hint by fingers and the greeting of the Christians is clapping by hands. The Prophet said : When a man reaches an assembly, he shall salute them. When he thinks good to sit, then he will sit. When he goes away, he will salute them. The first man has got no greater right than the last. Hazrat Omar said : I heard the Prophet say: When two Muslims meet with each other and one of them greets another and handshakes with him, one hundred mercies are showered on them, ninety for one who first greets and ten for one who handshakes. Hazrat Hasan Basri said: Handshake increases love. The Prophet said: Handshake among you perfects greeting. The Prophet said: Handshake is like kissing of a Muslim to his brother. There is no harm in kissing the hand of a religious man and an honourable man out of respect. Ibn Omar said : We used to kiss the hands of the Prophet. A desert Arab came and said: O Messenger of God! give me permission to kiss your head and hands. On permission being given, he kissed his head and hands. Hazrat Bara'a b. Azib reported that when he saluted the Prophet at the time of ablution, he did not respond to it till he finished his ablution. Then he responded to him and handshaked with him. He said: This is the practice of the foreigners. The Prophet said: When two Muslims meet with each other and handshake, their sins fall down.

It is prohibited to bow the head at the time of greeting. Hazrat Anas said : We asked the Prophet: O Messenger of God! shall we bow our head for one another ? He said: No. They said: Shall we kiss one another? He said : No. They said–Shall we handshake with one another? He said : Yes. Hazrat Abu Zarr said: Whenever I met the Prophet, he handshaked with me. Once during my absence he enquired of me. When I heard it, I came to him and found him sitting in a *Khatia*. He got up from it and embraced me. "This shows that embracing is good. It is *Makruh* to stand up for a man thinking him great but to stand in his honour is not *Makruh*. Hazrat Anas said that nobody was dearer to the companions than the Prophet. When they saw him, they used not to stand up, because they knew that the Prophet disliked it. The Prophet once said to them: When you see me, don't stand up as the foreigners do. The Prophet said : Let one seek his abode in Hell who is pleased with the standing of others for him. The Prophet said : Let nobody take the seat of another person after asking him to get up, rather he should make it spacious. One day a man saluted the Prophet while he was passing urine. He did not respond to him and disliked it. He said : When one of you meets his brother, let him say 'Peace be on you and God's mercy.' If he does not get space after greeting, let him not go but take seat behind the rows, The Prophet said : If two Muslims handshake with each other after meeting, God forgives them before they part away.

(19) To help the distressed : Save your Muslim brother from oppression on his honour, wealth and life, remove it and help him, because it is binding on account of the brotherhood of Islam. Once a man abused another before the Prophet to which another man protested. The Prophet said : If a man saves the honour of his brother Muslim, it stands as a screen of Hell. He said: If a Muslim saves the honour of another Muslim it becomes the duty of God to remove from him the fire of Hell on the Resurrection day. The Prophet said: If a Muslim is mentioned before his brother and the latter does not help him in spite of his ability to help, God will arrest him in the world and the next. If a Muslim is mentioned before his brother and he helps him, God will help him in this world and the next. The Prophet said: If a Muslim keeps alive the honour of his brother Muslim in this world, God will send to him an angel on the Resurrection day to save him from Hell-fire. He said: If a Muslim helps his brother Muslim in a place in which his honour is at stake, God will help him in such a place where he will be dependant on him for his help. On the otherhand, if a Muslim is about to disgrace his brother Muslim, and if another Muslim does not help him according to his ability and show no sympathy, God will disgrace and dishonour him in such a place where he will be waiting for help.

(20) Respond to sneezing : The prophet said: He who sneezes will say : God's praise in all circumstances and one who hears it will say: May God have mercy on you. The sneezer will then say : May God guide you and make your mind pure. Once the Prophet replied to a sneezer and did not reply to another. When asked the reason he said: One has praised God and another remained silent. The Prophet said: When a Muslim sneezes thrice, respond to him. If he increases more than thrice it is a disease. When the Prophet sneezed, he used to shut up his mouth with his hand or cloth. The Jews sneezed before the Prophet with the hope of geting a reply 'May God show you mercy.' He used to say : God guide you. The Prophet said: Sneezing comes from God and yawning from the devil. When one of you yawns, let him place his hand upon his mouth. Moses said: O Lord! art Thou near me, so that I may hold secret conversation with Thee? Art thou distant, so that I may speak loudly to Thee? He said: I am with one who remembers Me. He said: We are sometime in such a condition that to remember Thee is impertinence, such as in the state of impurity or at the times of calls of nature. He said : Remember me at all times.

(21) Help at the time of distress and calamities : God says : Remove evil with what is good. God says : They remove evil by good deeds. Hazrat Abu Abbas explained this evil by saying : Those who treat with *salam* and modesty in lieu of harm and harsh treatment. God says : If God would not have repelled one people by another, cloister etc. would have been destroyed. Hazrat Ibn Abbas said that the meaning of 'another' is a people with hope, fear, modesty and humble behaviour. The Prophet said : O Ayesha! the worst man on the Resurrection Day will be a man whom the people forsake for fear of his harm. He said : If a man keeps patience to save his honour after hearing abusive words, it will be an act of charity for him.

(22) Give up the company of the rich and take the company of the poor and show kindness on the orphans. The Prophet said : O God! let me live as a poor man let me die as a poor man and resurrect me with the poor. Whenever Hazrat Sulaiman saw a poor man, he sat with him and said: A poor man is sitting by the side of a poor man. It has been reported that nothing could please Jesus Christ so much as he was when addressed as a poor man. The sage Fuzail said : I heard that a Prophet said: O Lord! how can I know that you are pleased with me? He said : Look for it when the poor remain satisfied with you. The Prophet said : Be careful of the assemblies of the dead. He was asked: O Messenger of God! who are the dead? He said: The rich men. Moses asked God: O Lord! where shall I search for Thee? He said: Near the broken heart. The Prophet said : Don't be envious for the fortunes of the sinners, because you do not know what will be their condition. There is behind them one who enquires of them with haste.

Orphans : The Prophet said: Paradise is sure for one who maintains an. orphan after taking him from Muslim parents till he comes of age. He said : I and the care taker of an orphan will remain in Paradise like these two fingers. He hinted by joining his two fingers. He said: He who passes his hand out of sympathy on the hairs of an orphan will get virtues to the proportion of hairs on which his hand has passed. The Prophet said : The best house of the Muslims is one in which an orphan is well treated and the worst house of the Muslims is one in which an orphan is badly treated.

(23) Give advice to every Muslim. The Prophet said : A believer shall love for another believer what he loves for himself. He said : Nobody of you can be a believer till he loves for his brother what he loves for himself. He said : One of you is like a mirror for another. If he sees anything wrong in him, he should remove it from him. He said: He who fulfils the needs of his brother Muslim, has done divine service as it were for his whole life. He said: if a man destroys the honour of a believer, God will destroy his virtues on the Resurrection Day. He said : If a man spends one hour to relieve the sufferings of his brother Muslim day or night, it is better than two months *I'tikaf* (seclution in mosque), whether his sufferings are removed or not. The Prophet said : If a man removes the anxieties of a believer or helps an oppressed person, God forgives his seventy three sins. He said : Help your brother Muslim, he be oppressed or oppressor. He was asked: How can be help the oppressor? He said : He will prevent him from oppression. He said : The desirable thing to God is to incur pleasure to the mind of a believer, or to pay off his debt or to appease his hunger by giving food. The Prophet said: If a man saves a believer from the deceit of a hypocrite, God will send for him on the Resurrection Day an angel who will protect his flesh from Hell-fire. He said : There is no sin worse than two sins– (1) to set up partners with God and (2) to oppress God's servants. There is no virtue better than two virtues

(I) to have faith in God and (2) to do good to God's servants. The Prophet said : He whose mind is not moved with the sufferings of the Muslims, is not of them. The sage Ma'ruf Karkhi said : If one says everyday : O God! show mercy on the followers of Muhammad, God will include him in the class of *Abdals*. In another narration : If a man recites thrice everyday : O God! make the followers of Muhammad good, O God! relieve the sufferings of the followers of Muhammad, God enrols him as one of the *Abdals*.

(24) Call on the diseased : If a Muslim falls ill, call on him and nurse him. The following rules must be observed when you go to see a patient. (1) Sit for a short while before the patient, ask him few questions, take information of his health with soft mind and pray for his recovery. The Prophet said: If a man goes to a patient and places his hand on his forhead or asks the condition of his disease, his meeting with him becomes perfect. Handshaking perfects your greeting. The Prophet said : He who meets with a patient, sits by the side of Paradise. When he returns, he is entrusted with seventy thousand angels who pray for him upto night. He said: When a man goes to see a patient, he remains immerged in mercy. When he sits by his bed, it becomes permanent. He said : When a Muslim goes to see his brother, a diseased Muslim, or meets with him. God says Blessings on you, your steps are good. He said : When a man falls ill, God sends to him two angels saying : Look what he says to the patient. When he comes to him and praises God, they carry it to God and prays to Him. God says if I cause the death of this servant, I will admit him in Paradise. If I cure him, I will give him better flesh than this flesh, better blood than this blood and forgive his sins. The Prophet said : God gives disease to a man whom He loves. He said : The Prophet once came to see a patient and said : In the name of God, the most Compassionate, the

Most Merciful. I give you from the evil which I see to the refuge of God, the Unique, free from want. He begets not, nor is He begotten and there is none like him. The Prophet said : Visit a patient every alternate day and treat modestly with him.

(25) Join the funeral prayer of a Muslim : The Prophet said : He who follows the bier will get a *Qirat* of virtues. If he waits upto burial, he will get two *Qirats* of virtues. The Prophet said : One *Qirat* is like coins full of Uhud mountain. He said: Three things follow a dead man, two return and one does not return. His relatives and wealth return, but his actions do not return.

(26) Visit the graves of the dead : The object is to pray, to take lessons and to make the mind soft. The Prophet said : I have not seen a more horrible scenery than grave. The Prophet once went to the grave of his mother Amina. He said: I sought permission of God to visit her grave and He gave me permission. I sought His permission for her forgiveness but he refused it. He began to weep. He said : Grave is the first station out of the stations of the next world. If its inmate gets relief from it, what will occur after it will be easy. If he does not get relief from it, what will occur after it will be severe. Hazrat Abu Darda'a used to sit by graves. Being asked the reason, he said: I sit with such people who remind me of the next world. If I go away from them, they do not back-bite me. The Prophet said: There is no night in which a proclaimer does not proclaim: O inmates of the graves! whom do you envy? They say : We envy the inmates of mosques, as they fast and we do not fast, as they pray and we do not pray, as they remember God and we do not remember Him. Sufiyan Saori said : He who remembers grave much, will get a garden in Paradise out of His gardens. He who does not remember grave gets a hole in Hell out of its holes.

Rights of neighbours

As a Muslim has got rights over you, so a neighbour also has got rights over you. The Prophet said: There are three classes of neighbours. The first class neighbour has got one right; the second class two; and the third class three. He who is a neighbour, a Muslim and a relative has got three rights, one right of being a neighbour, one right of being a relative, and one right of being a Muslim. The second class neighbour has got two rights, one right of being a Muslim and one right of being a neighbour. The third class neighbour has got only one right – the right of being an infidel neighbour. The Prophet said: Treat well with your neighbour, you will be a Muslim. The Prophet said : Gabriel was insisting always to pay the right of the neighbour so much that I thought that he would give him the right of inheritance. The Prophet said : Let him who believes in God and the next world honour his neighbour. He said : He is not a believer from whose harms his neighbour is not safe. He said: The first two who will come as disputants on the Resurrection Day will be neighbours. He said : When you throw a stone at the dog of your neighbour, you cause trouble to his mind.

The Prophet once was said : A certain man fasts all day and prays all night, but he gives trouble to his neighbour. The Prophet said : He is in Hell. At another time, a man complained against his neighbour to the Prophet and he said: Have patience. When he said twice and thrice. The Prophet said : Throw your goods on the pathway. When he threw them, the people asked him : What is the matter with you? They were told that his neighbour was giving him trouble. They began to say : God's curse upon him. His neighbour came to him and said : By God! I will not treat with him further in such a manner. Once the Prophet said : Proclaim forty surrounding houses as houses of neighbours. He said: Fortune and misfortune lie in woman, house and conveyance. A woman is a cause of fortune when her dower is little, her marriage is easily performed and her character and conduct are good. The cause of her misfortune occurs when her dower is heavy, her marriage is solemnised with difficulty and her character and conduct are bad. Fortune regarding a house occurs when it is spacious and its neighbour is good and misfortune comes when it is narrow and its neighbour is bad. Fortune regarding a horse comes when it becomes submissive and has got a good figure and misfortune comes when it is disobedient and has got an ugly figure.

In short, the rights of a neighbour on you are the following: Salute him first, don't talk with him for long, don't ask about his condition long. Call on him when he is ill, show sympathy in his distress, be sorry in his sorrows, be happy in his happiness, share enjoyments in his happiness, pardon his faults, don't look at the inner side of his house from the top of your roof, don't trouble him by replacing your rafters on his wall, don't let water flow down, his courtyard, don't shut up the outflow of water of his house through your boundary, don't make the path to his house narrow, cover his fault if it is out, try to remove his distress as soon as possible, take care of his house in his absence, don't hear his back-biting talk with his sons and daughters with affection and read out to him what he is ignorant of the worldly and religious matters.

The Prophet said : Do you know about your duties towards your neighbour? Help him if he seeks your help, give him loan if he wants it, remove his wants if he is in wants, follow his bier if he is dead, give him joy if he gets good news, show him sympathy and express sorrow if he is in danger, don't raise up your building so high without his permission so as to obstruct his air, don't give him trouble. If you purchase some fruits, give him something. If you do not do it, take them secretly to your house. Don't allow your children to come out with them as it may cause displeasure of his children. Don't give him trouble by the smoke of your cook-shed. There is no harm in sending food cooked in your cook-shed to your neighbour's house. Then he said: Do you know the rights of a neighbour ? By One in whose hand there is my life, one on whom God shows mercy can fulfil these duties towards neighbours. Hasan Basri used to present the meat of *Qurbani* to his neighbours – Jews and Christians. Hazrat Abu Zarr said: My friend the Prophet gave me these instructions: When you cook curry, increase its soup and send something to your neighbour. Hazrat Ayesha said: O Messenger of God! I have got two neighbours, the house of one is near my house and the house of another is some distant. Whose right is greater? He said : The right of one whose house is nearer.

Hazrat Ayesha said: There are ten habits of an honourable man. They may be found in a man, but may not be found in his father. They may be found in his servant but may not be found in his master. God gives these to one whom He loves— (1) to speak the truth, (2) to treat good with the people, (3) to give charity to the beggars, (4) to help in domestic works, (5) to treat well with relatives, (6) to protect trust, (7) to perform the duties towards a neighbour, (8) to maintain friendship, (9) to entertain guests and (10) to keep shame. These are the foundations for all qualities. The Prophet said : O Muslim women! don't think insignificant to give your neighbours even a goat's cooked hoof. The Prophet said: The fortune of a Muslim is in spacious abode, good neighbour and satisfactory conveyance. One man asked : O Messenger of God! how shall I know whether a man is good or bad ? He said : When you hear your neighbour say : He is good, he is really good. If you hear him say 'he is bad', he is really bad. The Prophet said : If a man has got a share in a wall, he shall not sell it without asking his co-sharer. The Prophet said : A neighbour can place his rafter in the wall of his neighbour, whether he is willing or not. He said: Let none amongst you refuse his neighbour from placing rafter on his wall. The Prophet said: God gives sweetness to one whose good He wishes. He was asked : What is the meaning of sweetness? He said : He makes him dear to his neighbour.

Rights of relatives

The Prophet said : God says : I am *Rahim* (Merciful) and *I ham* (relationship) is derived from my name. I keep attached to one who joins it and I keep aloof from one who severs it. The Prophet said : If any man is pleased to prolong his life and to make his livelihood solvent, let him fear God and join the tie of relationship. The Prophet was once asked: Who is the best person? He said : One who fears God most, keeps best connection with his relatives, gives much advice for good deeds and prohibits bad deeds. Hazrat Abu Zarr said : My friend (Prophet) advised me to keep good relation with relatives even though they treat badly. He ordered me to speak the truth though bitter. The Prophet said : *Raham* (relationship) is hanging with the Throne. The man who fulfils his duties towards his relatives is not the real protector of relationship but he is one, who joins it after it is severed. He said : The rewards of keeping good relation with relatives are found more hastily than other rewards. His wealth and properties increase in spite of the inmates of his house being sinners and their numbers increase when they keep the relationship intact.

When the Prophet started for the conquest of Mecca, a man came to him and said: If you wish to marry a beautiful woman and to get a camel of red hue, start a campaign against the tribe of Mudlej. He said : God prohibited me to wage a campaign against them owing to my relationship with them.

The Prophet said : Charity to a poor man has got one merit and charity to a poor relative has good two merits. God says: You will never attain rightousness till you spend what you love. Hazrat Abu Talha was greatly satisfied on hearing the verse and wished to give in charity his garden of dates and said : O Prophet of God! I have gifted in charity this garden for the poor and the destitute. The Prophet of God said : Your reward from God has become sure. Distribute it among your near relatives. The Prophet said : The greatest reward is of that charity which you give to your relative who has got dispute with you. This can be understood from the following *Hadis*. The Prophet said : If a man joins the tie of relationship after it is severed and gives in charity to a man who deprives him, he will get the greatest reward. Hazrat Omar sent this order to his governors : Order relatives to meet one another.

Rights of parents and children

The nearer is the relation, the greater are the duties towards him. Parents are nearest to a man and so the duty towards them is greatest. The Prophet said : A son cannot fulfil his duties towards his father. He can, however, fulfil a part of it if he sees his father as a slave and liberates him. The Prophet said : To treat good with parents is better than prayer, fasting, pilgrimage, *zakat*, *Umrah* and *jihad* in the way of God. He said : If a man gets up at morn pleasing his parents, two doors of Paradise are opened up for him. If he gets up at dusk, he gets similar rewards. If he pleases one of them, one door is opened up for him even though the both oppress him (thrice). If a man gets up at dawn displeasing his parents two doors are opened up for him towards Hell. If a man does it at dusk, he will get similar punishment. If he displeases one of them; one door is opened up for him, even though they both oppress him (thrice). The Prophet said : The fragrance of Paradise will be smelt from five hundred years distance. He who is disobedient to parents and he who severs the tie of relationship will not get it. The Prophet said: Obey your mother, then your father, then your sister, your brother and then your nearest relatives and then the near relatives. God said to Moses : O Moses! if a man obeys his parents but commits sins, I enrol him as obedient to parents. If a man disobeys Me but is obedient to his parents, I enrol him as obedient to parents. It has been reported that when Hazrat Yaqub (Israil) went to Joseph, the latter did not stand up in his honour. God then revealed to him: Have you no stood up in honour of your father'? By oath of My glory, I will not make any Prophet out of your descendants.

The Prophet said : When a man wishes to give charity for his Muslim parents, his parents get its rewards without any reduction. Once a man asked the Prophet : O Messenger of God! is there any duty remaining towards parents after their death? He said : Yes, to invoke for them, to seek forgiveness for them, to fulfil their promise, to honour their friends and to preserve the tie of their relatives. The Prophet said : The best duty is to keep connection with those who were dear to them after their death. The Prophet said: The right of a mother is double than that of a father. He said : The invocation by a mother for her child is soon accepted. He was asked : What is its reason ? He said : She is more affectionate than father. The invocation of relatives does not go baffled. The Prophet was once asked : With whom shall I keep the tie of relationship? He said : With your parents. He said : I have got no parents. He said : Then with your children. As you have got duties towards your parents, so also you have got duties towards your children. The Prophet said : May God show mercy on the father who keeps his children to obey him. In other words, he does not help them by his evil actions to go to misguidance. The Prophet said : Treat equally with your children in the matter of charity. It has been said that a child is your flower and till he reaches the age of seven years, you will enjoy his fragrance. When he is seven years old, he becomes your servant and thereafter he becomes either your enemy or sharer in your works.

The Prophet said : Observe *Aqiqa* (birth ceremony) on the seventh day of child's birth, give him a name and remove from him uncleanliness. When the child is six years old, teach him good manners; when nine years old, separate his bed beat him when thirteen years old for saying prayer and get him married when sixteen years old. Then tell him catching his hands : I have taught you good manners, I have given you education and I have got you married. Now I pray to God that He may save you from dangers and difficulties and punishment of the next world. The Prophet said : The right of a son upon his father is that his father will teach him good manners and give him a good name. A man complained against his son to the Prophet. He asked : Have you invoked against him ? He said : Yes. He said : You have ruined him. It is commendable to show kindness to the son. Hazrat Aqra'a b. Habis saw the Prophet kissing his grandson Hasan and said: I have got ten children but I never kissed any of them. The Prophet said He who is not kind will not get kindness.

Once the Prophet was in prostration leading a prayer, when Hussain got upon his shoulder. The Prophet made such delay in prostration that the companions thought that revelation was coming to him. 'When he finished the prayer, the Prophet said : Hussain has made me his conveyance. I did not like to put him aside till he finished his work. The Prophet said : The fragrance of a child is the fragrance of Paradise. Once a man came from Yemen to join *jihad* to the Prophet who asked him: Have you got parents? He said : Yes. He asked : Have they given you permission for *jihad* ? He said : No. The Prophet said : Go to your parents and take their permission. If they do not give permission, serve them to your utmost, because of all the merits with which you will meet with God after *Tauhid*, the best is in the service of parents. At another time, a man sought advice from the Prophet about his joining *jihad*. He asked him : Have you got your mother ? He said : Yes. He said : Stay with her, as Paradise lies under her feet. At another time, a man came to give allegiance to the Prophet and said : My parents were weeping at the time when I was leaving them. The Prophet said : Go back and give them joy as you have made them weep. The Prophet said : The right of an elder brother over his younger brother is like the right of a father over his son.

Rights of slaves and servants

The last advice that the Prophet gave was regarding slaves–Fear God, give them food you eat, give them cloth you put on and don't inflict on them work beyond their strength. If you don't wish to keep them, ask them to go and don't inflict punishment on the servants of God. God has placed them under your control. If He wishes, He may place you under their control. The Prophet said : Give the slaves food and cloth with justice and don't engage them in works beyond their capacity. He said : The cheat, the proud, those who break trust and those who ill-treat the slaves will not enter Paradise. A man asked the Prophet : How many times shall I forgive the faults of a servant ? He remained silent for a while and then said : Forgive him seventy times every day. Once a companion of the Prophet beat a slave who began to raise loud cry. The Prophet came there and he stopped beating. The Prophet said : Why did you not pardon him before ? You have restrained your hand when you have seen me. He said :

O Messenger of God! I give manumission for the pleasure of God. The Prophet said : Had you not done it, Hell would have blackened your face. The Prophet said : When any slave serves his master and serves divine service well, double rewards are written for him.

The Prophet said : The first three persons who will enter Paradise and the first three persons who will enter Hell were presented to me. The first three persons who will enter Paradise are a martyr, then such a slave who does well his divine service and service to his master, then a needy man who refrains from begging although he has got a large family. The first three persons who will enter Hell are a tyrant ruler, then such a person of wealth who does not pay the dues of God and then the proud poor man. Hazrat Abu Mas'ud Ansari said : When I was beating my slave, I heard a sound from my back : O Abu Mas'ud! On turning back I found the Messenger of God. Immediately I threw the stick in my hand and he said: By God! God has got more power over you than your power over this slave. The Prophet said : When any servant comes to any of you with food, let him ask him to sit and take food with him. If he does not do it, let him give him a morsel of food. In another narration, when a slave prepares food for you and gives you relief from it, the vapour of that food and his labour are sufficient for you. Make him sit near you and take meal with him. If he does not do it, allow him to take some food therefrom and allow him to take something therefrom by hand or place some food in his hand and tell him : Eat. The Prophet said : He who takes care of his female slave and gets her married after setting her free, will get double rewards. The Prophet said : Everyone of you is a king and everyone will be asked about his subjects under his control.

The sum total of your duties towards servants and slaves are – Allow him to take share in your food and dress, don't give him work beyond his strength, don't look to him with an eye of hate and contempt, pardon his faults and think at the time of anger upon him that God has got power to punish you for your sins and guilts and that He has got more power than you. The Prophet said : Three persons will not be asked any question one who has brought separation in the united party, one who has become disobedient to his *Imam* (leader) and died as a sinner and the woman whom her husband left behind after relieving her from worldly needs and who after that shows her external beauty. No account will be taken of three persons. One who becomes partner in the screen, glory and honour of God, one who is not free from doubt about the existence of God and one who becomes despaired of the mercy of God.

CHAPTER VII

Rules of Living in Seclusion

There are differences of opinion regarding living in seclusion and living in society among the people. Those who supported the former opinion are the following sages Sufiyan Saori, Ibrahim b. Adham, Daud Tai, Fuzail b. Ayaz, Sulaiman Khawas, Yusuf b. Asbat, Huzaifa, Marashi, Bashar Hafi and others. Majority of *Tabeyins* (successors of companions) are supporters of living in society for the reason of doing good to others, establishing brotherhood, love and friendship among the believers and helping mutually for the sake of religion better than seclusion. The following are its supporters Sayeed b. Mosayyib, Shubi, Ibn Abi Laila, Hisham, b. Urwah, Ibn Shabramah, Shark b. Abdullah, Ibn Ayniah, Ibn Mubarak, Imam Shafayi, Imam Ahmed b. Hambal and others. Hazrat Omar said : Loneliness is like worship. Fuzail said : I am satisfied with God as an object of love, with the Qurān as a companion and with death as an admonisher. Hazrat Abu Daud and Tai said to Abu Rabi : Fast from the temptations of the world and break it in the next world. Flee from society as you flee from tiger. Hazrat Hasan Basri said : I have remembered from the Torah: You will be free from depending on men if you are satisfied with little, you will be safe if you keep distant from society, you will get the pleasure of freedom if you give up sexual passion, manliness will come out if you give up

hatred and you will get ever lasting happiness if you can refrain
from temporary greed. Wahab b. Ward said : I have heard that
wisdom has got ten parts, nine of which are in lonelines. Yusuf
b. Muslim said : I used to mix in society but did not hold any
talk with the people. Sufiyan Saori said: The present time is
the time of loneliness and staying in a corner of the house.
Hazrat Ibrahim Nakhyi said : Acquire learning and adopt
loneliness. Rabi b. Khasian said that Imam Malik used to be
present at funeral prayers, nurse the patients and pay the rights
of friends. He at last gradually gave up everything. Sayeed b.
Abi Waqqas and Sayeed b. Zaid used to live at Aqiq near
Madinah. They did not come to Madinah for Juma or for any
other thing and died at Aqiq. Sufiyan Saori said : Loneliness
has become lawful now. Bashar b. Abdullah said : Be
acquainted little with the people as you don't know what will
happen on the Resurrection Day. If you are disgraced, few
people will know you. A certain ruler asked Hatim Asam:
Have you got any requirement? He said : Yes. The ruler asked:
What is it? He said : Don't meet me and I shall not meet you
and don't be acquainted with me.

A certain man asked Sahal Tastari : I love to keep your
company. He said : When one of us dies, with whom will he
keep company? He said : With God. He said : Then it is better
at present to keep company with God. Fuzail said : The more
a man is acquainted with the people, the less is his wisdom.
Hazrat Abu Abbas said : Your assembly within your house is
the best assembly. You will not find anybody there and nobody
will find you. These are the sayings of those who love
loneliness.

Those who support living in society have got the following
proofs. God says : Don't be like those who differed and became
separate. God says : Then he united their hearts. These verses
speak of unity on the ground of love and speak of differences

regarding the Book of God. The second proof is said to be the saying of the Prophet : A believer loves an object of love and there is no good in one who does not love or get love. In this *Hadis*, condemnation of bad conduct is seen as it is a hindrance to love. There is another *Hadis* : He who separates from the united body even half a span shifts off the tie of Islam from his neck. He said : He who keeps separate from the united body dies the death of the days of ignorance. These are weak proofs of mixing in society. These speak of allegiance to one *Imam* or ruler and there is no mention of loneliness therein. The fourth proof cited is that the Prophet prohibited absence of meeting with the brother Muslim for more than three days. This proof is also weak as it contemplates previous quarrel. The fifth proof cited is that the Prophet said : Patience of one of you in a dangerous place of Islam is better than his worship of 40 years in a lonely place. This speaks of the time when Islam was in danger. At another time when a certain companion liked a lonely place where there was current of water the Prophet said: Don't do it, because the rank of one of you in the way of God is better than his divine service for sixty years. Don't you love that God should forgive you and you should enter Paradise? Make *Jihad* in the way of God, as one who fights in the way of God even for a short time, God will admit him in Paradise. Another proof is this *Hadis*. The Prophet said : The devil in men is like a tiger among a flock of sheep. The tiger attacks near and distant ones. Take care of hillocks and keep attached to united body, mosques and ordinary people. This means that loneliness is prohibited before the perfection of learning.

Merits and demerits of secluded living

That seclusion is good or bad depends upon the circumstances of each man. It is good for some people and bad for some people. The benefits of loneliness are as follows. The benefits are either worldly or religious. Benefits that are derived from loneliness are engagement in divine service, getting leisure for meditation or religious thoughts and relief from prohibited sins, such as show, back-biting, bad company with sinners and transgressors. The benefits of this world are that one can do his worldly matters with peaceful mind. So there are six benefits of loneliness.

(1) One can get sufficient leisure for divine service and deep contemplation of God's glory. The greatest ponder over divine matters is over the wonderful creations of God and of His sovereignty and power. In a society, that benefit cannot be availed of. A certain wise man said : It is not possible for anybody to take to loneliness unless he holds firmly the Qurān of God. Those who hold it firmly can enjoy time comforts of material and spiritual worlds. Those who remember God live in God's remembrance and die in God's remembrance and meet with God in God's remembrance. For this reason, the Prophet was immerged in deep meditation in the cave of Hira in early stages. For this reason, though he lived in society, his mind was always concentrated in the thoughts of God. Hazrat Junaid Baghdadi said : For the last 30 years, I am holding secret talks with God but the people think that I am speaking with them. A certain sage was asked: How can you keep patience in loneliness ? He said : I am not alone, God is my companion. When I wish that I should speak with Him secretly, I observe prayer. A certain sage was asked : What benefit have you derived from renunciation of the world ? He replied : God's love. Once Hasan Basri asked a sage : What things prevent you from mixing in society ? The man said : No time passes in which I am not in gifts or commit no sin. I remain busy for the gifts to express gratefulness to God and seek forgiveness to Him for the commission of sins. Zunnun Misri

said : The joy and taste of a believer lies in his invocation to his Lord. A certain wise man said – Love for the people is a sign of bankruptcy in religion.

(2) Second benefit : A man can get relief from the sins to be committed by living in a society by adopting loneliness. These sins are of four kinds– (1) to make back-biting and to hear back-biting, (2) to refrain from enjoining good deeds and from prohibiting bad deeds. (3) to work for show of people, (4) (a) and to enterain bad conduct and evil deeds. Except the truthful, nobody can be safe from back-biting. (b) Enjoining good deeds and prohibiting evil deeds is the basic principle of religion and compulsory. Once Hazrat Abu Bakr said at the time of Khutba: O people! you need this verse of God: O those who believe! take care of yourselves. When you find guidance, the misguided people cannot misguide you, but you do not use it in appropriate place. I have heard from the Prophet : If a man does not remove an evil deed of a man after seeing it, God sends punishment for it on all. The Prophet said : God take account of a servant, even He will ask this also : When you saw an evil deed being done, why did you not prevent it? When God will show proof to His servant, he will say : O Lord! I feared men and hoped for your pardon.

(3) Show : Show is an incurable disease and to remove it is very difficult on the part of the religious and pious men. Good feelings are required to be maintained in a society for which one feels inclined to make a show of his character and conduct. The Prophet said : The worst man is one who has got two faces – He comes with one face to one people and with another face to another people. A certain wise man said: If God loves a man, He wishes that his fame does not spread. Hazrat Taus went once to Caliph Hisham and said : O Hisham! how are you? He became displeased with him and said: Why have you not addressed me as 'Commander of the Faithful'?

Hazrat Taus said : The Muslims are unanimous against you. I fear that if I address you as Commander of the Faithful, I may be a liar. There is no fear for such a man to mix in society. The people once asked Jesus Christ : How are you? He said : I don't get in my possession what I hope and I have got no power to remove what I fear. I am busy with my affairs. All deeds are in the hand of another. There is nobody more in want than myself. A man asked Abu Darda'a : How are you? He said : I am well, provided I am released from Hell. Owais Qarni was once asked : How are you? He replied : How is the man who does not know whether he will live upto the next morning when evening comes to him, and when the dawn comes to him he does not know whether he will live upto evening.

(4) **Stealing of conduct :** You steal in your conduct what you see in the conduct of others. In other words, you follow their conducts. This is a secret disease from which even the wise men are not free, not to speak of the heedless ones. If one sees major sins being committed constantly around him, he takes them as of little consequence. For this reason, if you always look to the gifts of the rich, you will consider your own gifts as little. For this reason, you should take to the assemblies of the poor and the destitutes. You should took to the conduct and character of the religious people and not of those who are irreligious and commit sins and transgressions. The Prophet said: Mercy descends at the time of the discussion of the pious people. To be able to reach Paradise and to have sight of God mean mercy. It means that the beginning of mercy is good deeds and the beginning of good deeds is desire and the beginning of desire is discussion of the character of the pious men. Curse means to remain distant from God. The sins are the roots of being distant from God. The cause of curse is to go away from the remembrance of God and to be

busy with the worldly comforts. When such is the effect of discussion of the lives of the pious and the sinners, how is the condition when the pious and the sinners are met with? The Prophet said : A bad friend is for you like the hammer of a blacksmith. If the spark of the fire of heated iron does not even touch you, its vapour touches you just as its vapour touches you even when you do not know. The Prophet said: A good companion is like a seller of perfume, If he does not give you perfume, you get its fragrance. For this reason, it is unlawful for a man to disclose the faults of a learned man for two reasons – The first reason is that it will be back-biting him and the second reason is that the people will dare to commit the sins of the learned man when they see him committing them always. This is the machinations of the devil. God says with regard to those who oppose the devil: They hear words and follow what is good. The Prophet gave example of bad people. He said: The man who hears the words of wisdom and does not act but what is evil is like the person who says to a shepherd : Give me a stout and strong sheep from your flock. He then says : Choose the best one from the flock. Then he takes a dog by its ear from the flock. He who searches the faults of a leader is likewise. Seeing his bad deeds constantly, his abhorrence of evils drops from his hear.

Third benefit : The third benefit of loneliness is to get relief from quarrels and disputes and to save oneself from useless talks. The Prophet said : When you will see the people breaking their promises and trusts and when they become such (he thrusts the fingers of one hand into the fingers of another), they will remain busy with quarrels and disputes. A man asked: What will we do then? He said: Keep attached to your own houses keep the tongue under control and accept what you know and give up what you know not. Be busy then with your own affairs and give up the affairs of the people. The

Prophet said : The wealth of a Muslim in near future will be goats and sheep. He will roam in caves of hillocks and places of water. He will shift from one place to another with his religion from calamities. The Prophet said : In near future, such a time will come upon man when it will be difficult to save his religion. To save religion, he will flee away like a jackal from one cave to another and from one hillock to another. He was asked: O Prophet of God! when will it occur? He said : When you will not be able to earn livelihood without sin. When that time will come, one will be ruined at the hands of his parents, if he will have no parents, at the hands of his wife and children and in their absence, he will be ruined at the hands of his relatives. They asked : O Prophet of God! how will that come to pass? He said : They will abuse him for his insolvent condition. His parents will ask what is beyond the capacity of their son; as a result he will come to the position of ruin. The sage Sufiyan Saori said : Now seclusion has become lawful. Hazrat Sa'ad did not join the party of Muawiyah or the party of Hazrat Ali at the time when they were fighting for Caliphate. It has been narrated that when Hazrat Hussain was proceeding towards Iraq, Ibn Omar prevented him to proceed there but he refused on the ground that he had with him a letter of allegiance of the Iraqi people. Ibn Omar then recited a *Hadis* of the Prophet : Gabriel once came to the Holy Prophet and asked him to choose either of these two this world or the next world and the Prophet chose the latter. You are a piece of flesh of the Holy Prophet. By God! none of you will be the ruler of this material world which has been kept separate from you. In spite of this advice, Hazrat Hussain refused to turn back. He started with ten thousand men but there were no more than 40 persons with him at the time of battle.

Hazrat Tus kept attached to his own house. Being asked

the reason, he said : The dangers and calamities of this age and the oppression of the leaders compelled me to remain within the house. Hazrat Urwah erected a house at Aqiq for living and gave up coming to the Prophet's mosque. Being asked the reason, he said: On seeing your mosques as the place of sports and jokes, your bazars as the places of useless talks and your lanes as the places of obscene deeds, I have chosen to stay within the house wherein there is peace.

Fourth benefit : One can save himself from the harms of the people in case of secluded living. Hazrat Omar said Loneliness is better then a bad companion. Hazrat Samad said: One of our friends said: Men were like medicines with which they treated diseases. Men have turned now into diseases of which there is no cure. Flee away from them as you flee away from a tiger. Hazrat Hasan Basri said: Sabit Binani was the friend of God. When I intended to go on pilgrimage, he wished to accompany me. I said: If we live together, there may be such conduct between us which may lead us to hatred.

Another benefit of loneliness is mentioned here. It is to keep secrecy in religion, manliness, character and conduct, poverty and the remaining internal conditions. God praised such a man. The illiterate man thinks that they are rich owing to their abstinence from begging. Hazrat Abu Darda'a said : Man was before a leaf as it were with thorn, but at present he is a thorn without leaf. This was at the end of the first century. What is the condition now? Hazrat Sufiyan b. Ayniah said: Hazrat Sufiyan Saori in his life time and after his death in dream said to me : Make little acquaintance with the people as it is difficult to save oneself from them. This thought occurs in my mind that the sins I have earned are due to my mixing in society. A man was asked : Why have you abandoned society? He said : I feared that my religion would be robbed in my absence. Hazrat Abu Darda'a said : Fear God and fear society, because when they ride on a camel, they cause wound to it and the whip a horse when they ride on it and they cause harm to the mind of an unbeliever. A certain wise man said : Make little acquaintance, your religion and mind will remain safe and your duties will be less. The more the acquaintance, the more are the duties.

Fifth benefit is that the hopes of the people from you and your hopes from the people will vanish in case of secluded living as it is impossible to please all the people. So it is better to remain busy in purifying one's own character and conduct. Imam Shafayi said : To do benefit to the sinners is the root of every opposition. If one does not see the fineries of the world from the beginning, greed does not grow in him. For this reason, God said: Don't prolong your eyes towards what I have provided them of various kinds. The Prophet said : Look to those who are below you in respect of wealth and don't took to those who are superior to you in wealth, Otherwise you will consider the gifts of God on you as insignificant. Hazrat Aaon b. Abdullah said : I was at first in the company of the rich. I saw their dresses better than my dress, their conveyances better than mine. Then I kept company with the poor and I got then peace of mind.

Sixth benefit : If the idle and the fools take to loneliness, they get security from foolishness and heinous character. To meet with an idle man is like loss of sight. Hazrat A'mash was asked: How have you lost power of sight ? He said : Owing to my seeing the idle. Once Hazrat Abu Hanifa came to A'mash and said : The Prophet said : If God robs the sight of two eyes of a man. He gives him better than them in exchange. What thing has He given you in exchange of the loss of your eye sight ? Hazrat A'mash said jokingly : God has given me in its exchange the sight of the idle and you belong to that class. The wise Jalinaus said : Everything has got fever. Fever of soul comes at the sight of the idle. Imam Shafayi said : If I sit by the side of an idle man, the portion of my body which keeps near the idle man casts heaviness on me.

Benefits of Society

Know, O dear readers! that there are some religious matters which cannot be performed without mixing in society. The benefits which are gained by mixing in society are destroyed by loneliness. The benefits of society are the following :

(1) First benefit : By mixing in society, one can teach and learn religious learning which is the best divine service in this world. Education has got greater scope. Some education is compulsory and some optional. If loneliness is adopted without learning the compulsory education, it will be committing sin. If you have got ability to be expert in any branch of education, it will be a cause of harm if you adopt lonely living. For this reason, Ibrahim Nakhyi and other sages said : Acquire religious learning at first and then take to lonely habitation. If one remains busy in divine service for the whole day without acquirihg sufficient knowledge, his mind and body do not remain free from self-conceit and deceit. So education is the root of religion.

(2) Second benefit : Doing and taking benefit from the people mean to earn money by trading with them. Without mixing in society, it is not possible. If one is bound to earn his livelihood, it is compulsory for him to mix in society. To do benefit means to help the peoplè at the cost of life and property and to remove the wants of the Muslims.

(3) Third benefit : It is so make strenuous efforts and to gain the attribute of patience in the way of salvation. By mixing in society, man can earn the quality of patience at the harms and injuries inflicted by men. This leads to hard labour and extreme forbearance.

(4) Fourth benefit : It is to love and get love. Another benefit of mixing in society is that one can love another and one can get the love of another. The Prophet said: God is not vexed with you till you become vexed. Loneliness is not without undisturbed peace. The Prophet said : This religion is firm and take it with kindness. Hazrat Ibn Abbas said : Had I not feared random thoughts, I would not have mixed in society. He said : Who injures man except man ? The Prophet said : Man is upon the religion of his friend. So let him look with whom he befriends.

(5) Fifth benefit : It is to get virtues and give virtues. In a society, a man is required to be present at funeral prayers, call on patients, join *I'd* congregations etc.

(6) Sixth benefit : One can earn the quality of modesty and humility in a society while it cannot be gained in loneliness which sometimes creates pride. It is reported that a man of Israil dynasty wrote nearly 360 books on wisdom and thought that he got some rank to God for this. God then revealed to the Prophet of that age : Tell the man : You have filled up the world with hypocrisy. I will not accept any portion of your hypocrisy. Then he gave up writing books and took refuge in a grave and thought : I have now gained the pleasure of God. God then revealed to His Prophet tell him: You cannot gain My pleasure till you mix in society and bear their harms and troubles. Afterwards, he mixed in society. Then God revealed to His Prophet : tell him, now you have gained My pleasure. Hazrat Ali used to carry daily necessaries of the family from bazar and say: The perfection of a perfect man is not reduced if he carries anything for his benefit. Hazrat Abu Hurairah, Huzaifah, Obai and Ibn Masud and others used to carry fuels and food stuffs on their backs. Hazrat Abu Hurairah was the governor of Madinah at one time. He used to say while carrying loads of fuel : Give way to your ruler. The Prophet used also to carry his necessary things from the bazar. Some companions asked him : Give me the load to bear. He then said : The owner of the load has got right to carry it.

Hazrat Hasan, son of Hazrat Ali, while passing by the poor, used to sit with them and they used to say to him : O descendant of the Messenger of God! take share in our food. Then he used to get down from his conveyance and share with them their meal and said : God does not love the proud. Another reason is that one who remains busy in rendering pleasure of the people falls in error, because if he knows God perfectly, he will appreciate that there is no good in the pleasure of the people without the pleasure of God and all harms and benefits are in the hand of God. There is no benefactor and destroyer except He. He who incurs the pleasure of men by incurring the displeasure of God, God becomes displeased with him and keeps the people dissatisfied with him. If the object is only to incur the pleasure of the people, it is not fulfilled. God is the object of love and search. Imam Shafayi said : There is no such man as has got no friend and foe. When it is such, keep company with the pious. Hazrat Moses invoked God : O Lord! save me from the tongue of the people. He said : O Moses! I am also not free in this matter. So how can I make you free from their tongue? God revealed to Wazair: I will not enrol you as one of the humble ones near Me if you do not remain satisfied with the chewed matter in the mouth of the chewers.

(7) Seventh benefit is the gaining of experience which is gained by mixing in society. One whose natural intellect is not sufficient to understand the good of this material and spiritual world, loneliness is not good for him. If a boy without experience adopts loneliness, he will be misguided. He should, therefore, remain busy in educating himself. Every experience of loneliness is secret. Those who walk in the path of the next world search for purification of heart and allow themselves in the fiery tests. If they feel pride in their hearts, they try to remove it. Even some of them carry the skin of water or bundle of fuel and necessary articles from the markets. Thereby they gain experience and pride goes away. So the great benefit of mixing in society is that the faults of one come out. For this reason, it has been said that journey discloses the character and conduct of a man, as it is a result of mixing in society.

So what has been described above about the benefits and harms of seclusion, it is clear that loneliness is sometimes good and sometimes bad according to the special circumstances of each man and the surroundings he lives in. This depends on his friends and companions. A certain wise man said : To keep separate from society is a cause of enmity and to mix in society means sometimes company with the bad people: So be not separate and do not also mix, rather adopt the path of loneliness in mixing in society.

Rules and regulations of secluded living

(1) One should intend by loneliness to save himself from the harms of men. (2) He will seek safety from the harms of other people. (3) He will intend to be free from the faults in fulfilling the duties to the Muslims. (4) He will intend to prefer loneliness for divine services. (5) He shall engage himself in learning – *zikr, fikr* and other divine services. (6) He will not allow the people to mix with him. (7) He will not allow others to put questions to him. (8) He will not ask the news of any place or any man. (9) He will remain satisfied with little. (10) He will remain patient at the harms of his neighbours, if any. (11) He will be deaf in hearing the praise of others. (12) He shall know the merits of the path of the next world. In other words, he shall follow the rules and regulations of *zikr* with humility of mind, think of the wonderful creations

of God, the heavens and the earth, sun, moon, stars and of the sovereignty of God, think of life and death and of the conditions in grave after death.

If you do not give up the passions and temptations of the world, your patience in secluded living will not become perfect. The heart cannot be cleansed of impurities making short of your hopes and passions as you have got no power to prolong life. Think after getting up from bed in the morning that you will not be able to reach evening. In this way, you will be able to curtail your hopes and check passions. Know it for certain that he who cannot earn the love of God in his mind and His remembrance will not be able to bear loneliness after death. He who earns this attribute will be able to bear it, as death cannot destroy the place of God's love and remembrance. He will live in the midst of mercy of God. For this reason, God said about the martyrs : Don't think that those who have been killed in the way of God are dead, but they are alive near their Lord and get provisions.

CHAPTER VIII

Rules and Regulations of Journey

Journey is a means to ward off undesirable thing or to get objects of love, it is of two kinds – (1) Physical journey from one's native place to a distant country and (2) mental or spiritual journey to God in heaven. The latter is better, but it is fraught with dangers and difficulties and the path is unknown and unacquainted. The sojourners are indifferent to the wealth of this path. Hence the sojourners in this path are few. God says of this path : I shall show them My signs in the vacant regions and in yourselves. God says : There are signs in the world and in yourselves for the believers. Don't you mind ? He who keeps away from this journey is said by God in the following verse as an unbeliever : You pass by these signs morning and evening. Don't you understand ? God says: How many signs there are in the heavens and the earth which appear to them always but they remain heedless from them. He who remains satisfied with this journey, roam in such a Paradise cheerfully which extends to the heavens and the earth, though his body remains in his house.

Rules of journey from beginning to end

Journey means to go from one place to another. There are benefits and harms of journey. One is to shift from his place of residence on account of religion or for search of livelihood. There are therefore two kinds of objects of search – worldly and next worldly. Name and fame, wealth and riches, power and influence etc. are the worldly objects of search. Acquisition of knowledge is a religious matter and the journey for this purpose is of two kinds. Journey for acquisition of religious knowledge and for correction of one's own character and conduct or journey for acquisition of knowledge of the wonderful creations of God, such as journey of Alexander. Journey for actions with learning is of two kinds, to visit the holy places, such as Mecca, Madinah, Baitul-Muqaddas or journey for defense of the frontiers of Islamic state. Journeys are also undertaken for visiting the holy shrines of the religious leaders and friends of God and of those religious people who are alive. Thus it is seen that there are different purposes of journey.

(1) **Journey for acquisition knowledge** is of two kinds– Compulsory and Optional. When acquisition of knowledge is compulsory, journey for that is also compulsory. When it is optional, journey for that is also optional. The Prophet said: He who comes out of his house for acquisition of knowledge remains in the path of God till he returns home. The Prophet said : If a man crosses a path in search of learning, God makes his path to Paradise easy. Hazrat Sayeed b. Musayyib travelled many days in search of one *Hadis*. Hazrat Shubi said : If a man travels from Syria to the distant Yemen to hear a sermon, his journey will not be fruitless. Hazrat Zakir b. Abdullah travelled from Madinah to Egypt for one month and heard a *Hadis* from Abdullah b. Anis Ansari.

(2) **Journey for correction of one's character and conduct** : To walk in the path of the next world is not possible without character and conduct. He who does not enquire into his hidden faults cannot purify his heart. The name journey means to turn away from bad character and conduct of the people for which God reveals the secrets of heaven and earth.

In journey, a man's character is disclosed. When a person was brought before Hazrat Omar as a witness, he asked him: Were you with anybody in a journey for which you have known his character ? He said : I was not. Hazrat Omar said: Then I think you do not know him. Hazrat Bashar Hafi said: O learned men! if you would have come out in journey, you would have been purified, because if water is logged in a place, it becomes polluted and if it is flowing, it is made pure. In short, if a man remains confined in house, his character and conduct are kept limited there and his bad character is not disclosed as no opportunity arises in his case to see things opposed to his nature.

(3) Journey for seeing the wonderful creations of God: There is food for reflection in the wonderful creations of God. There is nothing in the world-mountains, seas, heaven and various kinds of creations which do not testify to the unity of God. He who appreciates it can see and hear them and he who does not pay attention to them cannot appreciate it. By hearing, we mean the hearing of heart. Ear cannot hear without sound and it appreciates the present condition. It is just like the saying of a man who narrates the story of wall and nail. The wall says to the nail : Don't give me trouble. The nail says : Ask one who beats me. The rod which is behind me beats me. Why does he not give me up ? There is no sign in the heaven and earth which does not bear testimony to the uniqueness and unity of God. It is its *Tauhid*. Various kinds of things glorify His name. Nobody understands their glorification or *Tasbeeh* as they do not undertake mental journey. If it was not possible. Solomon would not have understood the words of birds and Moses the talks of God. Those talks have got no words or sounds. The signs of writing that are on the backs of lifeless things can be appreciated by a man of deep insight. His outward journey is not required. Only his mental journey is necessary. Such a man has got object of joy in hearing and he can command the sun, moon and stars. The sun, moon and stars roam in the cycle of time– once, twice or many times in months or years. If a man goes round of mosque other than the *Ka'ba* for which he is ordered, his action would be considered as wonderful. If one who has been ordered to roam round the sky roams round the earth, his action will be considered wonderful. So a sojourner who cannot roam in the material world remains within the station of his own house without crossing the various stations to reach God. For this reason, a pious man said : Man says, open your eyes, you will see the wonderful creations of God. But I say : Close your eyes and you will see them. Both the views are true. The first man gives the news of the first station near the house and the second man gives the news of the distant stations. Without the satisfied soul of the sojourner, the distant stations cannot be crossed. Sometimes he roams for many years in one station. Sometimes God's grace shows him the straight path and there are few who can catch this favour. Those who cross these stations by the light of God's grace, can earn lasting fortune. The sovereignty of the spiritual world is like that of this world. Firstly, those who search it are few and out of them many remain with face of destruction and they decrease considerably while the goal is reached. Those who are coward cannot get this sovereignty. In order to get the high rank, one is to labour hard and pass many sleepless nights. God does not give it to those who are idle and coward.

Second kind of journey : It is the journey for divine service, such as pilgrimage, *Jihad* etc, visit of the shrines of Prophets, companions of Prophets and other sages. The merits which are gained by calling on the living sages can be obtained by vising their graves. Journey for such purpose is allowed and the following *Hadis* is not an obstacle to that. The Prophet said : Don't tie your camel in any place except in three mosques – this mosque of mine, the mosque of *Ka'ba* and the distant mosque (*Baitul-Muqaddas*). Except these three mosques, all other mosques are equal in rank. The merits in meeting the living sages are greater than meeting of those who are dead. There is written in the Torah : Meet with your brother Muslim for the sake of God after walking even four miles. We have been informed about the merits of visiting the mosque of Madinah and *Ka'ba*. The merits of visiting *Baitul-Muqaddas* are also great. Once Hazrat Ibn Omar travelled from Madinah for *Baitul-Muquddas* and prayed five times within the mosque. Hazrat Solomon prayed to God : O Lord! If a man wishes to visit the mosque and does not wish nothing except praying therein, let him not lose Thy mercy till he remains there in. When he goes out of the mosque, take him out of his sins as on the day his mother gave birth to him. God accepted his invocation.

Third kind of journey : It is good to make journey to get free from the causes obstructing religion. It is the way of the Prophets to flee for getting free from work which is beyond one's capacity. It is also compulsory to flee away for freeing the mind from engagement in actions, name and fame and power. Unless the mind is freed from things other than God, the religion does not become perfect. If it is not possible, the more one gets free from troubles, the better it is for the mind to be free from such thoughts. The mind can be made light or heavy. Those who can reduce their worldly anxieties get salvation, and those who increase them are ruined. It is not safe for a worldly man to get relief from anxieties unless he makes journey to a distant place and frees his mind from all sorts of worldly anxieties. Mind has got no space both for the Creator and also for the created. There are some men like Prophets and sages who are mentally strong like those who are physically strong. There are differences even in their physical strength. How many persons there are who can carry two and a half maunds of loads but it cannot be carried by a weak man. The strength can be increased by gradual and constant efforts. Similar is the condition of mental strength. In order to reach the high spiritual stage, continued and sustained efforts are necessary. For this reason, the early sages used to stay far away from their own houses. Sufiyan Saori said : The present time is very perilous. When the unknown persons suffer loss at present, what is the condition of those who have got name and fame ? So the present people should change their residences in order that they may not be known to the people. Hazrat Abu Nayeem said : I saw once Sufiyan Saori going with one pitcher in one hand and one bag of leather full of articles in another. On being asked, he said : I am going to such a place where commodities are cheap. Live where these things are cheap as it is safe for your religion and light for your anxieties. Hazrat Ibrahim Khaolan used not to reside in any place for more than forty days.

Fourth kind of journey : There is no fault in taking journey to another place for saving oneself from epidemic diseases like small pox, cholera, plague etc. or where commodities are cheap. Sometimes such journey becomes compulsory and sometimes commendable. If there in outbreak of epidemics in a certain locality, the people should not shift to another place as the Prophet said : Some people were punished with epidemic disease before you. It remained in the world after that. It comes sometimes and goes away sometimes. When it breaks out in any place, don't go near it. When it breaks out in such a place where you live in, don't go out of it fleeing. The Prophet said : My people will be destroyed by attack and epidemic diseases. Hazrat Ayesha asked: What is attack ? He said : It is an epidemic disease like the plague of camels. It grows in their sinews. He who dies of this disease dies a martyr. He who stays therein is like a prisoner in the way of God. He who flees away from if flees away as it were from *jihad*. The Prophet said to one of his companions : Don't set up any partner with God even though you are punished and threatened. Obey your parents. If they tell you to go out of your properties, you will go. Don't give up any prayer willingly. He who gives up a prayer willingly gets free from the security of God. Don't drink wine as it is the key to all sins. Give up sin as it displeases God. Don't flee away from *Jihad*. If an epidemic disease attacks the people among whom you live, stay with them. Spend from your wealth for your family but do not lift your stick from them and generate fear in them. It appears from the above *Hadis* that to flee away from an epidemic disease and also to come to it are prohibited.

From what has been described, it is found that journey is of different kinds – good, bad and lawful. What is bad becomes sometimes unlawful as the fleeing away of a slave or of a rebel. What is not good is to flee away from epidemic diseases. What is good is sometimes compulsory and sometimes commendable. Journey for pilgrimage and learning are compulsory and for meeting with sages and visiting their graves is commendable. What is lawful depends on *niyyat* or intention. If journey is undertaken for earning money by abstaining from begging, to protect the honour of oneself and his family or to give charity, it is lawful as they are intended within the actions of the next world. The Prophet said : All actions are judged by intention. This *Hadis* is applicable to compulsory, commendable and lawful journeys. A wise man said : God appoints angels to sojourners. They look to their intentions and they are given blessing according to their intentions.

Rules to be observed in journey

(1) Pay compensation of oppression and the debts and loans, provide the maintenance of those who are dependant on you and return the trusts deposited with you. Take lawful and good things for the journey and take sufficient money so that you may help others also in their needs. Hazrat Ibn Omar said : To help a man in journey with lawful money is to honour him. Treat well with, the fellow pilgrims in journey. Give them food from you and disclose your good conduct to them as journey discloses the secret faults of mind. A wise man said : If a man is praised by his fellow trader or fellow sojourner, there is no doubt that he is a good man. A wise man said : Three men cannot be blamed for their anxiety – a fasting man, a patient man and a sojourner. The conduct of a fellow traveller becomes perfect if he treats well with his fellow travellers, helps them in their needs, shows sympathy with them and helps them in their loading and unloading luggages and loads.

(2) To take good companion in journey. Take such a companion in journey who will help you in your actions and religion. When you forget, he will remind you. When you want help, he will help you as every man upon the religion of his friend. The Prophet prohibited to take journey alone, he said : Three persons form congregation. He said : When three of you form a company in journey, choose one of you as a leader. The companions used to do it and say : This man is our leader. The Prophet then appointed him as leader. Make such a man as leader who is best among you in character and conduct, most kind to his companions and places the needs of companions more than his own needs. The affairs of the world are best done if one is entrusted with the management as one God manages the affairs of the universe. Had there been two Gods, they would have quarrelled and all affairs of

the world would have been mismanaged. The duties of a leader should be learn from the following example.

Two friends Abdullah and Abu Ali Rabati once started on a journey. Abdullah said to Rabati : You are my leader. Rabati said to Abdullah: You are my leader. Then Abdullah was made leader of the two. Thereafter he carried his own luggage and the luggage of Rabati upon his back. One night, there fell profuse rain. Abdullah held a blanket over his companion for the whole night. Whenever Rabati said : 'Don't do it' Abdullah said : Have you not selected me as your leader? So don't order me and don't do other than what I order you to do. Rabati then said : I wished then that I should have been dead and that I should not have said to him : You are my leader. This should be the duty of a leader in journey or in administration. The Prophet said : It is better to have four companions in journey. There is surely some good in what the Prophet said. There are two duties of a traveller to protect the luggages and to go for taking necessary things. These can well be done if there are four persons in a company in journey.

(3) Take leave of relatives and friends. At the time of starting, recite the following : I entrust to God your religion, your trust and the results of your action. The Prophet used to recite it. The Prophet said : When anyone of you wishes to take journey, he should pray for his friends, because God gives good to them on account of his prayer. The Prophet said : When you take leave of any man, say : May God give you provision of God-fear, forgive your sins and give you good wherever you go. He who stays at home should say this to the traveller. Hazrat Musa b. Ward said : One day I intended to go on a journey and came to Abu Hurairah to take leave of him. He said : O cousin! shall I not teach you what the Prophet had taught me at the time of farewell ? I said : Yes. He said: I entrust you to God who does not break His trust. One day a

man came to the Prophet and said : I intend to go on a journey. Give me advice. The Prophet said to him : In the protection and upkeep of God. May God give you provision of God-fear, pardon your sins and direct you to good wherever you are, When you entrust to God, entrust everything to Him and not a particular thing. The result of entrustment of a particular thing is found in the following story. A certain man with his son came to Hazrat Omar at the time of distribution of money among the people. Hazrat Omar said to him : The appearance of the boy is exactly like yours. I have never found such similarity. The man said : O Commander of the faithful! I am narrating his story to you. When he was in his mother's womb, I was in a journey. When starting, I said to his mother : I am entrusting the child in your womb to God. Then I went abroad. When I returned, I saw that my wife had died. When I went to her grave, I found a fire burning over her grave. I asked the people : Why is the fire ? They said : This is the grave of your wife. Every night, we are seeing this fire. I dug her grave and found a lamp burning there and this child was playing with the lamp. Then I heard a voice from heaven : You have entrusted this child to Me. Had you entrusted his mother also to Me, you would have found her after your return.

(4) **Pray *Istikhara* prayer before starting :** A man came to the Prophet and said: I have made vow for a journey but I have written a death instruction. Tell me with whom I shall keep it. With my son, father or brother ? The Prophet said : If a man prays four *rak'ats* in his house before starting on a journey he cannot leave a better thing than it. He shall pray these four *rak'ats* after putting on his dress of journey reciting therein chapter *Ikhlas* and then say : O God! I am seeking Thy nearness by this prayer. So make this prayer as my successor for my family and property. Then the prayer becomes his successor in place of his family and property and guards round his house till he returns.

(5) Recite this invocation at the door of the house at the time of coming out for journey : In the name of God, I depend on God and there is no might and strength except in God. O Lord! I seek refuge to Thee that I may not be misguided and that I may misguide nobody, that I may not slip and that I may not make another slip, that I may not oppress or I may not be oppressed ; that I may not make anybody ignorant or that nobody may make me ignorant. When you walk on, say: O God! I have come out with Thy help, on Thee I depend, I consider Thee as my protector and to Thee I turn my face. O God! you are my object of trust and you are my hope. You are sufficient for what troubles me and what you know of me. It is glory to live in Thy neighbourhood, Thy presence is sufficient. There is no deity but Thee. O God! increase my God-fear, pardon my sins, guide me towards good wherever I go

(6) Come out in the morning for journey : The Prophet came out in the morning for journey to Tabuk and said : O God! give blessing to my people in the morning of Thursday. It is commendable to come out for journey on Thursday morning. The Prophet seldom came out on a journey except on Thursday. The Prophet said : Give blessing to my people in the morning of Saturday. When the Prophet sent any expedition, he sent in the early part of the day. The Prophet said : Give blessing of morning to my people. Journey should not be undertaken in the morning of Friday. The Prophet said: To go with the warriors in the way of God a few steps and to take care of their conveyance morning and evening are dearer to me than the world and its riches.

(7) Not to alight except in the mid-day is *Sunnat* : Most part of the Prophet's journey was at night. The Prophet said : You should take to journey during night because the earth is not so straitened at day as it does at night. When you alight at a station, pray two *rak'ats* and say : O God! I seek refuge to Thee with the help of Thy perfect words from the evils Thou hast created.

(8) Don't separate yourself from the company as you may be murdered : There shall be a guard at the time of sleep at night. When the Prophet slept at the first part of night, he spread out his hands and when he slept at the latter part of night, he placed his head upon his hand. He used to do that to stop over-sleeping. If there are two companions, one shall guard the other.

(9) Show mercy to a riding animal and don't give loads to it beyond its capacity : Don't beat it on its face as it is prohibited. Don't sleep over its back as it gives trouble to the riding animal. The Prophet said : Don't take up the backs of your riding animals as a seat for comfort. It is commendable to alight from the animal morning and evening, thereby the animal is given rest.

(10) Take six things in journey : Hazrat Ayesha reported that when the Prophet went out on a journey, he used to take with him five things – mirror, antimony, scissors, tooth-stick and comb. In another narration six things – mirror, urinal, tooth–stick, scissors, antimony and comb. Sa'ad said : The Prophet always used to take mirror and antimony with him in journey. The Prophet said : At the time of going to bed, you should use antimony, as it increases eye-sight and grows eye-lids. It has been reported that the Prophet used to apply antimony thrice in each eye.

(11) Rules of returning from journey : Whenever the Prophet returned from expedition, pilgrimage, *umrah* and at the end of other actions, he recited *Takbir* three times at the time of crossing any elevated place and said : There is no deity but God, He is one, there is no partner for Him, sovereignty is His, praise is His and He is powerful over everything. Thereafter send news of your arrival through a man to your family. Don't come to them all at once, lest you may see any undesirable thing. Nobody should come to his family from journey at night. The Prophet prohibited it. Whenever he returned from journey, he used to enter first in the mosque, pray there two *rak'ats* and then enter his house and say I have returned home being repentant to our Lord. I am making such repentance which leaves no remainder of sin. It is *sunnat* to take some delicious eatables for the members of the family. It has been reported in *Hadis* : If one is unable to take anything with him, he should take at least a piece of stone in his bag. He laid a great emphasis to this as it cements love and affection.

Secret rules of journey : Nobody should take journey except to increase the progress of religion. If there is chance of loss of any portion of religion, he should return home. Whenever you go out, intend to meet the religious people of that place and try to get benefit from them. Don't stay in one place for more than a week or ten days. If you wish to meet your relatives there, don't stay with him for more than three days which is the limit of entertainment of guests.

Some matters before journey

The matters which should be known before journey are divided into two classes– (1) to know the rules of religion made easy for journey (2) and to know about the *Qibla* and fixed times of prayer. In ablution, two things have been made easy in journey, to wipe over socks and to make *Tayammum*. Prayer also has been made easy in some matters to make prayer short, to unite two compulsory prayers, to pray on conveyance and to pray while walking on foot. In journey, it is not compulsory to fast. These seven rules have been made easy in a journey.

(1) To wipe over socks : Hazrat Safwan b. Asal said When we were in a journey, the Prophet ordered us not to open socks of leather for three days and three nights. In residence, one can wipe over socks for one day and one night. Socks must be put on after full ablution. The socks must not be turned in any place and they are not to be opened during the limited time. They are to be wiped over the portions of ablution only.

(2) To make *Tayammum* : *Tayammum* is allowed in journey when water is at a distance from where sound are not heard or there are ferocious beasts near water. The palms of two hands must be thrust upon the earth and with the palms, face is to be wiped and then the palms will again be thrust upon earth and therewith the hands upto joints will be wiped out. One compulsory prayer is to be performed with one *Tayammum* along with *sunnat* and optional prayer.

(3) To make compulsory prayer short : The noon, afternoon and night prayer may be made short by two *rak'ats*. It is to be performed in due time with *niyyat* of *Qasr* and under no Imam who performs full four *rak'ats*. According to Hanafi law, *Qasr* may be performed after crossing a distance of 48 miles from residence.

(4) To unite two compulsory prayers : Noon prayer may be delayed upto afternoon prayer or the latter may be prayed along with noon prayer in journey. Similar is the case with evening and night prayers which can be said together. The evening prayer may be said with the night prayer or the night prayer with the evening prayer. It is lawful to give up *Juma* prayer in journey.

(5) *Qibla* : The Prophet prayed *sunnat* prayers towards the direction of his riding animal while riding on it. Thereon prayers were said by hints in bending and prostration. One need not turn towards *Qibla* at the start of prayer.

(6) It is allowed to perform *sunnat* prayer while walking on foot by hints and jestures without sitting at the time of *Tahayyiat*.

(7) It is allowed for a sojourner not to fast. It may be kept on other days.

CHAPTER IX

Music and Ecstasy

Heart is the seat of secret wealth and it is the invaluable mine of jewels. There lies in it the most valuable jewel, just as fire lies secretly in stone and iron. It lies hidden in such a way as water lies in the lowest bottom of earth. There is no means of waking it up from sleep without sweet sounds. There is no path of sound entering into heart without the door of ear. The feelings that lie hidden in heart are brought out by sweet, melodious and rhymed sounds. These do not come out of heart without movement as what is in cauldron does not fall without being heated. Melodious song takes out what is hidden in heart and creates a wonderful feeling. When heart is controlled by songs, they take out from its qualities and guilts. So it is necessary to discuss about songs in the light of the teachings of Islam.

Different opinions regarding
(Sama) songs

We shall discuss now about religious songs and ecstasy that arise spontaneously. As a result of these songs, the organs of the body tremble. Imam Shafayi, Malik, Abu Hanifa, Sufiyan Saori and other learned men used such words regarding sama or religious songs which show that it is

unlawful. Imam Shafayi in his book '*Adabe Qaza*' said that
Sama is *Makruh* as it resembles void things. He who remains
busy in *sama* songs is a fool and his deposition is not
acceptable. Qazi Abu *Tayyib* said : To hear *sama* from such a
woman who can be married is not lawful according to the
disciples of Imam Shafayi. Imam Shafayi said that it is *Makruh*
to ring musical instruments by stick and that the Zindings
have discovered *sama* from the Qurān in order to divert the
attention of the people. Imam Malik prohibited songs. He said:
It is your duty to cancel the sale of a female slave who is
found after purchase to be a singer. Imam Abu Hanifa said
that *sama* is *Makruh* and to hear songs is sin. Hazrat Sufiyan
Saori, Hammad, Ibrahim Shubi and other learned men of Kufa
gave similar opinion. Abu Talib Makki after quoting the
opinions of many learned men said that *sama* is lawful. He
said that Hazrat Abdullah, Muawiyah and other companions
used to hear *sama*. He said that on fixed days of blessings,
the Meccans used to hear *sama*. The Medinites also used to
hear them. The sage Attar had two female slaves of melodious
sounds. His friends used to hear *sama* from them. The saints
Junaid Baghdadi, Sirri Saqti, Zunnun Misri and Haris
Mohasabi, Ibne Hasan Askalani used to hear *sama*.

Mumshad Dinawari said : I asked the Prophet in dream
O Messenger of God! do you dislike anything of *sama* ? He
said : I don't dislike it, but tell them that they should begin it
with a verse of the Qurān and finish it with its verse. Tahir b.
Bilal saw the Prophet in dream who was sitting in a corner of
a mosque with Hazrat Abu Bakr by his side. The latter was
reciting poetries and the Prophet was hearing. The Prophet
said : This is the truth in exchange of truth. Hazrat Junaid
said : In three places, mercy is bestowed on those people – at
the time of meal as they do not eat unless hungry, at the time
of *Zikr* as they make *Zikr* staying upon the high rank of the

Truthful and at the time of hearing *sama*, as they hear it being engrossed with love and see truth with veritable eye.

Proof that *Sama* is lawful

Shariat means the sayings and doings of the Prophet and the inferences therefrom. These things do not prove that *sama* or religious songs are unlawful.

Proof of inference from the Prophet's sayings and doings. *Gina* means songs which includes *sama* or religious songs. Ordinarily it means sweet sound. Sweet sound is of two kinds–rhythmical sound and simple sound. Rhythmical sounds are of two kinds: understandable like poetry or not understandable like the sounds of animals. *Sama* means religious songs with sweet voice. It cannot be unlawful, rather it is lawful according to the traditions.

Rhythmless sweet sound : Ear has been created to hear resounding of sweet sounds of *sama*. Man has got five organs and intellect and every organ has got a natural attribute of the sensation of the taste of joy. The natural attribute of eye is to see. It enjoys joy at the sight of beautiful things, such as various kinds of leaves and plants, flowing stream, beautiful face. In one word, all beautiful colours and sceneries are dear to eye. Sight of ugly colours is displeasing to eye. Then nose has been created to take smell. It loves to take sweet scent and fragrance and dislikes bad smell and stench of rotten things. Take the case of tongue. It likes sweet and greasy things and dislikes bitter and distasteful foods. Hands like smooth things more than hard and uneven things. Take the case of intellect. It feels comfort in knowledge and dislikes illiteracy and ignorance. Similar is the case of ear. The sound which the ears hear is of two kinds – sweet sounds like the sounds of nightingale and sweet songs and displeasing sounds like the sounds of an ass. What is true of other organs is true also of ears. *Hadis* allows hearing of sweet sounds. God says: He increases in creation what He wishes. This increase is said to mean sweet sound. The Prophet said : God did not send any Prophet without sweet sound. He also said : If a man recites the Qurãn with sweet sound, God hears his recitation more than one hears the songs of his female singer. One *Hadis* praised the Prophet David by saying : David used to sing with so melodious sound that men, jinn, beasts and birds gathered together spell bound to hear it. Nearly four hundred persons expired thus by hearing his songs. The Prophet once praised his companion Abu Musa Ash'ari saying : He has been given the musical instruments of songs of the family of David. God says the worst of sounds is surely the sound of an ass. This verse also praises sweet sound. If *sama* is held unlawful, then to hear the sound of nightingale is also unlawful. If to hear the sound of nightingale is lawful, then will it not be lawful to hear sweet and melodious sounds which have got wisdom and good meanings ?

Sweet sounds with rhythm. There is rhythm in sweet sound. There are many sweet sounds which have got no rhythm and many sounds with rhythm which have got no sweetness. Rythmical sweet sounds are of three kinds from the points of the places of utterances. Firstly, it comes out from material things, such as musical instruments and drums or the sounds of stick-beatings over instruments. Secondly, it comes out from the throats of animals including men, nightingale and other animals. It is naturally sound with rythm for which it is sweet. The source of the sound of animal is its throat. Sweet sound has been discovered by following the sweet sounds of animals. There is nothing in God's creation which is not followed by men. So how will the sounds, melodious or not melodious be unlawful for the ears ? Nobody says that the sweet sounds of birds are unlawful. The sound of an animal with life is not separate from the sound of a lifeless instrument. So to hear the sound of a man in whatever form it comes out of his throat is not unlawful except to hear the sounds of such instruments which *Shariat* expressly prohibited – *Kuba, Mazamir* and *Autar*. These are not made unlawful as they emit sweet sounds. If it would have been made unlawful for this reason, all things which man enjoys would have been unlawful. The reason of being unlawful is that they were connected with wine which was made unlawful. These instruments helped the drinking of wine, as to live with an unknown woman in a room is unlawful as it helps cohabitation. These instrument also reminded them with wine-drinking. The flute of shepherds, pilgrims, drummers which emit sweet sounds are not unlawful as they are not connected with the drunkards. God says : Say, who has prohibited God's beautiful things which He created for His servants and good provisions ? So these sounds with rythm are not unlawful.

Third kind of *Sama* which are easily understood : These are poetries which come out from the throat of men. They are lawful. Words which are easily understood and sweet sounds with rythm are not unlawful when they are separately lawful, they cannot be unlawful when they are united. If there are any objectionable words in them, they are unlawful, whether attended with sweet sounds or not. Imam Shafayi said – Poetry are words only. The good of them is good and the bad of them is bad. When recitation of poetry without sound and rythm is lawful, then to recite them with sound and rythm is lawful. When poetries were recited before the Prophet, he used to say : There is surely wisdom in poetry. When constructing the mosque of Madinah, the Prophet used to hear materials with his other companions and recite poetry. He recited at another time these poetries : O God! life is the life of the Hereafter, so below mercy on *Ansars* and *Muhajrins*.

The Prophet erected a pulpit within the mosque for the poet Hassan b. Sabit. He used to stand upon it and recite poetry deprecating the unbelievers and praising the Prophet. The Prophet then said : God is helping Hassan with the Holy Spirit till he declares glory on behalf of the Prophet and disputes. Once the poet Nabigah recited some of his poetries before the Prophet who prayed for him saying : May God not break your teeth. Hazrat Ayesha said that the companions used to recite poetry before the Prophet who only smiled. Amr b. Sharid reported from his father who said : I recited before the Prophet one hundred poetries of Omayya b. Salt. Each time he said : Repeat it.

Fourth stage : *Sama* wakes up the mind. What remains strong in mind, is awakened by *Sama*. I say that sweet song with ryhm is a secret thing of God for sout. It creates a wonderful feeling in mind. Some sound gives pleasure, some pain, some brings sleep, some excites passion some moves the organs of the body. Mind becomes such if the rings of songs sound in the innermost recess of the heart. A suckling child often is lulled into sleep or his cries stopped by sweet songs. Camels are so influenced by songs that even heavy load seem light to them. Once a slave was conducting a camel to a distant place. It was heavily loaded. The slave had a melodious sound. The camel was so impressed by his song that it crossed in one day three days' journey. When loads were taken from it expired. This shows that the effect of songs in mind is wonderful. For this reason, even birds used to sit on the head of Prophet David on hearing his songs.

In seven places, songs are commendable.

(1) Songs of pilgrims : They roam from one country to another with songs and flutes. These songs are lawful, and they describe poetry relating to *Ka'ba*, Black Stone Hateem,

Zamzam and other signs. These arouse feelings for visiting the *Ka'ba* and other holy places.

(2) The warriors should be given impetus to fight against the enemies by songs. It is lawful to call towards bravery and to lay down life for the cause of God.

(3) If two warriors meet in the battlefield, what they recite of songs and poetry of bravery is lawful, because they incite them to fight. It is lawful in lawful fights and not in unlawful fights.

(4) Songs of mornings : It is of two kinds: commendable and not commendable. It is not commendable to recite songs which increase sorrow for past mishaps, calamities. The Qurãn says :–'lets you do not grieve for what missed you.' To express sorrow for the dead falls within this class of songs, as it expresses dissatisfaction at the order of God.

Morning songs are commendable when men express sorrow for past sins. For this sin, Adam wept for forgiveness and Prophet David's songs were for forgiveness. Owing to his melodious songs, many people expired. This action is praiseworthy and to give encouragement for this is also praiseworthy.

(5) Songs at the time of festivals : It increases joy and happiness at the time of festivals and other days of expressing happiness, for this happens at the time of two *I'ds*, marriage festivals, birth ceremony, when a child is born, circumcision. When the Prophet returned to Madinah after the expedition of Ridwan, the women from the top of the roof were singing.

"Full moon rises above us from Saniyyatul Wadayi,

compulsory on us to express gratefulness to God Almighty."

This joy was expressed at the arrival of the Prophet to

Madinah from the expedition. This is commendable. Hazrat
Ayesha reported : I was seeing the sports of the Abyssinian
boys standing within the mosque on the day of *I'd*, The Prophet
covered me with his sheet. She was then of immature age.
One day Hazrat Ayesha saw that two girls were beating '*Daf*'
at Mina and the Prophet covered her face with his sheet. When
Hazrat Abu Bakr came there, the Prophet removed the sheet
from the face of Ayesha and said : O Abu Bakr! leave her as it
is an *I'd* day. One day the Prophet asked Ayesha : What are
these dolls ? She said : These are my daughters and in the
midst of them there is the horse. He asked : What are these
two over the horse ? She said : Two wings. The Prophet said:
Two wings of a horse ? Ayesha said : Have you not heard that
Sulaiman, son of David, had a horse with two wings?
Thereafter the Prophet laughed, so much so that his teeth were
visible. Hazrat Ayesha reported – The Prophet one day came
to me at the time when two girls were singing near me the
songs of Boas battle. He got up and turned her face towards
them. Abu Bakr then came and threatened me and said : The
instruments of songs before the Prophet ? The Prophet
advanced towards Abu Bakr and said : Leave them both. These
traditions in Sahih Bukhari and Muslim prove that songs and
plays and sports are not unlawful.

(6) **Songs of the lovers** : These increase love towards
God and give satisfaction and pleasure to mind. It is also
lawful. If the union with a strange girl or woman is unlawful,
songs for her love is also unlawful.

(7) **Songs on the part of one who seeks the love and
pleasure of God** and to meet with Him is lawful. *Sama* brings
out from the recess of his heart the power of sight of different
matters and a deep feeling and unspeakable taste which can
only be felt and not disclosed. This taste cannot be obtained
by any other organ of the body. The condition of intoxication

is termed by the Sufis as *Wajd* or ecstasy. This appears in mind as an effect of religious songs which did not exist before. The fire of ecstasy arising in mind burns the uncleanliness of mind as fire removes the accumulated refuges on invaluable jewels and diamonds. The result is the shining of mind in which *Mushahida* and *Mukashifa* appear. In other words, his inner eye is opened by which he sees the secrets of nature. This is the goal of the lovers of God and the last stage of their search. He who can reach that stage gains nearness of God. It is possible only by *Sama* songs. He who is stupid expresses wonder at the taste of ecstasy as an important man expresses wonder at the pleasure of cohabition or as a boy at the taste of power and fame. How he whose mind is not perfect for feeling can have taste and how he who has got no power of taste can taste ? How can he who has got no power of intellect get the taste of intellect ? He who earned the knowledge of recognition of God loves Him beyond doubt. This love deepens in proportion to his knowledge of God. This deep love or the Prophet for God kept him confined in the cave of Hira in deep meditation.

Know, O dear readers! that every beauty is dear to the organ of that beauty. God is ever beautiful and He loves beauty. If the beauty is of a material thing, it can be seen by the material eye and if that beauty is of glory, attributes and good character, it can be appreciated by the organ of mind. The word beauty has been used practically to appreciate these attributes. It is therefore said : That man has got beautiful character and conduct. It does no speak of his figure but of his qualities. He is loved for these beautiful attributes as one is loved for his beautiful appearance. If this love is deep, It is called *Ishq*. Even more wonder is this that a dead man is loved not for his figure but for the innate qualities he had. Every beauty in the world is a spark of that permanent Beauty of God and a spark of His light. So how can be not love Him who is ever beautiful and the prime source of beauty ? He who realises it loves Him most. Nothing is compared to the beauty of sun and moon. God is the creator of these beautiful things. So how should He be loved ?

Love for a created thing has got defects. It is a sign of our ignorance. But one who knows Him with real eye of truth knows of no beauty except the Creator of a beauty. He who knows workmanship as the attribute of a workman does not go to anybody except to him. Everything in the world is the workmanship of God and the sign of His creation. So he realises Him though His creations and realises His attributes and His workmanship, just as one realises the qualities of a writer through his written book. A man of little intellect understands love as physical union or satisfaction of sexual lust.

The Prophet once mentioned of a youngman of Banu Israil. The young man asked his mother from the top of a hillock : Who has created this sky ? The mother replied – The Almighty God. He again asked : Who has created this earth? The mother replied : The Almighty God. In this way he asked about mountains and clouds and the mother replied as before. He said : Such is the glory of God. Saying this he jumped down from the hillock and soon expired. This is nothing but the ecstasy of love for God who is Almighty and Great.

Sama is unlawful in five cases

(1) To hear *sama* from a woman whose look excites sexual passion. Beardless boys may also be included in this category if sexual passion is aroused at their sight. This illegality is not for songs but for women and beardless boys.

(2) Instruments of songs of drunkards are unlawful as they remind of unlawful thing and incite unlawful action of wine-

drinking and intoxicants. These are *Mazamir*, *Autar* and *Kuba* but not *Daf*, flute and other musical instruments.

(3) Obscene talks in *sama* are unlawful. If there is any obscene talks in poetry, useless talks and accusations against God, His Prophets and companions, they are unlawful. If there are descriptions of a particular woman and not of women in general, and narrations of the beauties of a particular woman before the people, they are unlawful.

(4) If any evil or immoral desire arises in mind or by hearing songs, it will be unlawful.

(5) If habit is formed for hearing *sama*, it is unlawful. Excess of anything is bad. If too much food is taken, it is bad for health. If too much oil is besmeared on face, it looks ugly. So, also if too much *sama* songs are heard, it forms into a habit which is bad. After strenuous efforts and hard labour, *Sama* songs and innocent enjoyments are not bad.

Question. From your arguments, it seems that *Sama* is lawful in some cases and unlawful in some cases. Then why did you say at the beginning that *Sama* is lawful?

Answer. In answer to that, know that if a person questions whether honey is lawful or unlawful, I must say at the beginning that honey is lawful but it is unlawful for a man of hot temper. If you ask me about wine, I must say in the beginning that it is unlawful, but it is lawful for a man in whose throat a morsel of food has stuck. These are the exemptions and not the general rule. So at the beginning the general rule has been mentioned by saying that *Sama* is lawful and wine is unlawful. Songs are not unlawful for musical sounds but for other measures. Imam Shafayi does not generally make *Sama* unlawful. He says that he who takes it as a profession, his evidence is not acceptable. The reason is that song is included within plays and sports and it is connected with useless things. God will not punish for useless things and plays and sports and they are not unlawful. God says : God will not punish you for vain talks in your oath. If oath is taken in the name of God and without being firm on it and without being opposed to *Shariat*, it is lawful.

Answers to those who say that *Sama* is unlawful

They recite the verse of the Qurān : There are men who sell useless talks. Hazrat Ibn Masud, Hasan Basri, Nakhayi and others say that useless talks here mean songs. The Prophet said : God made unlawful the trade of singing slave girls, taking their price and teaching them songs. The word '*Qaina*' or singing slave girl is used here to mean one who sings before the drunkards. We have mentioned before that if there is fear of sin as a result of singing, by women, it is unlawful. This is supported by the songs of slave girls in the house of Ayesha in presence of the Prophet. If useless talks are purchased in lieu of religion, it leads to misguidance and for that it is unlawful. This is the meaning of useless talk in the above verse.

(2) Another proof of illegality of *Sama* is said to be this verse : Do you wonder and laugh at this talk and don't weep while you are singing? If this verse makes song unlawful, then to laugh and weep also as mentioned in this verse are unlawful. God says: As for poets, the misguided ones follow them. By this verse, only the infidel poets have been mentioned. It is not understood from this that good poetry has been banned.

(3) Another proof is a *Hadis* in which the Prophet said *Iblis* was the first who sang mourning songs and the first who sang songs. This does not ban songs as the Prophet David used to sing mourning songs for sins. The Prophet heard this song when he returned from an expedition "The full moon alighted on us from the valley of Saniyyatul Wadayi."

(4) Another proof is a *Hadis* which the Prophet said : If a man raises high his voice in a song, God sends for him two devils. They climb upon his shoulders, place their feet on his chest and move them till he stops. This *Hadis* applies to the bad and obscene songs which we have narrated above and which raise in mind sexual passion.

(5) Another *Hadis* cited is as follows : Everything with which a man plays is void except his training of his house, his throwing of his arrows and playing with his wife. The word 'void' does not mean that everything except the three things are unlawful. It means want of benefit. To hear sweet songs of birds and to make innocent sports and enjoyments are not unlawful.

Effect of *Sama* and its rules

There are three stages of *sama* songs – (1) The first stage is the understanding of the meaning of *Sama* songs, (2) the second stage is ecstasy, and (3) the third stage is the movement of bodily limbs as a result of ecstasy.

(1) **First stage :** It is the understanding of the meaning of *Sama* songs. There is difference in understanding according to the condition of hearers of songs. (a) **The first** condition is the natural state of mind, to hear songs and not to have any taste except the taste of hearing songs. This is the lowest stage as birds and beasts take share in this stage. (b) **The second** condition is to appreciate after understanding the meaning of songs and to apply the object of songs to a particular man. The young men fall to this condition as their sexual passion is aroused by these songs. (c) **The third** condition is whatever the hearer hears of songs in relation to God and the change of condition of mind, he applies it to his own condition. At the initial stage the sojourners to the path of God fall to this condition and their only object is to gain knowledge of God.

They raise up their inner feelings and the hearers take the meaning of songs according to their own conditions. I am giving some instances here. A certain Sufi heard a man singing– 'The ambassador says : See me tomorrow.' At once his ecstasy was raised up and he fell down senseless. When he regained his senses, he was asked the reason of his swoon and he said : I remembered then the saying of the Prophet The inmates of Paradise will see their Lord once a week. The sage Rabi b. Daraj said : Ibn Mufti and I went by a beautiful palace on the bank of Tigris. We found a slave girl upon it singing and a beautiful youngman looking at her and saying O girl! repeat this song to me. When she repeated the song, the young man exclaimed : It has coincided with my thought. Suddenly he raised a loud shriek and expired. The owner of the palace gave her release from slavery, gifted away the palace, gave up everything and left for an unknown destination and his whereabouts were not afterwards found. His ecstasy was so strong as wine intoxicates a man.

Once Khizr was asked about songs. He said : Surely it is such a slippery stone upon which the feet of the learned cannot remain firm. Song arouses the hidden feelings of a man as intoxicants raise the passion of man. But he is saved whom God saves by the light of His guidance.

The poet Sa'labi said with regard to the world in the first meaning of *Sama* in the following poems :

Leave the world, keep it not in your connection.
Benefits therefrom are less than its harms.
Remember always the angel of death, cruel and hard.
Many statements are there about the word's cruel nature,
But it is good to me all life long, who will understand ?
It has beautiful face which charms all men.
But its heart is filled up with destructive poison.

In the second meaning of *Sama,* these poems can be applied well to oneself, that is, to his condition of mind. God says : They don't fear God and He ought to be feared. In this case, he fears God for show and not out of fear or love for Him. In other words, he is not placed on a high spiritual plane. For this reason, the Prophet said : O God! I am unable to count Thy glory. Thou art as Thou praised Thyself. He also said : I pray to God for forgiveness seventy times everyday and night. This forgiveness is for reaching a higher plane of spirituality from its lower plane. In the third meaning of song, a man considers his present condition as little after seeing the advanced condition of others. This depends upon the proportion of the purity of his mind and his intellect. The more his mind is pure, the more he is advanced to spirituality by hearing songs.

(d) The fourth condition is that of the hearer of songs who reached the highest stage of *Ma'arifat* after crossing different conditions and different stages. He is lost to everything except the knowledge of God. Even he loses his own personality, his own condition and his own actions and deeds. He is like a man who is tossing in the ocean being submerged therein. His condition is that of the women who cut their hands unknowingly seeing the exquisite beauty of Joseph. Thus the *Sufi* loses himself and enters the stage of *Fana Fillah,* immergence in God. He loses himself from all things around him. Those who love God deeply cannot look to things other than God. He is like that intoxicated man who loses sense of all things.

The sage Abul Hasan Nuri said that he heard a man singing this song :–

> O darling! I seek from thee lasting love.
> When it comes, intellect goes from me.

He at once got up and immerged in ecstasy. He went to an open field and began to run in it when sugarcanes were cut leaving the roots erect. His feet got wounded and he began to run upto next morning. As a result his feet began to bleed and after some days he expired. This is the highest stage of a *Siddiq* which can be gained only by some songs. That is the end of human attributes. The perfect stage is such a condition that one forgets therein his own life and conditions. Such a man hears songs for God and hears knowledge about God and from God. This rank is for one who immerges himself with rays of truth and crosses the boundary of conditions and actions. His *Fana* is not *Fana* of his body but of his soul. By soul, I don't mean his heart of blood and flesh but *Latifa* or essence connected with God and which is a spiritual thing. This essence is a clean mirror which has got no colour of its own. It takes whatever colour is presented to it. Similar by transparent glass has got no colour of its own. It takes the colour of whatever is put in it. It has got no form and it takes the form of whatever thing it is made of. Similarly whatever thing is put in *Latifa*, it takes its form and colour. So a poet sings :–

Cup and wine – both are liquid,
Both are one, both are soft.
It seems it is wine, not a cup of wine.
It seems it is cup, without wine.

This is a stage out of the stages of spiritual learning. From it arises a mistaken idea of those persons who claim *Hulul* (transfiguration) and *Ittehad* (transmigration). *Hulul* means change of condition or transfiguration. Its another name is *Ittehad* or transmigration. This is near the claim of the Christians who claim *Lahut* with *Nasut* or godhood with manhood. This is just like the saying of that man who, seeing the red colour in mirror says that the colour of mirror is red.

(2) Second stage of *Sama*–Ecstasy *(Wujd)*

After the understanding of songs, the stage of ecstasy comes. Zunnun Misri said that *Sama* songs bring truth. Abu Hussain Darraj said : In *Sama*, there is connection of ecstasy which is a deep feeling in mind arising out of the effect of songs. He said : *Sama* has taken me to the field of beauty and given me drink of sweets in the cup of purity and thereby I gained the station of contentment. Shibli said : The open form of *Sama* creates disputes and its internal form gives instructions. A wise man said : Song is food to the soul of a spiritual man. Hazrat Amr b. Usman Makki said : No word can explain ecstasy because it is a secret thing of God to the believers and men of firm faith. Abu Sayeed b. Arabi said that the meaning of ecstasy is lifting a screen, meeting with Lord, seeing of unseen things, appearance of secret words. He said : Ecstasy comes at the time of violent *Zikr*, at the time of heart-piercing fear, or subtle event, or at the time of getting benefit, or at the time of serious slip, at the time of seeing unseen things, grief over lost thing, repentance for past sins.

Wujd means presentation of an open thing, a secret thing before a secret thing, an unseen thing before an unseen thing. Then there is walk without feet and *zikr* without open *zikr*.

Meaning of Ecstasy : It arises out of mental condition which is of two kinds : One kind is *Mukashifa* and *Mushahida* which lead to unseen and unthinkable knowledge. Another kind leads to unthinkable change, fear and repentance. Songs only awaken these conditions. If there is change of open bodily limbs as a result of songs, it is called ecstscy or *Wujd*. Muslim Abadani said : Once the sages Saleh Mari, Otbatul Gulam, Abdul Wahid and Muslim Aswari alighted near us on the bank of sea. I invited them to a feast one night. When they came. I placed before them the feast. Soon after, a singer sang:

Those who are kept forgetful of next world by delicious food,

Will be thrown into Hell, it will be of no use.

On hearing this, Otbatul Gulam at once raised a loud shriek and fell senseless. They did not take any food and I took away the feast served before them. When the heart is pure and clean, it hears the message of heaven and sees also Khizr as he appears for men having experience of soul in different forms. In these conditions, the angels descended upon the Prophets with figures. The Prophet saw Gabriel twice in his natural form which occupied the whole space of heaven. The knowledge which is generated in man in the uncommon condition of heart is called *Tafarros* (inherent spiritual knowledge). The Prophet said : Fear the uncommon and unseen knowledge of a believer as he sees with the rays of God. The Prophet gives hint to this *Kashf* by saying : Had not the devil roamed over the hearts of the children of Adam, they would have surely seen the sovereignty of heaven. Heart is the ground of the devil and his forces except those hearts which are pure and clean as God says 'Except those servants among them who are sincere.' God says : You will have no control over My servants.

Different kinds of *kashf* (spiritual knowledge)

(1) If ecstasy goes away, *kashf* may be explained, (2) it cannot be explained as it is an unseen thing from the unseen world. Ecstasy is of two kinds– (1) that which arises spontaneously and (2) that which is brought with difficulty. The Prophet said : O God! give me grace of loving Thee and the grace of loving those who love Thee and who bring near Thy love. Trembling and softness of heart owing to fear are songs of ecstasy. God says : The believers are those whose hearts become fearful when God is remembered to them. God

says : If I had revealed this Qurān to the mountain, you would have found it fearful and perturbed owing to fear of God. So from the point of circumstances, the God-fear is called ecstasy. The Prophet said : Adorn the recitation of the Qurān with your sweet voice. He said to Abu Musa Ash'ari : You have been given an instrument out of those of the family of David. Many a time, the Sufis fell into ecstasy after hearing the melodious recitation of the Qurān. The Prophet said : The chapter *Hud* and similar chapters have made me grey-haired. This is nothing but ecstasy. The Prophet once was reading a verse of the Qurān and at once he fell down senseless. The Prophet once was reading : If you punish them, they are merely your servants, he began to weep. God praised such persons of ecstasy by saying : When they hear what has been revealed to the Prophet, you will see their eyes shedding tears as they perceived truth. It has been reported that when the Prophet prayed, voice could be heard from his chest like the sound of heated cauldron.

Ecstasy of companions and their successors

Hazrat Jarah b. Ali Aufa led prayers in the most humble spirit. One day when he was reciting 'Remember when the trumpet will be blown,' he at once fell down senseless and expired immediately. Hazrat Omar once heard a man reciting this verse : The punishment of your Lord must come and there is nobody to remove it. He at once raised a loud shriek and fell down senseless. He was brought to his house and he suffered for nearly one month. Hazrat Abu Zarr once heard a verse recited by Saleh Mari and raised a shriek and then breathed his last. Imam Shafayi once heard a Qazi reciting this verse : 'It is such a day when they will not talk and they will not be given permission to raise an excuse'. At once he fell down unconscious. Hazrat Ali b. Fuzail once heard a man reciting this verse–the day when the people will stand up before the Lord of the universe, he fell down senseless. This is the condition of the *Sufis* also. The sage Shibli was praying behind an *Imam* in *Ramazan* and the *Imam* was reciting : If I will, I can take back surely what I revealed to you. Immediately Shibli raised a shriek and his face became changed. The sage Junaid said : I said once that a man remained unconcious before the sage Sirri Saqti. He said to me : This man fell senseless on hearing the verses of the Qurān. I said : Recite to him the verses again. When they were recited, he regained consciousness. Shibli said to him : Where have you found this ? I said : Israil lost his sight owing to the loss of his son and regained it by reason of his son. Shibli thought it good and hinted at the poetry recited by Junaid :

I drank it again and found my salvation.
I got taste and drank with satisfaction.

A certain sage said : One night, I was reading this verse, 'Every life shall taste of death'. I recited it again and again. Suddenly an unknown voice said to me : How long will you read this verse ? You have killed thereby thirty four jinn who did not raise their heads upwards from their birth till now. Whenever Hazrat Ibrahim b. Adham heard any man reciting this verse –'When the sky will be rent asunder' his limbs trembled till he was restored to his former position.

If the recitation of the verses of the Qurān does not cause any effect in mind, he is like a man who hears nothing though he is called and said something. He is deaf, dumb and ignorant.

It has been stated that Abul Hasan Nuri was once in a company who were quarrelling about a matter. He was then silent. Afterwards he raised up his head and recited the following poem –

At mid-day, who is singing heart captivating songs,

Roaming from branch to branch with broken heart.
It brings to mind the love of the days of joy,
It brings tears as he sheds tears telling woeful tales,
My weeping sometimes makes his mind soft
I complain it to him, but he understands it not.
His complaint also becomes useless, I understand it not.
I can know him, if he understands the pangs of my grieved soul,
He also cannot forget me even in times of great sorrow

The narrator stated that after hearing this song, there was none in the company who did not stand up as a result of ecstasy. The dispute among them could not arouse their ecstasy.

Third stage of *Sama* (song)

This is the third stage of outward expression of the effect of religious songs, namely to fall in swoon, trembling of bodily limbs, tearing of clothes etc. It has got five rules.

(1) First rule : It is connected with the time, place and hearing of the sayings of friends. It means that *Sama* causes no effect at the time of a serious work such as eating, praying etc. The time when a mind is not engaged is fit for hearing religious songs. Regarding place also, care should be taken not to hold it in public roads, in dark room, in undesirable place where attention cannot remain fixed. Regarding friends, it appears that ecstasy seldom arises in their presence though it becomes a matter of amusement to them. In such an assembly, there is mostly a show of ecstasy and not real ecstasy.

(2) Second rule : A spiritual guide with his disciples should not hear songs as it may cause them injury for three reasons. The first reason is that some disciples are not so thirsty for spiritual drink that they can quench their thirst from such songs. They should engage themselves in *zikr*. The second reason is that the hearts of some of them are not so much broken as they can find taste in it and escape its injury. The third reason is that sometimes song brings greater harm than benefit to some disciples and they do not look to lawful and unlawful things. The sage Sahal Tastari said : The ecstasy which does not support the Book of God and *Sunnat* of the Prophet is void. The sage Junaid said : I once saw the devil in dream and asked him : Do you exercise any influence on my disciples ? He said : I do at two times – at the time of song and at the time of look. I enter in them at these two times.

Third rule : It is to hear attentively the religious songs, not to look to the audience, not to express outward signs of ecstasy as far as possible such as raising shriek, trembling of limbs, dancing etc. It is reported that while Moses was narrating the stories of the children of Israil, a man present tore his cloth to pieces. God then revealed to Moses : Tell the man : Break your heart and not cloth.

Fourth rule : At the time of hearing religious songs, don't stand up, cry hoarse but restrain yourself from these acts. It has been reported from many companions that they danced out of joy. After the death of Hazrat Hamza, a quarrel ensued among Hazrat Ali, Jafar and Zaid regarding the maintenance of the children of Jafar. The Prophet said to Hazrat Ali : You are from me and I am from you. At this good news, Hazrat Ali began to dance. The Prophet said to Jafar : You resemble me in character and conduct. At this, Jafar also began to dance in joy. He said to the slave Zaid : You are our brother and chief. He also danced in joy. Then the Prophet gave charge of the children of Hamza to Jafar as the wife of Jafar was the maternal uncle of the children and a maternal uncle is like mother. In another narration, it has been reported that the Prophet allowed Ayesha to see the dance of some Abyssinian slaves. Ecstasy sometimes becomes so strong that one cannot restrain himself and does act contrary to his habits.

Fifth rule : If anyone stands up out of ecstasy among a group, others also should stand up as it is a rule of good manners of association.

Sixth rule : There is another sort of ecstasy namely ecstasy for show which is illegal and should not be shown in any respect.

So from what has been stated above, songs sometimes become lawful and sometimes unlawful according to the circumstances of each case. Sometimes it becomes undesirable. It is unlawful for those youths whose sexual passion is strong as it increases their hidden voices in their minds. It is not illegal for those who enjoy good moral songs and it is commendable for those religious persons who are engrossed in divine love. God knows best.

CHAPTER X

Enjoining Good and Forbidding Evil

Enjoining good and prohibiting evil is the basic subject of religion. It is such a necessity for which all the Prophets were sent to the world. Had it been closed, Prophethood would have been meaningless, religion lost, idleness reigned, ignorance spread, disturbance prevailed, dangers and calamities appeared and mankind destroyed. It will be discussed in four sections – (1) merits of enjoining good and prohibiting evil, (2) its rules and conditions, (3) narration of prevalent corrupt practices in society, (4) and discussion about enjoining good and prohibiting evil to the rulers, administrators and those who are invested with powers.

SECTION (1)

Merits of enjoining good and prohibiting evil

It appears from the Qurānic verses and sayings of the Holy Prophet and of the sages and saints that enjoining good and prohibiting evil is compulsory.

Qurān : God says : There shall be a party from you who will call towards good and prohibit evil and they shall be successful (3: 105). This is *Farze Kifayah* and not *Farze Ain.* In other words, if some people do it, other Muslims will be absolved from its sin, but if none does it, all will be sinners. God says : All the people of the Book are not equal. A party of them recite standing in prayer all night, make prostration and have faith in God and the next world and vie with one another in good deeds. They are included within the religious people. God says : 'The believing men and believing women are friends to one another. They enjoin good on one another and prohibit evil and establish prayer.' They have been praised by God as they adopt these measures. Those who do not do these are out of the category of believers. God says : Those who are unbelievers among the children of Israil are cursed by the tongues of David and Jesus Christ, son of Mary. This is because they committed sins and transgressed. They did not prohibit them to divert from evil deeds. Evil is what they did. In this verse, God says that they are fit for curse as they gave up prohibiting the evil doings.

God says : 'You are the best of nations created for mankind. You enjoin good and prohibit evils.' In this verse God says that the Muslims are the best nation only for this that they enjoin good and prohibit evils. God says : When they were reminded, they forgot. I gave salvation to those who prohibited evils. God says in this verse clearly that they got salvation, because they used to prohibit evils and this verse also proves the compulsory character of this matter. God says: If I establish them in the world, they establish prayer, pay *Zakat*, enjoin good and prohibit evil. God praised the companions in the above verse. God says : Help one another in righteousness and God-fear and don't help in sin and transgression. This is an open order of God to enjoin good and forbid evil. God says : O believers! keep firm on justice, bearing witness for God even though it is against yourselves, parents and near relatives. This verse speaks of enjoining good to parents and relatives. God says : There is no good in most of their secret talks, except those of the man who enjoins on giving charity, doing good deeds or doing good to the people. I will give ample reward to one who does it for pleasure of God. God says : If two parties of the believers fight with each other, make peace between them. This peace means to prohibit them to make rebellion and bring them back to allegiance. If it cannot be done God ordered to kill those who do not submit. He said : Fight with one who rebels till he returns to the command of God.

Sayings of the Holy Prophet : The Prophet said : If some people commit sins and if there are other persons fit to prohibit them and still they do not do it, they do not do any religious act. Soon punishment from God will fall on all of them. The companion Abu Sa'labah asked the Prophet about the explanation of this verse. If you have found guidance, the misguided cannot do you any harm. He said in reply : O Abu Sa'labah! enjoin good and prohibit evil. When you will find the people following greed and passions, love the world and give opinion according to every wise man, be busy then with yourself and give up the affairs of the public, because disasters and calamities will come behind you back like full dark night. He who remains firm like you, will get the rewards of fifty of you. He was asked : "O Messenger of God! will he get rewards of fifty of them? He said : No, the rewards of fifty of you because you are getting help for good deeds, while they will not get any helper therefore.

Hazrat Ibn Masud was asked the explanation of the above *Hadis* and he said : This is not that age. At the present age, enjoining good and forbidding evil are accepted, but soon there will come an age when you will enjoin good but the people will give you trouble for that. If you say anything, it will not be accepted from you. When you get guidance, the misguided people cannot misguide you. The Prophet said : O

mankind! God said : Before you make invocation, enjoin good
and prohibit evil, or else your invocation will not be accepted.
The Prophet said : In comparison with *Jihad* in the way of
God, the good deeds are nothing but like a puff of breath in a
deep sea. All good deeds and *Jihad* in the way of God are
nothing but a puff of breath in the deep sea in comparison
with enjoining good and prohibiting evil.

The Prophet said : God will ask a servant : Who prevented
you to prohibit a person from doing evil when you saw it
being done ? If God would have taught him to reply, he would
have replied thus : O Lord! I entertained hope of Thee and
feared men.

The Prophet said : Be careful of sitting on the pathway.
The companions asked : We have got no alternative but to sit
on the pathways and we hold discussion there. He said : 'If
you are compelled to do it, fulfil the rights of the pathway.'
They asked : What are the rights of the pathways? He said :
To shut up eye-sight, to have patience at harms, to respond to
salutation, to enjoin good and to forbid evil. The Prophet said:
Except enjoining good and forbidding evil and making *Zikr*
of God, every word of man does harm to him and not benefit.
Then the Prophet said : God will not surely punish the pious
men for the sins of the people so long as they prevent them
from wrong doing. The Prophet said : When your women
will become disobedient, your young men will commit great
sins and you will give up *Jihad*, what will then be your
condition ? The companions asked : O Messenger of God!
will it happen ? He said : Yes, by One in whose hand there is
my life, a more serious thing than that will happen. The
companions asked : What is that serious thing ? He said
When you will not enjoin good and forbid evil, what will be
your condition ? They asked : O Messenger of God! will it
happen ? He said : Yes, by One in whose hand there is my

life, a more serious thing will happen. They asked : What is
that thing ? He said : When you will take the good deeds as
evil and evil deeds as good, what will be your condition ?
The companions asked : Will it happen ? He said : Yes. By
One in whose hand there is my life, a more serious thing will
happen. The companions asked : What is that thing ? He said:
When you will be ordered to do evil things and prohibited
from doing good deeds, what will be your condition then ?
They said : Will it happen ? He said : Yes. By One in whose
hand there is my life, a worse matter than that will happen.
God will say : I take oath by Myself that I will create such
disasters and calamities for them in which those who are
patient will be puzzled or perplexed.

The Prophet said : Don't wait near a man at the time when
he is unjustly killed, because God's curse falls upon that man
also who, being present there, does not prevent it. The Prophet
said : If a man be present at a place where there is danger, he
shall not speak there but truth, because he will not die before
his fixed time and he will neither be deprived of his fixed
provision. From this *Hadis*, it appears that it is not lawful to
enter a place of oppression and sin and be present where sins
are being committed if he is not able to prevent it. The Prophet
said : 'Curse descends upon that person who remains present
there.' To be present at a place where a sin is being committed
is unlawful in case he is unable to prevent it. For this reason,
a party of earlier sages used to take to loneliness, so that evil
deeds did not fall to their eyes in markets, festivals and
assemblies as they understood that they were unable to remove
it.

The Prophet said : 'When a man is present at the time of
commission of a sin and he hates it, he remains as it were
absent from it. When a man remains absent at the time of
commission of a sin but he loves it, he remains as it were

present there. His presence there is accidental and not out of volition as it is prohibited. The Prophet said: The Almighty God did not send any Prophet who had no disciples. He lived among them till God wished that he should live among them to instruct them to follow His injunctions and the Book. Afterwards He took his life. After him, his disciples used to act according to God's Book and His command and the ways of the Prophet. When they died, there came after them a party of men who used to deliver sermon upon pulpits but they themselves did bad deeds. When you will see it, then it will become the duty of every believer to fight with his hand. If he is unable to do it, he will fight with his tongue. Without this, his Islam does not remain.

Hazrat Ibn Abbas said : The Prophet was once asked : O Messenger of God! will any place be destroyed if there are pious men therein ? He said : Yes. He was asked : What is its reasons ? He said : They will neglect their duties and they will remain silent though they will see them committing sins. For that, they will be destroyed. The Prophet said : The Almigty God ordered an angel : Throw this place upside down upon its inhabitants. A man said : O Lord! there is a certain servant of Thee in this place. He did not commit a single sin for a moment. He said : Throw this place on that man and those people, as he did not turn his face to them even for a moment.

The Prophet said : God sent punishments on the inhabitants of a place which numbered eighteen thousands. Their worship was like the worship of the Prophets. The companions asked : O Messenger of God! why has it occurred? He said : They did not express anger for the sake of God, did not enjoin them good and prohibit them evil. Moses once asked God : O Lord! who is dearest to Thee ? He said : That servant who humbly comes towards My will as a vulture rushes towards its object, that servant who remains ready to help My pious servants in such a way just as a suckling child keeps attached to its mother's breast and that servant who gets angry when an unlawful thing comes to him in such a way just as a leopard does not care when angry whether the people are many or few. It appears that the merits of enjoining good or forbidding evil are great in the face of such great dangers.

Hazrat Abu Bakr Siddiq asked : O Messenger of God! is there any *Jihad* except *Jihad* with the unbelievers ? The Prophet said : Yes. O Abu Bakr! the *Mujahids* in the way of God are better than the martyrs. They are given provision and they are alive. They roam about in the world and God praises them before the angels. Paradise has been adorned for them. Hazrat Abu Bakr asked : O Messenger of God! who are they? He said: They enjoin good and forbid evil, love one another for the sake of God and give up hatred for one another for sake of God. Then he said : By One in whose hand there is my life! one of them will live in such a palace which is placed above all other palaces and above all the palaces of the martyrs. That palace, will have three lac doors. Each door is most valuable and made of emeralds and jewels of green colour and every door will have light. In that palace, he will have three lac Hurs who will look with askance eyes. Whenever any Hur will look at a person, he will say : Do you remember such and such a day when you enjoined good and forbade evil ?

Hazrat Abu Obaidah said I asked : O Prophet of God! who is the most honourable near God among the martyrs ? He said : The martyr who stands before a tyrant ruler and enjoins him to do good and prohibit evil and for which he is killed. If the tyrant ruler does not kill him, pen will be shut up for him till he lives. The Prophet said : The greatest martyr among my followers will be that person who, standing before a tyrant ruler, enjoins him to do good and prohibits him to do evils, as a result of which the ruler kills him. His place will be between Hamaza and Ja'far. Hazrat Omar said : I heard the Prophet say : Those persons of the present age are bad who do not do justice and who do not enjoin good and prohibit evil.

Wise sayings

Hazrat Abu Darda'a said : You shall enjoin good and prohibit evil, or else God will place over you such a tyrant ruler who will not show honour to your elders and show kindness to your juniors. The religious men among you will pray against them but God will not accept their prayer. They will seek help against them but they will not be helped. They will seek forgiveness but they will not be forgiven. God revealed to the Prophet Ushu b. Nun : I will destroy from your followers forty thousand religious men and sixty thousand sinners. He said : O Lord! I have understood the reason of the destruction of the sinners, but what is the fault of the religious men ? He said : They were not dissatisfied with them when I remained dissatisfied and they used to take their meals with the sinners. Hazrat Ali said : The *Jihad* which begins before you are the *Jihads* of your hands and then the *Jihad* of your tongue and then the *Jihad* of your heart. When your heart does not enjoin good and prohibit evil, it becomes enveloped with darkness and its upper portion goes towards its lower portion.

SECTION 2

Duties of enjoining good and prohibiting evil

There are four heads of this matter – (1) one who prevents sins, (2) one who commit sins, (3) the sin which is prevented, (4) and the mode of prevention of sin. Each head has got rules and conditions.

(1) One who prevents sins : One who prohibits evils must have some qualifications. He must be wise and must have strength and ability to do the same. An insane man, an unbeliever and disqualified man go out of this rule and are unfit to prohibit evils. The ordinary people also are unfit for it unless they get orders from the rulers. A slave, a woman and a transgressor are unfit to perform their function. (a) So one must be mature of age and wise. (b) He must be a believer. He who disbelieves the basis of religion is not for this purpose. (c) He must have sense of justice. God says : Do you enjoin men to do good and forget it for yourselves ? God says : It is a most reprehensible thing to God that you say what you do not do. The Prophet said : While passing by a party of men in the night of ascention to haven, I saw that their lips were cut by the scissors of fire. I asked : Who are you ? They said : We used to enjoin good, but we ourselves used not to do it. We used to prohibit evils, but we ourselves used to do them. God revealed to Jesus Christ : Give advice first to yourself. When you follow that advice, give advice to others or else you will be put to shame before Me. Imam Ghazzali said that it is lawful for a great sinner to enjoin good and forbid evil.

Five stages

There are five stages of enjoining good and forbidding evil. (1) The first stage is giving simple advice, (2) the second stage is to give sermon with sweet words. (3) the third stage is to abuse and mete out harsh treatment, (4) the fourth stage is to apply force and prevent one from doing a sinful act, such as to throw wine from its pot, to snatch away dress of silk and stolen articles and to return them to rightful owner and (5) the fifth stage is to assault, beat and threaten one from doing a sinful act. Except in the fifth stage, a man is not required to obtain permission of the authorities to do such works in the four stages.

Some examples of giving advice to the rulers

(1) Once Caliph Marwan b. Hakam was delivering sermon before *I'd* prayer. A man said to him : Sermon is generally held after *I'd* prayer. *Marwan* said to him : Leave this word. He said : The Prophet said : If anyone of you sees a bad thing, let him prevent it by his hand. If he cannot do it, let him prohibit him by his tongue. If cannot do it also, let him cherish hatred for it in his mind. This is the weakest faith. The rulers are also included in this advice.

(2) Once Caliph Mehdi came to Mecca and stayed there for many days. At the time of *Tawaf* of the *Ka'ba* it was cleared of the public. Once Abdullah b. Mazruq jumped up and said to the Caliph : Look at! what you are doing. Who has given you more right regarding the *Ka'ba* than that of one who comes from a distant place. God says : The man who stays therein and the man who comes from a distant place are all equal. Who has given you power to drive out the people ? The Caliph recognised him as one of his officers and brought him to Baghdad after arrest and confined him in a stable. His men tied him with a horse for killing him. God subdued the horse to him. Baffled at this, they locked him in a room with the key in Caliph's hand. Three days after this, he was found to the amazement of all eating vegetables in a garden. He was taken to the Caliph and asked : Who has taken you out of this

room ? The Caliph raised aloud his cry and asked him : Don't you fear that I can kill you ? He was laughing and said: I would have feared you if you would have been the owner of life and death. Afterwards he remained in jail upto the death of Mahdi. When he was released afterwards, he went to Mecca and sacrificed one hundred camels to fulfil the vow of his release.

(3) The following story has been narrated by Habban b. Abdullah. While travelling in a certain place with Sulaiman, Caliph Harun Rashid said : You have got a beautiful singing female slave. Tell her to sing before me. When she came, the Caliph told him to bring musical instrument. When he was taking it to the Caliph, he met a hermit on the way. The hermit took the instrument and broke it into pieces. The man complained about it to the Caliph who called the hermit out of anger. When the hermit entered the Caliph's darbar with a bag of small pebbles, the Caliph asked him why he had broken the musical instrument. The hermit said : I heard your father and his predecessors to recite this verse on the pulpit : God orders you to do justice, to show kindness, to give charity to the near relatives and prohibits you from evils and rebellion. I saw evil and broke the musical instrument to pieces. The Caliph remained silent and allowed the hermit to go. When the hermit went away out of the Caliph's darbar, the latter gave a purse of money to a man and said : Follow this hermit. If you hear him say : I have told the Caliph such and such, don't give it to him. If you find him silent, give it to him. When the hermit went out, he went to the place of date-stones and remained silent. The man gave the purse to him. The hermit said to the man : Tell the Commander of the faithful to return the money wherefrom he took it. Then he begain to pick up date-stones and recite the following poems :-

"I see the worldly addicted engrossed in anxieties,

Along with the increase of their wealth, sorrows increase.
The world gives to the honourable troubles and disgrace,
It gives him who submits to it an honourable place.
Give up what is useless to you and unnecessary,
And take to what is to you absolutely necessary."

(4) The sage Sufiyan Saori said : Caliph Mehdi once went on a pilgrimage in 166 Hijri. I found him at *Jamrah Aqabah* to throw stones and then the people were pushed back on all sides by sticks. I waited there for sometime and said to the Caliph : "O man! having beautiful face, I heard the narrator say this *Hadis* : I saw the Messenger of God on the Day of sacrifice to throw stones here in which there was no beating, no driving out of the people, no assault by sticks and in which it was not said : Go back all around." But you are driving the people from left, right and front. The Caliph asked : Who is the man? He was told that he was Sufiyan Saori. The Caliph said : O Sufiyan! had there been Caliph Mansur, you would not have dared to say this. He said : If you had seen the disasters that fell on Caliph Mansur, the condition wherein you are now would have been less.

(5) Once a man was found enjoining good and forbidding evil without permission of the then Caliph Mamun. When the man was brought before the Caliph he said : O Commander of the faithful! we help you in your task. God said : The believing men and women are friends to one another. They enjoin good etc. The Prophet also said : A believer in relation to another is like a building one portion of which strengthens the other. Hearing this, the Caliph became pleased with him and said : You are a fit person to undertake this task.

(6) One who gives advice should have strength and power. He who is unable to undertake this task should entertain hatred for sinful acts. Inability here means to fear injury and harm from the person to whom advice is given. God says : Don't meet destruction by your own hands. There are three kinds of sin – (1) major sin for which there are prescribed punishments in the Qurãn and to prevent them is compulsory; (2) such sins which are done continuously, such as wine drinking, wearing silk dresses, using cups of gold and silver and to prevent them is compulsory; (3) and such sins which are expected to be committed in future. There are **four conditions** for prevention of these evils. The **first condition** is that it must be an evil action in the eye of *Shariat* and it must be unlawful. The **second condition** is that it is to be prevented in the course of its commission. If a man has finished drinking wine, it is not applicable in the case except by way of advice. (3) The **third condition** is that it must be known to the man preventing it as a sinful act without enquiry. If a man commits a sin after closing the door of his house, to enquire about it secretly is not lawful. Once Hazrat Omar secretly entered a house and found a man committing a sinful act. The man said on being asked : If I have committed one sin, you have committed three sins. Being asked about them, he said : God says : Don't spy into the secrets of another but you have done it. God says : Don't enter the houses by their backs, you have come after overriding the wall. God says: Don't enter a house except with permission of the owner and without salutation, you have neither taken permission, nor saluted its inmates. After this, Hazrat Omar let him off after imposing on him the condition of repentance. (4) The **fourth condition** is that the evil must be known to be evil without efforts. If otherwise, there is no forbidding of evil. These relate to the minor details of different sects. One sect gives opinion that a particular act like eating lizard is an evil, while according to another sect, it is not an evil.

Third mode

The man who should be prevented from sin

The sin which should be prevented must be such as is fit

to be prevented according to *Shariat*. If a man is seen drinking wine, he should be prevented from drinking it and it is compulsory. So in the case of a mad man if seen to commit adultery with a woman. If a man is seen damaging the crops of another, he should he prevented from doing it for two reasons, first to fulfil the duty towards God and secondly towards the man wronged. The law of a lost thing found is that if it is susceptible of damage, one is not bound to take it.

Fourth matter
Modes of prevention of sin

Know, O dear readers! that there are different modes of prevention of sins in different stages. The **first stage** is to know the condition of the sinner; the **second stage** is to inform him of the harm of sin; the **third stage** is to prevent him from doing the sinful act; the **fourth stage** is to advise him, and give him admonition; the **fifth stage** is to rebuke him and use harsh words; the **sixth stage** is to apply force; the **seventh stage** is to give him threat of beating; the **eight stage** is to actually beat him; the **ninth stage** is to use weapons against him and the **tenth stage** is to fight against him with followers and soldiers.

(1) First stage : To pry into the secrets of a sinner is prohibited. So one should not enquire what is occurring in a house. But if anyone informs you that a certain man is drinking wine or doing some unlawful act, it then becomes your duty to prevent it. So the first thing is to enquire about the condition of the sinner.

(2) Second stage is to inform the sinner that he is committing or going to commit a sin. Many men do sinful acts out of ignorance. If warning is given, they may themselves desist from the sinful acts. For instance an illiterate man

observes his prayer but does not bow and prostrate well or
prays with unclean cloth. Had he known them, he would not
have prayed thus. Man is not born learned. Learning shall
have to be acquired.

(3) Third stage is to prohibit a sinner by sermon,
admonition and showing fear of God. If a man commits sin
after knowing it to be a sin, he should be given sermon and
shown fear of God's punishment. He should be informed of
the traditions of the Prophet which deal with punishments of
the crime. The Muslims are like one soul and so the destructive
faults should be removed from the soul. One who gives advice
should take precaution whether he himself is free from that
vice. He should then remember what God said to Jesus Christ:
O son of Mary! first take advice to yourself. If you obey it,
then give advice to the people or else you will become ashamed
of Me. Once a man asked the sage Daud Tai about the
condition of a person who enjoins good and forbids evil to a
ruler or a man in power. He said : I fear whipping by him.
The man said : If the person can bear it ? He said : I fear
death. The man said : If he can bear it ? He said : I fear for
him self-praise begotten by praise of the people.

(4) Fourth stage is abuse and using harsh words. If there
is good result in the use of soft words with the wrong doer.
harsh words should not be resorted to. When it fails, then use
harsh words and abuse him. This is like the words of Prophet
Abraham : Woe to you and what you worship except God.
Use such words to him : O fool! don't you fear God ? O sinner,
O ignorant man ! The wise man is he who has been described
by the Prophet in the following words : The wise man is he
who humbles himself and acts for what is after death and the
fool is he who follows low desires and hopes for forgiveness
of God. There are two rules in this stage. (1) Don't abuse
except when necessary and use harsh words when necessary.

If appreciable result is not seen by the measure, express anger by turning away from him.

(5) Fifth stage is to correct evils by hand, such as pouring down wine, taking off silk dress from the body, ejecting from a land unlawfully occupied. This method should be adopted after the failure of the first four stages. Keep correction within limit and don't exceed what is necessary.

(6) Sixth stage is to threaten and warn. If all the previous modes of correction fail, this method should be adopted. For instance, one should say to the drunkard : Throw away the wine, otherwise I shall break your head and I shall strike your neck or I shall put you to disgrace.

(7) Seventh stage is to assault by hand or stick in case the previous modes of correction fail.

(8) Eighth stage is to fight with followers being armed. Many a time, people with arms are necessary to ward off evil. because many a time the wrong door with his party- men remain ready to fight. When the two parties meet, fight begins and it is necessary for pleasure of God and to remove the injuries of sinful actions. It is allowed for the warriors against the unbelievers. Similarly it is necessary to bring the great transgressors under control.

Qualifications of one preventing wrongs

One who prevents wrongs and evils should have the following qualifications

(1) knowledge that the act is wrong, (2) God fear and (3) good conduct. Regarding knowledge, the place, limit and order for prevention of wrongful act should be known and should remain confined within the rules of *Shariat*. Without such knowledge, one cannot distinguish between right and wrong. God-fear is necessary for one who prevents evil

because one who prevents it should not act for self-interest but for the sake of God. Such a man should possess also good conduct, kindness and humanity. When anger arises, good conduct only can control it.

If one who prevents evils possess these three qualities, he can earn merits for preventing sins. If he does not possess these qualities he exceeds many a time the limits of *Shariat*. The Prophet said : He who is not patient in enjoining good and forbidding evil and has got no knowledge of enjoining good and forbidding evil shall not enjoin good and prohibit evil. So it appears that knowledge, patience and kindness are necessary in the matter of advice.

Hazrat Hasan Basri said : If you are an adviser for good deeds, first fulfil them yourself or else you will be ruined. Anas reported : We asked the Messenger of God : O Messenger of God! shall we cease to enjoin good and prohibit evil to others if we do not act fully according to our sermons and refrain from doing evils ? The Prophet said : If you are unable to act fully according to your sermons, still you will enjoin good. If you are unable to give up fully what you prohibit, still you will prohibit it. A certain sage advised his sons : If anyone amongst you wishes to enjoin good, he should advise himself first with good qualities of patience and hope for rewards from God. He who hopes for rewards of God will not find any difficulty therein. One rule of *Hasbat* or advice is to remain satisfied with patience. For this reason, God kept patience attached with advice. The wise Luqman advised his son : O dear son! establish prayer, enjoin good and prohibit evil. Be patient at the danger that will befall on you for this.

(4) Absence of greed : One who takes up the mission of advice should not keep much connection with the world and should not have fear. He who depends on men will not be able to prevent sins. Once a speaker advised Caliph Mamun and spoke harshly with him. The Caliph said to him : O gentleman! be modest as he who was better than you was sent by God to people worse than yourself with the instruction of advising them with soft words. God says : Tell him soft words, so that he may take lesson and fear. Once a slave came to the Prophet and said : Give me permission to commit fornication. At this, the companions raised a loud cry. The Prophet said : Bring him to me. When he sat before the Prophet, he said : Do you like that somebody should commit fornication with your mother ? He said : Never. The Prophet said : So nobody likes that another should commit fornication with his mother. He thus asked him whether he liked fornication with his daughter, sister, nice and aunt and each time he replied in the negative. The Prophet then touched his chest with his hand and prayed : O God! purify his mind, pardon his sins and his private parts. From that time, there was no action more heinous in his sight than fornication.

Fateh b. Sakhraf said : Once a man with dagger in hand was dragging a woman by force. Nobody dared to go near him for fear of being murdered. The woman was raising loud cries being confined in his hand. Suddenly the sage Bashr Hafi was passing by that way. He went to him and touched his shoulder. As a result, the man fell down senseless and the sage then left the place. The woman also went away. When the man regained his senses, the people asked him – What has happened to you ? He said : I don't know anything, but I remember this much that a man came to me and said after touching me : Certainly God sees you and your action. On hearing his words, fear came in my mind and my feet got paralysed. I don't know the man. They said : He is Bashr Hafi. On that very day, he was attacked with fever which ultimately led him to the grave.

Evil actions prevalent in society

All evil actions are of two kinds – *Harâm* (unlawful) and *Makruh* (not commendable). To prevent what is unlawful is compulsory and to remain silent at the time of its commission is unlawful. To prevent what is *Makruh* is *Mustahab* or commendable and to remain silent at the time of its commission is not good but not unlawful.

The following are some of the evil actions in mosques. To make bow and prostration not in a good manner, to recite the Qurãn in a melodious voice, to prolong the prayer call, putting on by the *Imam* of a black robe or of a robe consisting mostly of silk, to tell stories in Friday sermon, to buy or sell at the time of *Juma* prayer.

The following are some of evils in markets – to tell lies to the customers; to conceal the defects of commodities and articles of sale, to increase or reduce the weights and measures, to sell toys of animals and buy them, to sell articles of gold and silver, silk dresses etc. Some of the evils in pathways are the following. To construct shops in the pathways, to encroach the pathway by extending the verandah of a building, to tie animals obstructing the pathway of the people, to sacrifice animals on the pathway, to throw refuges, to allow water of a building to fall on the pathway or by extending a pipe. The following are some of the evils in feasts. To spread cushions of silk, to serve in cups of gold and silver, to beat drums, or to sing songs, to serve unlawful foods and drinks, to arouse laughter by telling false stories, to spend lavishly in various kinds of food. The following are some of the evils in buildings. To spend unnecessary expenses in the construction of buildings because to spend money without benefit is to destroy it. If a man has got only one hundred dinars without any other property and it is necessary for the maintenance of his family members, his spending it in a marriage will be considered as misuse and to prevent him from it is compulsory. God says Don't spread your hand to its utmost spreading lest you sit down condemned and despaired. God says : Don't be extravagant in expense. The extravagant are the brothers of the devils. God says : When they spend, they are not extravagant, nor miser. To prevent miserliness and extravagance is compulsory.

Advice to the Rulers

In case of enjoining good to the rulers and kings and forbidding them evils, only the first two modes should be adopted and not the other modes of harsh treatment, abuse, assault and fight. In other words, they should be advised with sweet words with full possession of knowledge of their evil actions. To apply other modes in their case is unlawful as it creates disturbance and loss of peace and tranquility. To take risk personally and individually is not unlawful without risking the people in general into dangers and difficulties, because the Prophet said : Hamza, son of Abdul Muttalib, is best among the martyrs and then the next best is he who standing before a ruler enjoins him good and forbids him evil for which he is killed by him. His rank is lower than Hamza. The Prophet said : The best *Jihad* is to speak right words before a tyrant ruler. The Prophet praised Hazrat Omar by saying : He is an iron man and the defamation of a back-biter cannot divert him from the matters of God. Those who had firm and certain faith approached the rulers with truth and enjoined them good and forbade evils even at the risk of their lives, properties and honour in order to be blessed with martyrdom.

(1) When the Quraish leaders wished to take revenge on the Prophet, Hazrat Abu Bakr raised protest. Hazrat Urwah said : I asked Abdullah b. Amr : What was the greatest trouble which the Quraish gave to the Prophet ? He said : I went once

to the Quraish who were then discussing about the Prophet
sitting in the *Ka'ba* and saying : This man has made us fool,
abused our forefathers and our religion. He has disorganised our
unity, abused our idols and we have shown patience in a great
task. Suddenly the Prophet appeared there, kissed the Black
Stone and made *Tawaf* round the *Ka'ba*. The Quraish began to
abuse him each time when he was passing by them in the
round. Then the Prophet said : O Quraish! don't you hear ?
Beware, by One in whose hand there is my life, I have not come
to you with a sacrificial animal. The Quraish then bent down
their heads and one of them said : How sweet is this word. He
gave consolation to the Prophet and said : O Abul Qasim! go
away, by God, we are not ignorant. Then the Prophet went away
from that place. Next morning, one of the Quraish threw a sheet
of cloth round the neck of the Prophet and began to drag him by
force. Hazrat Abu Bakr went to him and said crying : Woe to
you ; Will you kill this man ? He only said : My lord is God.
They then let off the Prophet.

In another narration, it was reported that Abdullah b. Omar
said : When the Prophet was in the precints of the *Ka'ba*,
Oqbah b. Obay caught hold of his neck with a sheet of cloth
and began to drag him therewith with force. Hazrat Abu Bakr
came there and drove him out and said : Will you kill such a
man who says : God is my Lord ? He has come to you with
clear message from your Lord.

(2) It was reported that Caliph Muawiyah kept the
allowance of the Muslims in abeyance for sometime. When
he was delivering sermon on a pulpit, Abu Muslim Khaolani
stood up and said : O Muawiah! these allowances are not
your paternal properties, nor were they acquired by your father
and mother. The Caliph then grew into rage, got down from
the pulpit and said to them : Sit down in your own place.
Then he went to a bathroom, took bath and came again and

said : Abu Muslim uttered such words which enkinded my rage. I heard the Prophet say : Wrath comes from the devil and the devil was created of fire and fire can be extinguished by water. When someone of you gets angry, take bath. Therefore I took bath and Abu Muslim uttered the truth that these properties were not acquired by my wealth or by my parents. Take now your allowances.

(3) Hazrat Zart b. Mehsan reported : Hazrat Abu Musa Ash'ari was our governor at Basra. When he read khutba, he used first to praise God and send blessings on the Prophet and thereafter he used to pray for Hazrat Omar. I did not like that Hazrat Abu Bakr should be omitted from the prayer. I stood up and said to him : Why don't you pray for the first Caliph Hazrat Abu Bakr ? He did not pay any heed to my request but complained against me to Hazrat Omar. The latter summoned me. I was then sent to Hazrat Omar to Madinah. The latter asked me : What has occurred between you and my governor Abu Musa Ash'ari ? He said : When he reads *khutba*, he prays for you only. I was dissatisfied at it and said to him: Why don't you pray also for Hazrat Abu Bakr and why do you give superiority of Omar over him ? In spite of this, he complained against me to you. At this, Hazrat Omar began to weep and said : You are more fit for the post of governor than my governor and more guided towards truth. Forgive me and God will forgive you. I said : O Commander of the faithful! God has forgiven you. Hazrat Omar began to weep and said : By God, shall I not inform you of Abu Bakr's one night and one day ? 'Yes'. I said : 'tell me'.

Hazrat Omar said : When the Prophet with Abu Bakr came out one night to migrate to Madinah, he was guarding the Prophet from all sides. When the Prophet was feeling pain in his toes for walking long, Abu Bakr raised him up to his shoulder and carried him till he reached the cave of Saur and said to the Prophet : Don't enter this cave till I first enter it. If there is any injurious animal in it, it will first attack me. When he entered into the cave and found nothing, he carried the Prophet into it. There was a small hole in the cave and Abu Bakr closed it by one of his feet. A little after a snake stung the foot of Abu Bakr who began to shed tears at the pain caused by the poison of the snake. The Prophet saw it and asked him : O Abu Bakr! don't weep. Surely God is with us. This is one night of Hazrat Abu Bakr.

Regarding his one day, I may let you know that when the Prophet expired, some desert Arabs raised the standard of rebellion. Some of them said : We shall observe prayer but we shall not pay *Zakat*. I came to Abu Bakr and advised him to be kind to the rebels. He said to me : You were powerful during the days of ignorance but you have become fearful in Islam. Why should I show kindness to them ? When the Prophet expired and revelation stopped, they stopped payment of *Zakat*. They used to pay it to the Prophet but before this he fought against them for this. So we shall fight against them in this matter. By God, it is he who has shown us the true path. This is Abu Bakr's one day. Then Hazrat Omar sent a letter to his governor rebuking him for not praying for Abu Bakr in his *khutba*.

(4) The sage Ata b. Ribah once went to Caliph Abdul Malik b. Marwan at Mecca. When the Caliph saw the sage Ata, he stood in his honour and asked him : Have you got any necessity? The sage said : O Commander of the faithful! fear this sacred place of God and His Prophet, keep its purity, fear God in the matters of the descendants of *Muhajirs* and *Ansars*, as by their help you are sitting in this throne. Fear God regarding the soldiers guarding the frontiers as they are the forts of the Muslims and take care of the affairs of the Muslims. You will be asked about these matters. Don't be indifferent to

those who are under your control and don't shut up your doors against them. The Caliph said : I will try to follow your advice.

(5) Once the sage was brought before the Caliph Walid b. Abdul Malik. He said to the Caliph : I heard that there is a well named Habhab in Hell. The well has been reserved by God for every tyrant ruler. On hearing this. Walid raised a cry and fell senseless.

(6) The sage Ibn Ali Shamelah was famous for his wisdom and good treatment. Once he went to Caliph Abdul Malik b. Marwan who requested him to tell him some words of advice. He said : O Commander of the Faithful! on the Resurrection Day, mankind will not be saved from its grievous punishment and serious condition. Only he who pleases God displeasing himself will be safe. The Caliph wept at this and said : I will keep the advice as the object of my life till I live.

(7) The tyrant Governor Hajjaj once called the learned men of Basra and Kufa including the sage Hasan Basri. Hajjaj began to condemn Hazrat Ali. Ibn Ayesha said : We began to support him. Hazrat Hasan Basri began to cut his thumb and remained silent. Hajjaj said to him : Why do I see you silent? What is your opinion regarding Ali? Hasan Basri said : God said regarding Hazrat Ali : I have fixed the *Qibla* to what you are accustomed only to examine those who follow the Apostle from amongs those who turn on their heels (2 : 143). Hazrat Ali was one of those believers whom God gave guidance. My opinion about him is that he was cousin and son-in-law of the Prophet and he was dearest to him. God adorned him with many virtues. You or anybody else will not be able to attain those vitues and nobody will be able to enter into his attributes. My opinion is that God is sufficient for any fault that he might have got. At this, the face of Hajjaj became reddish and he stood up in rage. Then he entered his house and we went away.

One day, Hajjaj summoned the sage Hasan Basri and said: Do you say that God will destroy those who kill the servants of God for money ? He replied : Yes. Hajjaj asked : Why do you say this ? He said : The cause is that God took promise from the learned that they would make the people understand the words of religion and not conceal them. Hajjaj said : O Hasan! hold your tongue, I warn you that you should not make me listen to what I don't like. There is a great deal of difference between your body and mind.

(9) The sage Hatil Jayyat once came to Hajjaj who asked him : Are you Hatil ? He said : Yes, ask me what you wish. I have taken promise for three matters to God near *Maqame Ibrahim* – (1) I will speak truth whoever asks me anything, (2) I will have patience if anybody throws me into danger and (3) I will express gratefulness if anybody pardons me. Then Hajjaj said : What do you say about me ? He said : You are the enemy of God in the earth, you destroy the honour of the people and kill them at your whim. Hajjaj said : What do you say about Caliph About Malik b. Merwan? He said : He is a greater sinner than you. Among his sins, you are one. On hearing this, Hajjaj ordered : Punish this man. Then inflicting whipping on him, the whip of the executioner broke. Then the executioner tied him with a rope and began to cut his flesh with a knife, but he did not utter even '*uf*'. Hajjaj was informed that the man's end was nearing to which he said : If he expires, throw his body into the market. Jafar said : I and one of his friends came to him and said to him : O Hatil! have you got any necessity ? He said : One handful water. When they brought water to him, he drank it and soon expired. His age was then only 18 years.

(10) Omar b. Hubairah was governor of Basra, Kufa, Madinah and Syria. He called to his court Shafi of Kufa and Hasan Basri of Basra. He said to Shafi : I wish to cancel the

allowances of some persons about whom I heard that they say many things against me. My wish is that they should return to my allegiance. What do you say ? He said : A ruler is like a father. Sometimes he is right and sometimes he commits mistakes for which he incurs no sin. The ruler was pleased to hear my advice. Then he said to the sage Hasan Basri : What do you say about it ? He replied : I heard the companion Abdur Rahman reporting that the Prophet said : God will make Paradise unlawful for one who, being appointed to rule over the people, does not look to their welfare and provision. Regarding the cancellation of allowances of the people I say that to preserve the right of God is more an important duty than to preserve your right. God is more fit to be obeyed. There is no permission to show allegiance to the created being disobedient to God. The letter of the commander of the Faithful cannot be placed above the Book of God. Accept it if it is in concord with the Book of God and throw it if it is contrary to it. O Ibn Hubairah! fear God. Perchance a messenger may come to you from the Lord of the universe. He may take you to the grave and remove you from the palace. The governor Ibn Hubairah said : O Shaikh! don't say these words. God selected the commander of the Faithful as a ruler. Hasan asri said : He who gives you better advice regarding religion is better than one who hopes to incur your pleasure. Shubi then said : I did never see a man more brave and learned than Hasan Basri.

(11) Ibn Ali Jubair was once present before the Caliph Mansur. Hasan b. Zaid was then governor of Madinah. Some people complained against the governor Hasan to the Caliph. The latter asked Ibn Ali Jubair about the governor. He said : Hasan conducts his affairs according to his whim and does not do justice. The Caliph then asked him : What do you say about me ? He said : I bear witness that you have seized power

unjustly and there is injustice prevalent in your rule. Then the Caliph Mansur caught hold of his neck and said : Had I not been here, Persia, Byzantium, Dailam and Turkey would have snatched this place from you. After this, the Caliph released him and said : By God! had I not known that you are a truthful man, I would have killed you.

(12) Hazrat Aozayi reported : Caliph Mansur once called me and said : Advise me. I said : O Commander of the Faithful! the Prophet said : God made Paradise unlawful for the ruler who dies being displeased with his subjects. He who dislikes truth hates God as He is the open Truth. It is just that you should upkeep the honour of your subjects, establish justice among them, not shut up your doors against them, be happy in their happiness and sorry in their sorrows. There are the foreigners, the unbelievers and the Muslims under your rule and upon you is the duty of doing justice among them.

O Commander of the Faithful! once there was stick of grape in the hand of the Prophet. He used to cleanse his teeth and threaten the hypocrites therewith. The Prophet said : Then Gabriel came down and said : O Muhammad! why is this stick ? you have broken the hearts of your people and created terror in their minds on its account, Now think of those who shed the blood of their subjects, destroyed their houses and banished them from their countries.

Once the Prophet assaulted a desert Arab very unwillingly with his own hand. Then Gabriel came down and said : O Muhammad! God has not sent you either as an oppressor or as a proud man. Then the Prophet called the desert Arab and said : Take retaliation on me. The desert Arab said : My parents be sacrificed to you, I have forgiven you. I will never do it, if you have killed me. I would have still prayed good for you.

O Commander of the faithful! the Prophet said : The place of even an arrow in Paradise for one of you is better than the world and its wealth. Your rule will not last for ever as it did not last for your predecessors. I have heard that Hazrat Omar said : If any young one of a goat perishes by the side of the river Tigris, I fear I may be asked about it also. How will it be if a man comes to your court for justice and returns despaired? Do you know about the verse revealed to Prophet Daud : O Daud! I have appointed you Caliph (vicegerent) in this world. So establish justice among them and don't follow your low desires, lest it may misguide you from the way of God.

God says in the Zabur : O David! when two parties come to you for justice, don't think in your mind that judgment will be given in favour of one to whom your mind inclines and he will be vicorious over his adversary. In that case, your name will be cut off from the register of Prophethood and you will not be fit to represent Me. O David! I have sent my Prophets to take care of My servants as a shepherd takes care of his flock of sheep. They have been given knowledge of that care and burden of administration, so that they may tie the broken things and make alive the weak by provision. O Commander of the Faithful! you are tried by such a thing, which if placed upon heaven and earth, they would have refused to bear it and would have been fearful.

O Commander of the Faithful! I heard that Hazrat Omar appointed a man to collect *Zakat* from the Ansars. After some days Omar heard that he stayed in his house and therefore he asked him : Why have you not gone out to discharge your duty ? Don't you know that you will get rewards of one warrior in the way of God ? He said : I have heard that the Prophet said : If any man is entrusted with an office of the public, he will be raised up on the Resurrection Day with his hands tied up to his neck. Nothing will unloosen it except justice. Then he will wait upon a bridge of fire. It will break down with him and as a result all his limbs will be broken. Then he will be brought and accounts will be taken. If he be pious, he will get salvation for his good deeds. If he be a sinner, he will be raised along with it and will fall down to the abyss of Hell. Hazrat Omar asked him : From whom have you heard this _Hadis_ ? He said : From Abu Zarr and Salman Farsi. When they were brought, they admitted it and then Hazrat Omar said : Woe to me, who will take the power of administration when there are such evils in it ? Abu Zarr said : That man will take it whose nose will be cut by God, whose face will be powdered to dust by Him. Then he began to weep.

Then I said : O Commander of the Faithful! your grand-father Abbas wanted governorship of Mecca, but the Prophet said to him : O Abbas! uncle of the Prophet, keep yourself away from this trouble. It is better than the burden of administration. You cannot conceive it. The Prophet said it out of kindness to his uncle. He told him that it would not be of any use to God. God then revealed to him : Warn your near relatives. The Prophet then said : O Abbas! O Sufia! O Fatima! (daughter of the Prophet)! I am not responsible for you to God. My actions will help me and your actions will help you.

Hazrat Omar said : The burden of administration devolves upon one who has got deep knowledge, who is firm in promise, whose evils cannot openly be spoken of, who does not fear his relatives and whom the slanders of the slanderers cannot move. Hazrat Omar said : There are four classes of rulers— (1) a powerful ruler who keeps himself and his officers engaged. They are like warriors in the way of God. The hand of mercy is upon them. (2) A weak ruler who does not make efforts in administrative matters and owing to his weakness his officers pass time in comforts. He will be ruined and will not get salvation. (3) A ruler who keeps his officers busy in duties but himself remains in comforts. This is such a calamity about which the Prophet said : A bad shepherd is a danger and ruins himself. (4) A ruler who lives in comforts and his officers also live likewise. They are all ruined.

O Commander of the Faithful! I heard that Gabriel once came to the Prophet and said : When God passed order to enkindle the fire of Hell, I have come to you. Fire has been placed in Hell for the Resurrection Day. He asked : O Gabriel! describe the fire of Hell to me. He said : According to the orders of God, it burnt for one thousand years and then it assumed reddish hue. Then it burnt for another one thousand years and then it assumed yellowish colour. It burnt for another one thousand years and then it assumed black colour. The fire of Hell is at present dense black. Its fleak does not rise up, nor can it be extinguished. By One who sent you as a true Prophet, if a piece of cloth of the inmates of Hell would have been exposed to the inmates of the world, all would have expired owing to its stench. If an iron chain would have fallen in the world, all would have expired owing to its stench. When the Prophet heard it from Gabriel he wept and Gabriel also wept. Gabriel said : O Muhammad! why are you weeping ? Your past and future sins have all been forgiven. The Prophet said : Shall I not be a grateful servant ? O Gabriel! why are you weeping ? You are the trusted spirit and trustworthy in *Tauhid*. Gabriel said : I fear I may be tried as Harut and Marut were tried. I can't trust my rank near God. They both wept till a proclamation came from heaven : O Gabriel! O Muhammad. God made both of you safe from punishment. Muhammad's rank over all other Prophets is like that of Gabriel over the rest of the angels.

O Commander of the Faithful! I heard that Hazrat Omar said : Don't give me time even for a moment if two persons wait long before me seeking justice in the matter of their property. The greatest difficulty is to establish the duties towards God. The greatest honour near God is God-fear. God gives honour to one who seeks honour by doing divine service. God disgraces one who seeks honour by committing sins.

These are my advices to you, peace be on you. The Caliph Mansur then gave him the present of a purse. He did not accept it saying : I will not sell this advice in lieu of a temporary thing of the world.

(14) Once Caliph Mansur stayed sometime at *Darun Nadwa* at Mecca. He used to pray at the latter part of the night at the *Ka'ba* and go round it and nobody knew it. He then used to lead the morning prayer. One night while going round the *Ka'ba*, he heard a man saying : O God! I complain to you that disturbance, rebellion, oppression and injustice are going on in the country. After hearing it, the Caliph sat in a corner and the man was called to him. When he came, the Caliph said : I have heard you saying such and such. I am greatly disturbed to hear it. The man said : If you grant me security of life, I may tell you. The Caliph said : You have got no fear. The man then said : You are responsible for the disturbance and disorder in the country. The greed which finds place in you has not entered into any other person. God placed upon you the burden of administration over the Muslims. You are neglecting to do good to them and you are busy in misappropriating their properties. Between you and the public, there are the stumbling block of limes, bricks, iron doors and guards with arms. You have appointed such officers who oppress the people. You have given them power to take by oppression the properties of the people. You have issued orders prohibiting the entry of the public to you except some persons. You have made no provision for the oppressed, hungry, naked, weak and poor. When the people see that you have selected some special men for you and you do not give permission to anybody except those persons, they say that the Caliph has

broken the trust of God. So they say : Why should we not break our trust with him ?

During the reign of Banu Omayyah, whenever the oppressed reached the rulers, they at once meted out justice to them. You amass wealth for one of three reasons – (1) If you say : I amass wealth for my children, God advices you that when a child is born, it does not take wealth with it or food. God gives it out of His kindness provision and arranged it before hand in its mother's breast. (2) If you say : I am getting wealth to make my reign firm, God advises you that those who were before you amassed gold and silver, arms and ammunitions which did no benefit to them. When God intended to make you Caliph, you had no wealth. (3) If you say: I amass wealth in order to live more comfortably than what I lived before, I will say that the rank which is gained by good works is more than that in which you are now. What will you do with the reign which God has given you ? When the Almighty will snatch away your reign and call you to account, your pomp and grandeur will come of no use to you.

The Caliph Mansur, on hearing it, began to weep bitterly and then said : Alas! had I not been created. Had I been a thing not fit to be mentioned. Then the sage said : Keep near you some high classed leaders and guides from the learned. Then the sage went away after saying : If you recite morning and evening some invocations, it will give you the following results. Your faults will be forgiven, your joy will become lasting, your sins will be forgiven, your invocation will be accepted, your provision will increase, your hopes will become successful, and you will die as a martyr. The invocation is the following :–

O God! I bow to Thy glory. As Thou art gracious to the kind, so Thou art above the great with Thy greatness. As Thou

hast got knowledge of the things above Thy Throne, so Thou
hast knowledge of the things below the abyss of the earth. To
Thee, the machinations of mind is like open things. Thy
knowledge of express things is like secret things. Everything
before Thy glory is humble. Every powerful man is humble
to Thy power. All affairs in this world and in the next are in
Thy hands. Give me relief and a way out for the thoughts I
am entering with this evening. O God! pardon my sins, forgive
my faults and keep my undesirable things secret. Beget love
in me to invoke such things for which I am not fit for my sins.
I invoke Thee freedom from fear and for Thy pleasure. Thou
are doing so much good to me but I am committing sins. Thou
art giving me love through Thy mercy and I am causing your
anger by my sins. Put my firm faith in Thee, give me courage
to invoke Thy shower of mercy and blessings on me Thou art
Forgiving, the Compassionate. The above talks were held
between Mansur and Khizr (peace be on him).

(5) When Harun Rashid became Caliph, the learned men
met him and he fixed their annual allowances. Only his friend
Sufiyan Saori did not meet him. Then the Caliph wrote to
him a letter inviting him to come to his palace. When the
sage Sufiyan received the letter, he wrote in reply on its back:
From Sufiyan to Harun Rashid ; proud of wealth and deprived
of the taste of faith, I write to you that, I demolished the path
of love for you and cut off my love for you. I dislike action
for which you cite me as a witness as you have written that
you have opened your treasury for the Muslims. You are
spending it unjustly and against the provision of *Shariat*. You
are satisfied with what you have done. O Harun! you are
spending the wealth of the State extravagantly without the
consent of the people. Are the widows, orphans and learned
satisfied with your actions ? Know that you shall have to face
the Almighty very soon. You have taken your seat on the

Throne being dressed with silk robes. You have hung down long screens over your doors and kept your tyrant soldiers as guards. They drink wine but beat the drunkards. They commit fornication but mete out prescribed punishment on the fornicators. They steal but they cut off the hands of thiefs. Why don't you inflict punishment on them before they inflict punishment on others ?

He handed over the letter to the messenger of the Caliph without closing it in an envelope and without any seal. The messenger handed over the letter to the Caliph who accepted it cordially. He then used to keep it by his side and read it at the end of each prayer till his death.

(6) The Caliph Rashid stayed for some days at Kufa after pilgrimage. People then began to come to him. One Bahlul of deranged brain was one of them. When Harun came to him, he proclaimed loudly : O Commander of the Faithful! At this, Rashid uncovered his face and said : O Bahlul! *Labbaik!* Bahlul said : You should take to modesty and humility in your journey. At this the Caliph began to weep and said : Give me more advice. Bahlul said : O Commander of the Faithful! if any man spends something out of his God given wealth and gives charity, he is enrolled as a pious man. Then the Caliph presented him something which he refused to accept saying : I have got no need of it.

These are some of the examples of the previous sages and learned men in enjoining good and forbidding evil. They cared very little the powers of the rulers and depended entirely on God. They remained satisfied in the belief that God would grant them the benefit of martyrdom.

CHAPTER XI

Character and Conduct of Prophet

All praise is due to God who created the universe and taught His greatest Prophet Muhammad (P.H.) the best good manners, purified his character and conduct and adopted him as His friend. He gives grace to follow the Prophet to one who wishes to make his character and conduct beautiful. He deprives one to follow him whom He wishes to destroy. Open good conduct is the fountain of secret good conduct. The movements of the bodily limbs are the results of thoughts of mind and the external actions are the results of character and conduct. To make efforts in recognising God and the acquisition of wonderful secret powers are the fountains of actions. The light of this secret power is expressed outwardly and makes the body beautiful and gives rise to good attributes after removing evils. The man who has got no fear in mind has got no fear expressed in his bodily limbs. The beauty of the conduct of prophethood is not expressed in a man whose mind is not illumined with the light of God. I intended to gather together in this chapter the ways of the life of the Holy Prophet, but as I have mentioned some of his ways in the first and second parts of this book, I do not wish to repeat them here.

(1) **Prophet's learning through the Qurān**

The Prophet used to invoke and pray to the Almighty God to grant him good manners and good treatment with the people and to adorn him with good character and conduct. He used to say in his invocation : O God! make my constitution and conduct good. He used to pray : O God! save me from bad character and conduct. Acceptance of his prayer is seen in the following verse : Invoke me, I will respond to you (2:186). God revealed the Qurān on him and through it He taught him good manners. His character is the Qurān. Hazrat Sa'ad reported : Once I went to Ayesha and her father and asked them about the character and conduct of the Prophet to which Ayesha replied : Don't you read the Qurān ? I said : Yes. She said : The character of the Messenger of God is the Qurān. His conduct is expressed in the following verse : Take to pardon, enjoin good and turn away from the illiterate. God says : God enjoins justice, kindness, giving charity to the relatives and prohibits indecencies, evils and rebellion (16:90). God says : Have patience at the disasters that befall on you. It is a difficult task. God says : It is difficult to have patience and to forgive.

God says : Pardon and forgive them. God loves the doers of good. God says : Don't you like that God should forgive you ? God says : Remove evil with what is good, as a result the enmity that exists between you and him will be removed and he will become your friend. God says : Those who appease their wrath, those who pardon people, God loves the doers of good. God says : Give up conjectures in most cases, as some conjecture is sin. Don't spy and don't back-bite one another.

In the battle of Uhud, when the cover of the head of the Prophet fell down and he became separated from his companions, blood was oozing out from his face and he said wiping his blood : How will the people get salvation who dyed the face of the Prophet with blood while he calls them towards their Lord ? Then God revealed this verse : 'You have got no hand in the matter'. This was only for teaching him good manners. The verses concerning the teaching of good manners to the Prophet are many in the Qurãn. It was the first object of God to teach the Prophet good manners and good character and conduct. For this reason, the Prophet said: I have been sent to complete good conduct.

God praised the character of the Prophet by saying : "You are surely on sublime character". The Prophet explained it to the people : God loves good character and hates bad character. Hazrat Ali said : I wonder for a Muslim who does not do benefit to his brother Muslim who stands in need of it. If he hopes for rewards and fears punishment, he should hasten towards good conduct as it shows the path of salvation. A man asked Hazrat Ali : Have you heard it from the Prophet ? He said : Yes, I have heard better advice from him. When the prisoners of the tribe of Hatim Tai were brought to him, a girl came to him out of them and said : O Muhammad! if you wish, release me, but don't dishonour me before the tribe of the Arabs. I am the daughter of the leader of my people and my father was the care taker of my people. He used to set free the captives, feed the hungry, spread peace and did never return any beggar at the time of his need. I am the daughter of Hatim Tai. The Prophet said : O girl! what you have mentioned about his qualities are the attributes of a believer. The Prophet said to his companions: Let her be free as her father loved good character and conduct. Abu Burdah b. Niyar stood up and said : O Messenger of God! does God love good conduct? The Prophet replied : By One in whose hand there is my life: None shall enter Paradise except one who has got good conduct.

The Prophet said : God adorned Islam with good character

and beautiful actions. Good company, good manners, modest talk, doing good to others, feeding, spreading peace, visiting the ill pious or sinner, following the bier of a Muslim, treating good with a neighbour believer or non–believer, showing honour to a Muslim having honour, to accept invitation, to forgive, to settle disputes among the people, to give charity, to greet first, to pardon the faults of the people, to give up songs, instrument of songs and jests which Islam prohibited, not to backbite, to speak truth, to give up miserliness, greed, deceit, to give up bad treatment with enemy, not to cut off blood tie, to give up bad conduct, pride, glory, hanghtiness, indecencies, hatred, rebellion, enmity, oppression etc.– all these are the attributes of a believer.

Hazrat Anas reported that the Prophet did not give up good advice and enjoined us to stick to it. He used to warn us from backbiting and prohibited it. The following verse is sufficient to prove it : God loves justice and doing good to others. Hazrat Muaz said : The Prophet advised me thus : O Muaz! I advise you : fear God, speak the truth, fulfil promise, pay up trust, give up breach of trust, save your neighbour, show kindness to orphans, be modest in talk, spread peace, do good deeds, hope less, stick to faith, earn knowledge about the Qurãn, love the next world, fear rendering of accounts and lower your aim. O Muaz! I forbid you : Don't tell a truthful man liar, don't follow any sin, don't disobey any judge, don't be a leader, don't disobey a just judge, and don't create disorder in land. I give you instruction : Fear God while passing by each stone, tree, and heaps of earth. Make repentance anew after committing any sin. Repent secretly for secret sin and openly for open sin.

(2) Prophet's character and conduct

The Holy Prophet was the most patient among men, the

bravest, the best judge, and one who pardoned most. His hand did not touch any strange woman. He was the greatest charitable man. He did not pass a single night hoarding any *dirham* or *dinar*. Whenever any excess money came to him and if he did not then get anyone to accept it as charity, he did not return home till he gave it to the poor and the needy. He did not store up for more than a year the provision of his family members which God was pleased to give him. He used to take one-fifth of what easily came to him out of dates and wheat. What remained in excess, he used to give in charity. He used to give away in charity to him who begged of him of anything, even out of his stored up provision.

He used to repair his shoes, join his wives in their labours and cut meat with them. He was the most shameful among men and could not stare at anyone for long. He accepted invitation of slaves and free men and presentation of even a cup of milk. He did not use the properties of *Zakat* and used to accept the invitation of the widows and the poor. He used to speak the truth even though it was sometimes a cause of trouble to himself and his companions. He used to say : I don't accept any invitation of any infidel. He used to bind stones in his belly for appeasing his hunger and eat whatever he got. He did not return any present and did not take precaution in any lawful food. If he got dried grapes in lieu of bread, he ate them. If he got baked meat, he ate it. He used to eat whatever he got of bread, wheat, sweets and honey. He considered milk as sufficient if he did not get any other food. He used not to take food leaning against a pillow or upon a high table. Soles of his two feet served as his towel. He used not to eat bread consecutively for three days till he met God. It was a voluntary act on his part. He used to accept invitations of marriage, attend the sick and the diseased and attend the funerals. He was the most modest without pride and his tongue was most eloquent without prolongation of his speech.

His constitution was the most beautiful. No worldly duties could keep him busy. He used to put on whatever he got. His ring was made of silver and he used to put it on in the little finger of his right or left hand. He used to take his servant behind his back on any conveyance whether it was horse, camel or ass. Sometimes he walked bare footed, sometimes he had no turban or cap on his head. He used to go even to a distant place to see the sick, love scents and hate stench or bad smell, sit with the poor and the destitutes, eat with them, honour those possessing honour, advise them to do good deeds and show kindness to the relatives. He did not treat harshly with anybody and accepted excuse offered to him. He used at times to cut jokes without falsehood and not burst into laughter. He held innocent sports and plays as lawful, played with his wives and held races with them. He used to drink milk of camels and goats along with his family members and give them equal shares in foods and dresses. He passed no time uselessly except for God. He used to walk in the gardens of his companions for recreation. He did not hate the poor for their poverty nor fear the kings for their mighty power. He used to call the people, high or low, towards God. God adorned him with all the qualities and good administration although he was illiterate. His boyhood was spent along with the shepherds and he used to graze sheep and goats. He was an orphan and his parents died in his infancy.

(3) Prophet's good manners

If the Holy Prophet abused anybody, he used to give him compensation and show him kindness. He did never curse any woman or slave. Once when he was in the battle- field, he was asked : "O Messenger of God! it would have been better if you had cursed them. He said : God sent me as a mercy and not as a great curser." When he was asked once to curse a particular person or an unbeliever, he did not curse him but on the contrary prayed for his welfare. He never beat anybody with his own hand except in the way of God. He did not take any revenge for personal wrongs but he used to take it for preservation of the honour of God.

He used to select the easier of two things and keep away if there is any sin therein or anything to cut off relationship. He used to fulfil the needs of anyone who required his help, whether a slave or a free man. Hazrat Anas said : By One who sent him as a Prophet, he never said to me – Why have you done this' or 'why have you not done this'? His wives also did not rebuke me. If there was any bed of the Prophet, he used to sleep on it or else he used to sleep on the ground. God described the Prophet in the Torah – "Muhammad the Prophet of God! His chosen servant, without harshness, not roaming in the streets, not returning evil for evil. He is prone to pardon, He is forgiving. His birth is at Mecca, his migration to Ta'ba and his reign in Syria. He and his companions put on *Ijar* round their waists and call towards the Qurān and wisdom. He makes ablution of his bodily limbs." Similar is his description in *Injil* (New Testament).

Another trait of his character is that he used to salute first one whom he met with. He used to wait at a place where he was to meet a man. He used not to withdraw his hand from anybody till he first withdrew his hand. When he met with any of his companions, he used to handshake with him, hold his hand, enter his fingers unto his fingers and hold them firmly. He did not stand up or sit without remembering God. When anybody sat by him at the time of his prayer, he used to make it short and say to him : Have you got any need ? When he fulfilled his need, he returned to his prayer.

His assembly was not different from that of his companions, as he sat where he went. He was not found sitting among his companions spreading out his legs. He used to sit mostly facing the Ka'ba and honour one who came to him. Even he used to spread his own sheet of cloth for one with whom he had no relationship. He used to give his pillow to one who came to him and everyone thought that the Prophet honoured him more. Whoever came to him could see his face.

He used to call his companions by their surnames with honour and he used to give one surname to one who had no surname. He used to call the women by the names of their issues and call others by their surnames. He used to call the boys by their surnames for which their hearts were inclined to him. He used to get angry last of all and was very affectionate and kind in dealing with the people. Nobody could speak loudly in his assembly. He used to recite : "O God! Thou are pure, all praise is for Thee. I bear witness that there is no deity but Thee. I seek forgiveness from Thee and turn to Thee."

(4) Prophet's words and laughter

The Prophet was the greatest of the Arabs in oratory and sweet speech. He said : I am the greatest orator among the Arabs. He used to speak little. When he talked, he did not talk much. His talks fell gradually from his lips like pearls. Hazrat Ayesha said : The Messenger of God used to talk like you. They said : The Messenger of Allah used to talk little and every thing was expressed in this short talk. In his speech, there was no defect of excess or shortness. The words came one after another like pearls. Whoever heard them remembered them. He was sweetest in talk among his companions. He used to keep silent for long and have no talk without necessity. He used not to talk evil words and what he talked was just. He did not use ornamental words. His companions did never dispute before him. He used to say : Don't beat one verse of the Qurān by another as it has been revealed for many purposes. He used to smile much before his companions and his teeth then were exposed to view.

It was reported : Once a desert Arab came to the Prophet whose face became changed at seeing him. Seeing anger in his face, the Arab said : By One who sent him as a true Prophet, I will not ask him till he smiles. Then he said : O Messenger of God! we heard that *Dajjal* (Anti-Christ) will come with *Sarid* for the people. Then the people will remain hungry. My parents be sacrificed to you! Do you forbid me to eat it till I am destroyed ? Do you order me to eat it with satisfaction? Shall I talk infidelity after faith in God ? The Prophet laughed at this, so much so that his teeth were exposed to view. Then he said : It is not that, rather God will make you free from the food from which He made the believers free.

At the time when the Qurān was being revealed to him, he used not to smile most. When something happened, he entrusted it to God, kept himself free from his own strength and ability and said in invocation : O God! show me truth in a true manner or give me grace to give it up. Save me from doubt, so that I may not follow my passion without Thy guidance. Make my desire to obey Thee. Take pleasure from the peace of my mind. Show me the different shades of truth. Thou guidest to the straight path whomsoever Thou willeth.

(5) Prophet's manners in eating

The Holy Prophet ate whatever he got. To him, the best food was what all partook of. When the dining cloth was spread, he used to say : "In the name of God, O God! make it a gift to express gratefulness that there might be gifts in Paradise." Whenever the Prophet sat to eat, he used to sit as a praying man sits not placing one leg upon another and say : "I am a mere servant, I eat as a servant eats." He used not to take any hot food and said : "There is no grace in it and God will not feed us with fire." So make this food cold. He used to eat whatever was presented to him with three fingers with the help of the fourth finger at times. Once a tiffin made of clarified butter, honey and wheat presented to him. He ate it and said : How good it is! He used to eat bread, curry, dates and salt. Of all the fresh fruits, the dearest to him was grapes, cucumber and watermelon. He used to eat gourd with bread and sugar and sometimes with dates. His ordinary meal consisted of dates and water. Sometimes he mixed milk with dates. Meat was his most favourite curry. He said : Meat increases the power of hearing and is the king of foods in this world and the next. Had I prayed to my Lord for eating meat everyday. He would have granted it. He used to eat cooked meat with gourd. He liked gourd and said : It is the fruit of a plant of my brother Jonah. The Prophet said to me : O Ayesha! when you cook meat, mix therewith much water as it makes the broken hearted strong. He used to eat the meat of hunted birds but he did not himself hunt or follow game.

He used to eat bread with butter and like goat's neck and thigh. He liked gourd among curries, vinegar condiment, dried dates among dates. He prayed for three things and said : These have come from Paradise and they are medicines for poison and insomnia. He liked among curries creepers of yellow flower and carrot. He disliked the meat of reservoir of urine. He did not eat several things of goat–genital organ, female organ, blood, urinal meat, goitre, gall bladder etc. He did not eat onion and garlic, nor condemned them. He used to eat what he liked and did not eat what he did not like. He did not like to eat the meat of lizard and cockroach, neither did he prohibit them to be eaten. He used to lick up his dish with his hand and said : Most blessing is in the remnants of food. He used to lick up his fingers after meal so much so that they assumed reddish hue. He used not to cleanse his hands with towel till he licked up his fingers well and said : Nobody knows in which food there is blessing. When he finished his meal, he used to say : O God! for Thee is all praise. You have given me food and drink and given me satisfaction. So praise to Thee without expiation and farewell and being not free therefrom. He was accustomed to wipe his hand well and then wash his hands and mouth with excess water and take the name of God each time. He used to drink water in slow degrees and not hastily in one breath. He used not to blow breath in the cup of water at the time of drinking and supply food to one by his side. Once he was given milk and honey mixed together but he refused to drink it saying : Two drinks at the same time and two curries at the same time ! He said : I don't make them unlawful but I consider them bad for rendering accounts on the Resurrection Day as they are additional things in this world. I like modesty and God raises up one who humbles himself for God. He lived in his house more bashful than an unmarried girl. He used not to order for preparation of any food and eat whatever was given to him and remain silent if not given.

(6) Prophet's manners in dress

The Prophet used to put on sheet, gown, shirt and whatever he got. Green dress used to please him but most of his dresses were white. He said : Give your living men to dress with white garments and dress your dead therewith. He used to put on gown for *Jihad*. His shirt was long up to his thigh. He had only one shirt dyed with saffron with which he led prayers. Sometimes he put on only one shirt up to his thigh and say : I am only a slave. I put on garment as a slave puts on. He had two special garments for *Juma* prayer which he did not put on at other times. Sometimes he had only one garment with which he cohabited with his wives. He had a black garment which he gifted away. Umme Salma said : What fault has this black garment committed ? He replied : I had put it on. She said : You look more beautiful if the black garment mixes with your beautiful constitution. Sometimes, he used to go out putting on a seal tied with thread in his hand. He used to impress his letters with seal and say : It is better to put seal in letters than back-biting. He used to put on cap under his turban. If he had no turban, he used to put on cap. Sometimes, he put off his cap from his head and fixed it in front as a prayer-stake. When he had no turban and cap, he covered his head with a sheet of cloth. He had a turban named *Sahhab* which he presented to Hazrat Ali.

Whenever he put on a garment, he began from his right side and said : All praise is due to God who has given this garment to cover my private parts and to express adornment. When he wished to put off his garment, he began from his left side. When he put on a new garment, he gave his old cloth in charity to a poor man and said : If a Muslim gives his wearing garment to another Muslim, nobody except God will dress him. He remains in the custody of God till that cloth remains with him, be he alive or dead. His bed was made of grape-covers and refuges. It was two yards long and one yard and one cubit broad.

He had the habit of naming animals, arms and properties. The name of his standard was *Iqab*, he had his swords named *Zulfiqar, Makhzam, Rejab* and *Kazib*. The middle portion of his swords was moulded with silver. He used to wear belt of leather which had three rings of silver. The name of his arrow was *Katum*, of his shield *Kafur*, of his camel *Qaswah*, of his ass *Duldul*, another ass *Ekab* and of his goat *Aynah* whose milk he used to drink. He had an earthen pot which he used as an ablution pot and drink water therefrom.

(7) Prophet's pardon

The Holy Prophet was the most patient among men and the most forgiving inspite his having power to take retaliation. If anybody presented to him any necklace of gold or silver, he used to give it to some of his companions. One day, a desert Arab stood up and said : O Muhammad! if God ordered you to do justice, I don't see you doing it. He said : Woe to you ! Who will do better justice to you after me ? When he was about to go, the Prophet said : Take him to me with humility. The Prophet was taking silver coins for the people in the cloth of Bilal in the battle of Khaiber. One man said to him : O Messenger of God! do justice. The Prophet said to him : Woe to you, if I don't do justice, who will do justice after me ? If I do not do justice, I shall be ruined and suffer loss. Hazrat Omar then said : Should I not kill him as he is a hypocrite ? He said : May God save him ! In that case, people will say that I kill my companions.

Once the Prophet was in a certain *jihad*. At one time, the unbelievers found the Muslims heedless. So one of them raised a sword upon the head of the Prophet and asked him : Who will prevent me to kill you ? He at once replied : God! Immediately the sword fell down from his hand and the Prophet took it up and said : Who will prevent me to kill you? He said : Hold it firmly. The Prophet said : Say, I bear witness that there is no deity but God and that I am His Messenger. He said : I have got no envy against you, I shall not kill you. I shall not go with you and I shall not join those who fight against you. Then the Prophet set him free. The man went to his tribe and said : I have come to you today from the best man.

Hazrat Anas reported that a Jewess mixed poison in the food of the Prophet at Khaiber. When he began to eat it, he got smell of the poison and stopped eating. The woman was brought to the Prophet who asked her about the poisoned food. The woman said : I intended to kill you. He said : God will not give you that power. The companions exclaimed : Should we not kill her ? The Prophet said : Don't kill her.

One day a Jew enchanted the Prophet. Gabriel gave this information to the Prophet. He took out the enchanced thing and came round, but took no revenge against the Jew. Hazrat Ali said : The Prophet sent Jubair, Miqdad and myself to a certain place and said : Go on till you reach Raojakhak where you will find a woman with a letter which you must take from her. We then reached the place and told the woman to deliver the letter to us. The woman denied knowledge of any letter. She was then compelled to deliver the letter to us. We then came therewith to the Prophet. It was written therein 'From Hatib b. Abi Balta'a to the polytheists of Mecca' etc. This letter was written to inform them secretly the affairs of the Prophet. The Prophet said : O Hatib! what is the matter ? He said : O Messenger of God! don't hasten to inflict punishment on me. I have mixed with my people. The Refugees who are with you have got at Mecca their relatives who look after their families there. It was my object that though I have got no relationship with the Quraish, I would find such a man among them who will take care of my relatives there if I show kindness to them. I have not done it in a state of infidelity. I have not done it after accepting Islam being satisfied with infidelity. I have not done it being a retrogade. The Prophet said : This man has spoken the truth. Hazrat Omar said : Give us order to kill this hypocrite. The Prophet said : He joined the battle of Badr with us. Who will inform you that the Almighty God addressed the warriors of Badr saying: Do whatever you like. God has forgiven you.

Once the Prophet distributed the booties when an Ansar stood up and said : God is not pleased with this distribution.

When it was mentioned to the Prophet, his face turned red and he said : May God show you mercy. My brother Moses was given such troubles, but he remained patient. The Prophet said : Let nobody communicate anything of my companions, as I wish that at the time when I come to you, I come with a sound mind.

(8) Prophet's objects of dislike

The skin of the Prophet was thin and his interior and exterior were clean. His pleasure and wrath were exposed in his face. When he got very angry, he used to touch his head repeatedly. He used not to disclose to anybody what appeared to him bad. One day a man dyed with yellow colour came to the Prophet. He disliked it but did not say anything till he went. When he departed, he said to the people : If this man is asked to give up yellow colour, it would be better. Once a desert Arab passed water in presence of the Prophet within the mosque. The companions were about to assault him when the Prophet said to him : These mosques are not for passing urine and for uncleanliness.

Once a desert Arab came to the Prophet and begged something from him. He gave it to him and said : I have treated well with you. The desert Arab said : Never, you have not treated well with me. At this, the companions got angry but the Prophet prohibited them to do any harm to him. Then he went to his room and brought something for him to eat and said : I have done you benefit. Then he said : May God bless your family and relatives. The Prophet said to him : What you said first seemed unpleasant to my companions. If you like, say to them what you have said to me just now. What is in their mind will then vanish. He said: I shall say it to them. At another time, when the desert Arab came, the Prophet said: I added what the desert Arab told me. It seemed to me that he was pleased with it. I asked him : Are you satisfied? He said: Yes, may God bless your family and relatives. The Prophet said : The simile of the desert Arab in relation to me is like that of a man who had a camel which went out. It went faster fearing the people who followed it. The driver of the camel hinted : You all go away and leave the camel and myself alone. I know it better and shall show kindness to it. The driver of the camel gave it some food and called it towards him. When it came, he loaded it and rode upon it. When the desert Arab used harsh words, he would have entered Hell had I not prohibited you to take revenge upon him and assault him.

(9) Prophet's Generosity

The Holy Prophet was the greatest charitable man. His charity during *Ramazan* was greatest. Nothing could prevent him from it. Hazrat Ali narrated the qualities of the Prophet and said : His hand of charity was spread to its utmost and his tongue was the most truthful. His conduct was the most modest and he was the most honourable in lineage. Fear struck one who saw him first. Whoever mixed with him loved him. One who praised him said : I have never seen like him before and after him. Once a man begged something to the Prophet in the name of Islam and it was given to him. He begged him something further and it was also given to him. And that was one flock of sheep which were grazing between two hillocks. He went to his people and said : Accept Islam because Muhammad gives so much that he does not fear poverty for that. He did never deprive one who begged something from him.

Once 10,000 dirhams were brought to the Prophet which he distributed among his companions. After that a man came to him and begged him something. He said : I have got now nothing, but still I am giving you something after purchasing it. It was done accordingly. Hazrat Omar said: O Messenger of God! God has not imposed burden on you over which you have got no control. His words did not appear pleasing to the Prophet. That man said : Spend and do not fear poverty from God. The Prophet then smiled and pleasure was visible in his face. Once when he returned from the battlefield of Hunain, the desert Arabs came to him and begged from him so much that he was compelled to take shelter to a corner of a tree. They caught his sheet and he said : Give back my sheet to me. Had I had sheep to the number of these thorny plants, I would have distributed them all to you and you would not have found me a miser or a coward.

(10) Prophet's Bravery and Heroism

The Holy Prophet was the greatest hero and brave man. Hazrat Ali said : In the battle of Badr, we all stood surrounding the Prophet. He braved the enemies and we found him bravest on that day. He said: When fight began and friends and foes met with one another, we feared for the Prophet as he was closest to the enemies. Nobody went so near the enemies than him, When he passed order for fighting, he got pleased and prepared himself. He was seen at that time most superior in strength. Hazrat Imran said: The Prophet attacked the enemy who came to him first. The companions said that the Prophet had then a firm hold on the enemy. In the battle of Hunain, vhen the Prophet was surrounded by the enemies, he alighted from his mule and said : I am surely the Messenger of God. There is no untruth in it. I am the descendant of Abdul Muttalib. He was on that day the bravest of all.

(11) Prophet's modesty and humility

In spite of the lofty position of the Prophet, he was the most humble and modest. Hazrat lbn Amir reported : I saw the Prophet throwing stones at *Jamrah* riding on a camel. There was no assault in it, no driving out and no saying: Go aside, go aside. He sat on a sheet of cloth on the back of a mule and took someone behind him. He used to visit the sick, follow the biers, accept invitations of servants and slaves, repair shoes and sew garments. He used to help his family members in their household duties. His companions used not to stand up in his honour as they know his dislike for it. He used to salute the children when passing by them. One day a man was brought to the Prophet and he was afraid to see him. The Prophet said : Be quiet, I am not a king. I am the son of humble Quraish woman who used to eat gourd. He used to sit with his companions like an ordinary man. Whenever any stranger came to see him, he could not at first recognise him till he was introduced to him. Hazrat Ayesha said : May God sacrifice me to you! eat leaning as it is easier for you. The Prophet leaned towards the ground so much that it seemed that his head would touch the ground. He used to say : I shall take meal like the eating of a slave and sit like the sitting of a slave. He used not to eat in plates till he lived.

(12) Prophet's figure and Constitution

The Prophet was neither long statured nor short. When he walked alone, he appeared like a middle statured man. If a man of long stature walked with him, his figure looked longer. When two men of long stature walked by his two sides, he appeared longest, but when they became separate from him, the people called them long men. The Prophet was of middle stature. He was pretty, neither too white, nor too brown. He was of pure reddish hue. Someone praised him saying : His limbs which confronted the sun, such as face and neck, appeared more whitish than reddish colour. The sweats of his face were like pearls and more perfumed than musk. His hairs were very pretty, neither straight nor curly. When he combed them, they appeared like lines in sands. It is said that his hairs were kept flowing up to his two shoulders. Sometimes he parted his hairs into four parts and each two parts were let off through his two ears. Sometimes he kept his hairs above his ears and his neck then appeared shining like pearls. Grey hairs were found in his head and beard. Their number was not more than seventeen.

The Prophet had a most pretty constitution. Some gave the simile of his beauty to that of the full moon. His forehead was wide and the place between his eyebrows was bright like pure silver and eye-balls were black tinged with reddish hue. The hairs of his eye lashes were profuse. His nose was thin and his teeth were neither separated, nor united. When they were exposed at the time of his smile or laugh, they shone like lightning. His lip was most beautiful and the ends of his face was the most soft. His faces were smooth and nose not long. His beard was thick and he did not trim it. He used to clip his moushtache. His neck was the most beautiful, neither long, nor short. If the rays of the sun fell on his neck, it appeared like a cup of silver mixed with gold. His chest was broad. It was even like a mirror and white like the moonlight. There was a thin line of hairs extending from his chest upto the navel and there was no other hair over his belly. There were three lines in his belly. His wearing apparel covered one line. His shoulders were wide and there were hairs over them. The place between his shoulders was wide and therein there was impression or seal of prophethood inclined a little towards the right shoulder. Therein there was a spot mixed with black and yellow colours. There were hairs around it which appeared like the hairs of a horse.

He had hands full of flesh and his fingers were like silver sticks and his palms were softer than wool and were so full of scent that it seemed that otto was applied to them. Sweet scent was attached to the hand of a person who handshaked with the Prophet. If his pure hand touched the head of a boy, he could be recognised among boys owing to the sweet scent of his hand. His thighs were full of flesh and his constitution was proportionate and beautiful. In his later days, he became rather fleshy but he was without grease like his first stage of life.

The Prophet walked firmly and steadily. He said : Concerning constitution I am similar to Adam but in character and conduct I am similar to Abraham. He said : I have got ten names near my Lord – (a) Muhammad (praised), Ahmad (most praised), Mâhi (remover of infidelity), *Aqib* (coming last), Hashir (all appearing after me), messenger of mercy, messenger of repentance, messenger of fights, Muqfi (last of all prophets) and Qasim (embodiment of all virtues).

(13) Prophet's miracles

The character and conduct of the Holy Prophet, his actions, his habits, his management of affairs, his treatment with the different classes of people, his showing straight path to them, his wonderful answers to different difficult and subtle questions, his untiring efforts for the good of people, his good guidance regarding the open laws of *Shariat*. All these matters lead one to the conclusion that these were beyond the power of a man without the help of an unseen hand. It is impossible on the part of a hypocrite or a liar. The people testified by seeing his constitution and qualifications that he was a great truthful man sent by God. God gave him these qualities though he was illiterate and had no education and lived always with the illiterate Arabs. Being illiterate, orphan and weak, how could he acquire such good character and conduct, such knowledge about God without worldly knowledge ? His true and correct knowledge about the earlier Prophets show that he is a true messenger of God, because he knew these truths by revelations. How could he know what was beyond the power of man unless he received revelations? His miracles prove that he is a true Prophet of God. I am narrating a few of his miracles without prolonging it.

(1) When the Quraish of Mecca told the Prophet to divide the moon into two parts, the Prophet invoked God who split the moon into two portions and it was clearly visible to the people present.

(2) At the time of the seige of Madinah by the allied armies for more than one month, the Prophet supplied provision to all the people.

(3) At another time, he satisfied eighty people with food with only four *mudds* of maize and one little goat.

(4) Once the daughter of Bashir had a few dried grapes with which the Prophet fed all his soldiers to their satisfaction and there remained also something in excess.

(5) Once water began to gush forth from the fingers of the Prophet, so much so that his soldiers drank to their hearts content and made also ablution therewith.

(6) Once there was no water in a well at Tabuk and it dried up. The Prophet threw a little water of his ablution to the well and immediately it gushed forth so profuse water that thousands of soldiers drank it to their satisfaction.

(7) At another time, there was no water in a well at Hudaibiyah. The Prophet threw the remaining ablution water into it which immediately gushed forth abundant water. Fifteen hundred men drank it to their satisfaction.

(8) Once the Prophet threw a handful of dust towards the faces of his enemies as a result of which they instantly became

blind. Soon after this verse was revealed : When you throw, you did not throw, but God threw it.

(9) The Prophet used to deliver sermon standing on the trunk of a palm tree in the mosque. When it was replaced by another, the trunk began to emit mild sound which was heard by all his companions. When he touched it with his hand it became calm.

(10) Once the Prophet told the Jews to make *Mobahala* (that is whoever is a liar, he will die) but the jews gave the news next morning that they feared to make it for fear of their lives. This is mentioned in the Qurãn.

(11) The Prophet warned Hazrat Osman of great danger as a result of which he would enter Paradise. History bears testimony that he was murdered in his very house while he was reading the Qurãn. The Prophet told Ammar that a rebellious party would kill Osman. It is true that they murdered him.

(12) Once a man joined *Jihad* in the way of God. The Prophet said about him that he would enter Hell. Then it was seen that be committed suicide.

(13) When the Prophet was on his way towards Madinah on migration, one Suraqa b. Malik was following him to capture him in expectation of a reward, but the feet of his horse was sunk in dust in the act. When he sought the Prophet's help to escape from the danger, he prayed for him. This continued for three times and the Prophet prayed for him each time. After being released for the third time, the Prophet gave him this prophecy in his almost helpless condition that he would soon wear the bangles of Persian king Khusru. After the conquest of Persia by the Muslims, these bangles were procured from the king and were given to him for wearing.

(14) Aswad Ansari was a liar and claimed Prophethood

during the lifetime of the Prophet. He was a resident of Sana'a in Yemen. One night he was found assassinated in that town. In that very night, the Prophet gave his death news to the people and he named Feroze Daifami as his murderer.

(15) During the night of migration to Madinah, one hundred Quraish surrounded the house of the Prophet to kill him, but he went out of their clutches throwing dust on their heads for which they could not see him going out.

(16) Once the Prophet gave the prophecy to some of his companions : The last man among you will die of arson. It afterwards occurred that it came true.

(17) Once the Prophet called two trees to cover him to give him opportunity of urinating. The two trees shifted from their sites, covered him from public view and went away to their old sites after he finished his call of nature.

(18) The Prophet was of middle stature, but when he walked a two long men by his two sides, he was seen the longest of them.

(19) The Prophet said : I will kill Abu b. Hani in the battle of Uhud. In the battle, the Prophet inflited a minor injury on him and as a result he expired.

(20) Once the Prophet was given food mixed with poison to eat. He who ate it first expired, but the Prophet lived for four years even after taking that food. That food told the Prophet : There is poison in me.

(21) In the battle of Badr, the Prophet mentioned the fate of the leaders of the Quarish. This happened exactly as he said.

(22) The Prophet said to his daughter Fatima : You will meet me first after my death. She died six months after the Prophet.

(23) Once the Prophet said to his wives : She who is longer in hand will meet me first after my death. Hazrat Zainab was the most charitable among his wives died first after the Prophet.

(24) A certain camel had no milk in its udder. As soon as the Prophet touched its udder, it began to give milk. Abdullah b. Masud embraced Islam on seeing this miracle of the Prophet.

(25) Once one eye of a companion went out of its socket. The Prophet restored it to its site and his eyesight increased more.

(26) The greatest living miracle of the Holy Prophet is the Qurān which stands even today. He threw challenge to the people to produce a chapter like it. The Qurān says : "Say, if jinn and mankind gather together to bring a book like this Qurān, they won't be able to bring like it even though they help one another." So nobody was successful to bring a book or even a sentence like it upto this time. This alone is a sufficient and living testimony that the Holy Prophet Muhammad (peace to on him) is a true messenger of God.